Ageing, Independence and the Life Course

of related interest

Gerontology
Responding to an Ageing Society
Edited by Kevin Morgan
ISBN 1 85302 117 2

The Psychology of Ageing
An Introduction
Ian Stuart-Hamilton
ISBN 1 85302 063 X

Ageing, Independence and the Life Course

Edited by Sara Arber and Maria Evandrou

Jessica Kingsley Publishers
London and Bristol, Pennsylvania
in association with the British Society of Gerontology

First published in the United Kingdom in 1993 by
Jessica Kingsley Publishers Ltd
116 Pentonville Road
London N1 9JB
in association with the British Society of Gerontology

Copyright © 1993 Sara Arber and Maria Evandrou

British Library Cataloguing in Publication Data

Ageing, Independence and the Life Course
I. Arber, Sara II. Evandrou, Maria
155.67

ISBN 1-85302-180-6

Printed and Bound in Great Britain by
Cromwell Press, Melksham, Wiltshire

Contents

List of Figures

List of Tables

CHAPTER 1

Mapping the Territory
Ageing, Independence and the Life Course

Sara Arber and Maria Evandrou

All age groups, including those in later life, are constantly engaged in actively creating and recreating their lives, adjusting to changing circumstances, such as bereavement or retirement, in varying ways depending on their values, attitudes and biographical experience.

This book takes issue with approaches in social gerontology which see elderly people primarily in terms of their problems and welfare needs, and treat them as a distinct subgroup of the population with different needs and concerns from the rest of society. Such an approach instils an image of elderly people as in poor health, needing care, in poverty, role-less and socially desolate. Contributors to this book reject the ageism inherent within much social policy and writing on later life, by presenting research on the diversity amongst elderly people and their lifestyles. This is illuminated by embracing a life course approach.

The Life Course Approach

The life course approach provides a framework for analysing the various influences which contribute to the life experience of different groups of individuals at particular stages of their lives. It emphasises the interlinkage between phases of the life course, rather than seeing each phase in isolation.

> (T)he life course approach...views life transitions and changes in work status and family relations as a life process, rather than an isolated state or segment of human experience.... Rather than viewing any stage of life, such as childhood, youth and old age, or any age group in isolation, it is concerned with an understanding of the place of that state in an entire life continuum. (Hareven and Adams, 1982 p.xiii)

Elderly people pursue their life goals and attempt to come to terms with the transitions they experience within the structural constraints and cultural dictates of the society in which they live (Hareven and Adams, 1982). They seek to reconcile their own personal preferences with the cultural prescriptions of their family, peers and others in society. Their lives are interwoven with those of others.

The life course approach eschews a static view of old age in isolation, providing a dynamic framework which focuses on change and continuity. Elderly people are likely to retain many of the attitudes and traditions that were prevalent during their formative years. The present cohorts of elderly people have lived through historical periods which differ radically from contemporary society. Differences between the 1930s and the 1990s are enormous: for example, gender roles were more differentiated than they are today, housing standards and expectations about material assets and car ownership were lower, the welfare state with its free health service was unknown, elderly people were poorer and more likely to co-reside with younger family members, there were strong taboos about the open expression of sexuality, and quite different ideas about modesty and appropriate behaviour.

Elderly people who migrated to Britain will have had varying historical experiences. Some migrated from European countries, others were part of the post-war migration from Commonwealth countries. Their cultural traditions, experience of colonialism, language and expectations will have profoundly influenced their expectations and experiences of ageing in contemporary Britain. Some of these differences are explored in the chapter by Askham et al., contrasting the health expectations of elders from the Caribbean and from the Asian subcontinent.

The life course approach emphasises the interaction between the passage of individual time, family time, and historical time. The life experience of an elderly person will be created by that individual, within the context of actions by their family, and changes they have experienced in society over time. What seem like purely individual decisions, for example about when to retire, may be influenced by the retirement or health of other family members, and by the wider societal context, such as employers' policies to promote retirement before the statutory retirement age.

Older people are not a homogeneous group. A span of thirty years separates recently retired elderly people from those in their nineties. Most of the obstacles facing the achievement of a full life in old age are the same as those which confront individuals at any other stage in the life course. Elderly people have diverse biographies, affected by their gender, class position during adult life, and their ethnic background. These factors interact with one another and impact on the experience of ageing and the meanings attached to it. In particular, financial and material resources enjoyed during the middle stages of the life course influence perception of needs, as well as resources available at later stages of their lives. Similarly the housing experience and range of housing options available to people in later life are shaped by the tenure and quality of their earlier housing status, as illustrated in Chapters 8 and 9. What is emphasised throughout this book is the diversity of current status and of past experiences amongst older people.

Perceptions of Ageing

Negative images of elderly people as redundant, dependent, decrepit and inferior abound in our society (Comfort, 1977; Arber and Ginn, 1991a, 1991b). Attitudes and stereotypes orientate the actions of younger to older people, and provide cultural prescriptions which influence the self- perceptions of elderly people and their appropriate role behaviour. Gibson's chapter illustrates the ways in which the media and other cultural products portray the emotional and sexual needs of elderly people, leading to images of older people as having different needs and concerns from other age groups.

According to Oliver (1990), a dominant ideology within society is the 'personal tragedy theory of disability and ageing'. This centres on concepts of normality, able- bodiedness and able-mindedness. People who are elderly or disabled are seen as not living up to this 'normal' ideal, and because they fall short of this they are viewed in negative terms. This ideology assumes that the individual must adjust to the demands of society, which are predicated on able-bodiedness. In contrast the theory of social oppression sees the problems of disability as associated with the structure and institutions of society, and how they prevent elderly and disabled people from living as full lives as possible within the limits of their functional capacities (Oliver, 1990).

The medicalisation of ageing is exemplified by the medical profession's concern to return elderly people to 'normal physical functioning', with the ideal of a younger able-bodied person. The establishment of the speciality of 'geriatric medicine' exemplifies how older people are seen as patients, with age *per se* seen as pathological rather than ageing being a normal process. The medicalisation of ageing is also reflected in the use of age-specific criteria, such as the requirement that general practitioners invite all their patients over age 75 for annual screening, irrespective of their health or other characteristics. Similarly, general practitioners must certify elderly people as fit to drive or perform other activities. Such age-based criteria neglect other bases of differentiation in health and well-being, such as social class and gender.

Elderly people should not be seen as 'victims of tragedy' or as requiring charity or pity, but as having rights, like any other citizen (Twine, 1991, 1992). The aim should be to maximise independence and social participation. In order to achieve such objectives, it is necessary to change attitudes within society towards elderly people, and to reform the structures and institutions which reward people in terms of participation in an unequal labour market and which segregate elderly and disabled people from the rest of society.

A related concern is whether services should be provided according to citizenship or should respond to the special needs of particular groups of elderly people. The chapter by Askham and colleagues examines the perceptions of Asian and Afro-Caribbean elders about whether their ethnic background should lead to special treatment, and contrasts this with the views of health and social service professionals. Zarb's chapter explores how disabled people face a double disadvantage as they age; they often experience the ageing process earlier than other people and have to overcome the added threat of a second loss of independence, having previously overcome and adapted to the original limitations of their disability.

Ageing and Age-Based Transitions

In most Western countries, the last century has seen a profound change from viewing ageing as a natural process to viewing it as a distinct age-defined period of life characterised by decline, weakness and obsolescence (Hareven, 1982b). This contrasts with less industrial countries, such as Bosnia and Hercegovina, where Vincent and Mudrovcic (Chapter 6) demonstrate that ageing is still considered a natural process. Here, ageing does not commence at a fixed age but is identified by lack of vigour, relating to both physical and mental capacity, and lack of ability to participate in valued activities in the community. Ageing and old age as a category are culturally produced and socially structured.

In Britain the introduction of a state pension in 1908 marked the public and institutional formulation of old age as a distinct stage of life. It sharpened the boundaries between old age and middle age and opened the way for old age to be defined as a 'social problem' (Harper and Thane, 1989). The 'structured dependency thesis' argues that the institution of a fixed age for retirement has socially created dependency (Townsend, 1981; Phillipson, 1982; Walker, 1980, 1981; Macnicol, 1990).

We need to analyse whether chronological age is associated with entry to and exit from different social status positions, in terms of work, family status, household composition and extent of participation in the community. Some societies have very specific age-based transitions marked by rituals, such as initiation rites (Herdt, 1982; La Fontaine, 1985), but in most societies the association between chronological age and particular social statuses is much less clear cut.

In any society, there may be differences in the cultural valuation accorded to different phases of the life course and different work/family roles, and these evaluations change over time. Thus, how individuals experience specific transitions in their life course will be influenced by the valuation attached to occupancy of particular roles at that point in time. The life course approach suggests that chronological age is less important than the social status occupied by individuals.

We will briefly consider some of the life course transitions through which older people may pass as they age, focusing on the extent to which these transitions are associated with a particular chronological age, and the degree of convergence between the timing of each of these transitions. Three sets of transitions are considered: first, the transition from paid work, second, transitions in family roles and household living arrangements, and third, transitions in health status and caring needs.

Transitions from paid work

In Britain, the minimum age for receipt of the state retirement pension was set in 1908 at 70 and reduced to 65 in 1925; it was lowered to 60 for women in 1940 (Thane, 1978). The proportion of men over 65 who were still economically active was 60 per cent in 1921, falling to a third in 1931, and eight per cent in the late 1980s (Arber and Ginn, 1991a). The last two decades have seen a continuation of this trend (Laczko and Phillipson, 1991; Kohli *et al.* 1991), resulting in progressively earlier ages of exit from paid work, without any change to the age for receipt of a state pension. Thus, the institutionalised age-transition of pension receipt is only loosely associated with the actual age of labour market exit. Figure 1.1 shows that under three-quarters of British men aged 55–59 were in paid work in 1989, which fell to about half of men aged 60–64, and 11 per cent of men aged 65–69. The median age of men's exit from paid work is now below 65.

In 1989, half of British women in their late fifties were in paid employment, falling to a fifth in their early sixties (Figure 1.1). For women, there have been two contrasting trends over the last thirty years; first a higher proportion of women now participate in paid employment, and second a trend towards earlier labour force exit. Among women in their fifties, these trends tend to cancel each other out. The trends are in opposite directions for married and single women in their fifties; a higher proportion of married women are in paid work than twenty years ago, but fewer single women are working (Ginn and Arber, 1992a).

Despite the fact that only a minority of men and women are still in paid employment at state retirement age, work has remained a major source of social status, self-esteem and social contacts in society, as well as being the primary source of financial well-being. Many commentators have discussed how exit from paid work has segregated older people from others in society and increased perceptions of older people as socially redundant and a burden (Phillipson, 1982; Featherstone and Hepworth, 1990). Despite this trend to early exit from the labour market, there are well-known public examples of people in their seventies and beyond who command responsible and high-powered jobs within politics, the judiciary, the monarchy, media and journalism.

The meaning and experience of the transition out of paid employment may differ according to gender, class and ethnicity. For example, Mason (1987, 1988) shows that married women lose some of their independence and autonomy following their husband's retirement. To what extent retirees can spend their time on leisure pursuits, or other valued activities depends largely on their financial resources and health status, both of which are associated with class and gender (Arber and Ginn, 1991a). Laslett (1987,

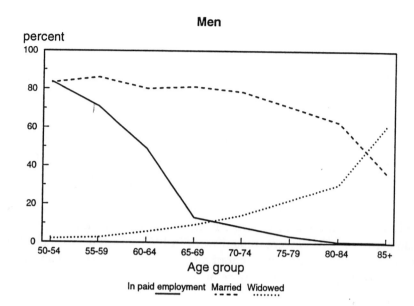

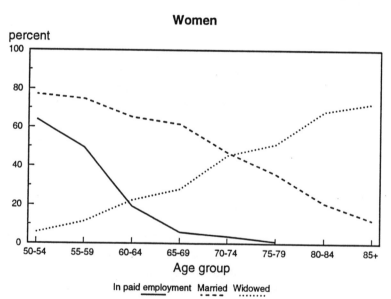

Source: Authors' own analysis 1989 General Household Survey

Figure 1.1 Transitions in later life: percentage in paid employment, married and widowed by age group and gender

1989) has coined the term 'the Third Age' to refer to the period between paid employment and physical dependency, emphasising the opportunities people can pursue during this new period of freedom from paid work while in relatively good health. However, Laslett has been criticised for having a middle class notion of this period of life and neglecting the material inequalities among older people. Illsley views the concept of the Third Age as an 'unrealistic portrayal of the lifestyle, time-scale, planning orientation, financial resources and aspirations of the mass of today's retiring non-intellectuals'. (Laslett, 1991 p.86).

The timing of the transition out of paid employment does not have a clear chronological relationship with the other two major transitions to which we now turn: transitions in family status, and health and caring needs.

Family status and household living arrangements

An important family status transition is grandparenthood. This often occurs many years before retirement from paid employment, belying the stereotype of the elderly grandparent. For example, all the men and all but one of the women were in paid employment in Cunningham-Burley's study (1984, 1985) of married couples around the time of the birth of their first grandchild. There is a lack of British data on the age of grandparenthood, or indeed of great-grandparenthood.

Once men have made the transition out of paid employment, those who survive are statistically unlikely to face any major status transition until their mid-eighties. There is no age at which the majority of men live alone, and only above age 85 are the majority (54 per cent) widowed (Figure 1.1). In contrast, the majority of women experience both the transition into widowhood and to living alone in their mid-seventies.

For men who outlive their wives, there is an interval averaging two and a half decades between retirement and widowhood, while for women this interval is under two decades. There is a gradual increase in the likelihood of widowhood with advancing age. Figure 1.1 shows that a tenth of women in their late 50s are widows, a fifth in their early 60s, over a third in their late 60s, nearly a half in their early 70s, and three-fifths in their late 70s. Other social characteristics, such as social class, influence the age of widowhood: people who were previously in higher middle class occupations on average are widowed later than those previously in working class occupations (see Chapter 10).

The transition to living alone is more likely to be experienced by elderly women than men. The proportion of elderly people who live alone largely mirrors the age gradient for widowhood shown in Figure 1.1, except that it reaches a peak of 66 per cent for women in their early eighties and then declines slightly. The proportion of men who live alone increases with age, reaching 37 per cent among men over 85. With advancing age and increased frailty some older people move to live with adult children or siblings (see

Arber and Ginn chapter) or into residential care (see Higgs and Victor chapter). Whether or not elderly people experience these transitions is influenced by their gender and class. Elderly people from ethnic minorities may experience household transitions in a different way and at different ages, but there is a lack of British data to answer these questions.

Table 1.1 Transitions in health status and institutional residence for elderly men and women by age

	% with Severe Disability* (6+)		% with Moderate Disability* (3+)		% Living in institutions	
	Men	Women	Men	Women	Men	Women
65–69	4	6	10	11	1.2	1.0
70–74	4	7	13	21	1.6	1.9
75–79	10	15	20	33	2.8	4.0
80–84	11	24	33	50	5.5	8.7
85+	24	43	53	69	12.2	20.3

* Disability of elderly people living in private households, based on activities of daily living, see Arber and Ginn (1991a)

Sources: Disability: *General Household Survey, 1985* (authors' analysis);
Institutional residence: OPCS (1984): Table 5.

Transitions into disability and the need for care

Among elderly people living in the community, only a minority of any age group are disabled to the extent that they need care on a daily basis (Table 1.1). Even among those over age 85, under half of women and a quarter of men experience this degree of incapacity. Disability is measured by the individual's ability to undertake activities of daily living (Arber and Ginn, 1991a); those who are 'severely disabled' would generally be unable to walk down the road unaided, bath themselves or go up and down stairs without help. Elderly people with 'moderate' disability would be able to accomplish these activities but only with difficulty. It is reasonable to assume that they would be in need of some informal care, but not necessarily on a daily basis. This lower threshold of disability applies to half of men over 85, and a fifth in their late seventies (Table 1.1). The proportions are higher for women, reaching two-thirds of women over 85 and a third of women in their late seventies. Although the likelihood of being physically disabled increases with age there is no specific age when it increases markedly. Other factors, as well as chronological age, have a major impact on the likelihood of disability, in particular earlier life course experiences relating to class position in the labour market (see Chapter 10).

The final transition experienced by some elderly people is entry into communal living, such as Local Authority residential care, a nursing home or long-stay hospital (see Chapter 12). Only a small percentage of elderly people live in a communal establishment, one per cent in their late sixties, rising to 12 per cent of men and 20 per cent of women over age 85 in 1981 (Table 1.1). Although the likelihood of institutional residence increases with age, this transition remains confined to a small minority of elderly people. Social class and capital resources may influence the timing of such a transition and the type of institution entered.

Methodological Issues in Life Course Research

Researchers aiming to adopt a life course approach face a number of methodological problems. The lack of British longitudinal surveys and life history data on older people makes the task difficult for researchers in sociology and other social sciences. Nevertheless, several chapters in this book show how researchers have adopted a life course approach using a variety of techniques.

In the previous section, cross-sectional survey data was used to map age-based transitions, focusing on the likelihood of being in particular statuses at specific chronological ages, using data mainly from our own analyses of the General Household Survey (GHS) (OPCS, 1990). This data only gives a partial picture because it is based on survivors and tells us little about the timing of these transitions for any one individual. The same individual may pass through each of these transitions within a few years or over several decades, many others will die before passing through particular transitions, especially the transition to institutional residence. We do not know what proportion of elderly people will become disabled at some point during their life or for how long they will remain disabled. Similarly we do not know what proportion will spend any time in residential care. Longitudinal studies of elderly people are needed to answer these questions, and in particular to disentangle time, period and cohort effects.

Longitudinal research or life history data would provide more precise figures on the timing and sequence of transitions among elderly people born in different cohorts and can take into account differential survivorship. For example, Guralnik (1991) used US longitudinal data to show that elderly people disabled in one or more activities of daily living have higher mortality over the following three years. The chapter by Bennett and Morgan provides an illustration of the value of longitudinal data, focusing on changes in levels of customary physical activity as elderly men and women age.

Several chapters use a qualitative life history approach; Clapham and his colleagues apply the concept of housing careers and evaluate the contribution of ethnographic and biographical approaches to a life course perspective; Vincent and Mudrovcic employ life history techniques to assess different perceptions of ageing; Gibson uses autobiographical accounts in discussing the emotional and sexual lives of older people; and in-depth interviewing is used by Gurney and Means to explore the relationship between life events and the meaning elderly people attach to 'home'.

The use of a life course approach for quantitative research is hampered by the lack of British longitudinal studies of ageing, although the OPCS Longitudinal Study (Goldblatt, 1990) provides valuable information based on census data, and is referred to in Chapters 10 and 12. The only large scale longitudinal dataset which includes the latter part of the life course is the British Household Panel Study at Essex University. All adults aged 16 and over were interviewed in 1991 in this nationally representative sample of 5000 households and will be reinterviewed annually for ten years (Rose *et al.* 1991). Social scientists in recent years have worked to overcome the lack of suitable data (Winter, 1991) by using cross-sectional datasets to simulate longitudinal profiles. Harding (1990) usefully details the various approaches that have been applied to date.

The most straightforward of these techniques is pseudo-cohort analysis. Pseudo-cohorts can be constructed by using successive years of cross-sectional data such as the GHS to track a particular cohort through time. Although the same individuals are not surveyed each year, individuals from the same cohort are. Thus the characteristics of one cohort (such as younger elderly people) can be compared with those of a group which represents them demographically ten years later. Taking the example of exploring how the experience of widowhood impacts on financial resources, different years of cross-sectional data could be used in the following way. Average equivalised household income of married couples aged 60–65 in 1975 could be compared to that of widows/widowers aged 75–80 in 1990, assuming that the latter group statistically represent the former in terms of life course progression. The analysis is limited in that it focuses on the average group characteristics or behaviour, rather than that of individuals, and fails to capture the various changes in people's circumstances over time. An alternative approach which attempts to understand more fully the diversity and change in individuals' experiences over the life course is provided by dynamic micro-simulation models, such as LIFEMOD (Falkingham and Lessof, 1992). Irrespective of the methodological technique employed, there is great value in being sensitised to the life course as an analytical framework within research.

Independence, Interdependence and Autonomy

Independence and dependence in the late twentieth century are terms which are rich in ideological connotations. 'Dependence' is often conceptualised in pejorative terms, equated with dependence on state services, with the implication that such dependence is illegitimate and fosters a 'dependency culture' (Johnson, 1990). How dependence is viewed is tied up with autonomy, control and power. We need to go beyond the negative connotations often associated with dependence, to understand the meaning of these terms to elderly people themselves.

The meaning of independence to elderly people has been the subject of surprisingly little research. A notable exception is Sixsmith (1986) who, in a study of the meaning and experience of home in later life, found that a recurrent theme was the significance of independence for most older people. Their perception of independence had three dimensions (Sixsmith, 1986 p.341):

1. Being able to look after one's self; that is, not being dependent on others for domestic, physical or personal care, which we shall term *physical independence.*

2. Capacity for self-direction, that is, being free to choose what to do, free from interference and free from being told what to do. We will term this *autonomy.*

3. Not being under an obligation to anyone, and not having to rely on charity. This signifies that independence is not threatened if support is based on *reciprocity or interdependence.*

Thus, physical independence is a value in itself, but if impairment results in dependence, this will not necessarily threaten self-esteem if it is perceived as part of a wider system of reciprocity or interdependence. Autonomy is a separate dimension from independence, since an individual may be dependent on another person for personal care, but still have autonomy. For example if they are able to go out when they choose because they have sufficient resources to pay for a hire car whenever required (see Chapter 3).

Dependence and independence should not be seen as dichotomies, but as part of a spectrum which involves interdependence and reciprocity. Complex industrial societies are founded on interdependence (Twine, 1991, 1992; Johnson, 1990). Periods of dependence are inevitable in rapidly changing societies, especially where there is a complex division of labour. For example, childhood has been socially created as an extended period of dependency, the costs of which are borne mainly by parents (especially mothers) and the state. This period of dependency is necessary if society as a whole is to benefit from a highly educated and skilled workforce. Twine (1992) argues that the state should recognise these life course interdependences and reward them with civil rights to life course transfers, for example, state pensions based on citizenship rather than the civil opportunity of success in the labour market, which is associated with class position.

The notion of dependence is highly symbolic, imbued with a range of cultural meanings which vary over time. We should reject the idea of dependence *per se*, and examine the perceptions of dependence. These perceptions are associated with ideologies prevalent within the individual's family and social group and in the wider society. Ideologies about dependence may be class, as well as gender-specific. For example, it is more acceptable for a man to be dependent on a female neighbour to cook him lunch than *vice versa* (see Chapter 4). The upper class may be more willing for others to take over their personal functions, such as bathing and dressing, since personal tasks in the past were performed by servants and thus personal care by a stranger may be less threatening to their self-esteem. Meanings will be influenced by the individual's biography, and the attitudes and values present during their formative years. Each cohort will vary in their attitudes towards the legitimacy of their rights to various welfare benefits.

Individuals are rarely totally dependent or independent, but are dependent in certain aspects and not in others. Two dimensions of dependence need to be considered. First, the nature of the services or resources they are dependent on, these may include financial resources, housing, health care, personal and social care, and support for emotional and/or sexual needs. Second, on whom the individual is dependent. This may include relatives, such as a partner, parents, or children; friends and neighbours; a paid employee; or the state. Both these dimensions will influence whether the relationship is perceived as one of dependence, and if so, the implications such as lowering the individual's self-esteem.

Independence in Four Spheres

We distinguish four inter-related spheres which promote independence; their absence or the provision of poor substitute support may result in dependence and adversely affect self-esteem:

1. Financial resources
2. Housing and home
3. Physical health (functional) resources
4. Social, emotional and sexual interdependence.s

Married couples often perceive themselves as having a single identity, acting as a unit rather than as individuals. This is exemplified by one of Sixsmith's respondents, 'I like to be independent – I don't want to be beholding (*sic*) to any man. We don't owe a penny between us – it is one of our principles'. (Sixsmith, 1986 p.341). He slips imperceptibly between *his* values (our assumption of gender) and *their* values as a couple. For couples, one of the key threats to independence is death of a partner. Access to each of the four spheres of support is conventionally seen as a legitimate right within the marital relationship, which is culturally assumed to be characterised by interdependence.

We examine each of the four spheres in turn highlighting the nature of dependencies in each sphere and how they are evaluated by elderly people and society in general.

Financial resources

In late twentieth century Britain, financial support in the form of the basic state (National Insurance) pension is considered a right, legitimated through employment contributions, and reflecting a societal acceptance of life course or inter-generational transfers, that is the interdependence of one generation on another. According to Twine (1992) both the basic state pension and SERPS (the State Earnings Related Pension Scheme) are seen as 'social rights', unlike occupational pensions, which he argues are 'civil opportunities' contingent on the vagaries of the labour market, and threatened by life course events beyond the control of the individual.

The chapter by Evandrou and Falkingham shows that the value of the basic state pension has declined in real terms, and the changes to SERPS have reduced its benefits for women and other groups less advantaged in the labour market (Arber and Ginn, 1991a; Groves, 1991). These reductions in 'social rights', together with the increasing acquisition of occupational and personal pensions will result in greater financial inequality among elderly people. Thus, the financial well-being of elderly people is intimately linked to their life course.

Financial resources are essential for the maintenance of independence and quality of life, as well as promoting autonomy. Dependence on informal carers or the state can be reduced if frail elderly people have sufficient resources to pay for aids and housing adaptations, or for their own domestic or personal care. Thus, whether a given level of functional impairment results in feelings of dependence and lack of autonomy is contingent on financial independence. However, Wilson (Chapter 3) argues that it is not purely the objective amount of money which an elderly person has but the meaning of that money and its symbolic value to them which determines whether a given level of income is used to reduce dependence.

Housing and home

The living arrangements of a person, whatever their age, are a key determinant of whether they perceive themselves as an autonomous and independent person. 'Home' means much more than the housing in which a person is living. It is important to people symbolically, representing the independent self, and instrumentally in materially enabling independent life (Sixsmith, 1986). The home is the private domain of the individual in which they can act as they wish, that is, with autonomy. It provides a physical barrier between the individual and outsiders. The dependencies and indignities of coping with a physical impairment can to some extent be excluded from view, if personal care and support are provided from within the home.

The dominant ideology of community care dichotomises 'home' as good and 'institutional living' as bad, but in either setting there may be varying degrees of independence or dependence. We need to be critical of this simple polarisation, and ask whether, from the point of view of the elderly person, living in an institution is preferable to continuing to live at 'home' or moving to live with a relative. For example, an elderly person living in their married child's home may be almost entirely dependent and lacking in autonomy. Similarly, a housebound elderly person reliant on state social care services may have a poorer quality of life than if they resided in an institution. Gavilan (1992) uses Goffman's (1963) framework to show that a housebound person may be 'institutionalised at home' in the sense of losing autonomy, being controlled by the 'care plans' and schedules of care workers, and having their self systematically mortified by the intrusion of care workers into the private areas of their home and personal belongings. They may live in their own home but lose control over it, becoming passive and dependent, as well as socially isolated.

Because of the central significance of home to the independence of elderly people, a number of chapters examine this sphere: Gurney and Means explore the meaning of home, Clapham *et al.* examine the interlinkage between housing and the life course, Higgs and Victor examine the role of institutional care versus care in the community, and Arber and Ginn analyse how class relates to different living arrangements within the community.

Physical health (functional) independence

Functional capacity is the major factor determining whether an individual of any age remains independent, rather than being dependent on care-givers. Such domestic and personal support is mainly required by people who need support over long periods, often the remainder of their life time. This contrasts with health care which all individuals require at various stages during their life course. Following acute medical intervention, individuals may need short-term domestic and personal care, but this differs from longer term support in terms of the management of reciprocities invoked by care- giving and receiving.

Access to free state health care is seen as a universal right, with a high level of popular support (Taylor-Gooby, 1985). This contrasts with state social welfare services which people generally do not see as a right, and about which changes in their level and manner of provision have little resonance with the wider public. Welfare services which are means-tested are less likely to be seen as rights and more likely to be experienced as stigmatising and as denoting dependence. However, younger cohorts who grew up after the introduction of the welfare state may have a wider conception of their rights to social welfare services than the present cohorts of elderly people.

Changes associated with the 1990 Community Care Act (DoH, 1989) have shifted the responsibility and funding of what is now termed 'social care' to Local Authority social service departments (see Chapter 12). Social care involves assisting with personal and domestic tasks and other aspects of daily living. A key component of the new community care policy is the provision of 'services that intervene no more than is necessary to foster independence' (DoH, 1989: para 1.10). The emphasis is on providing care by the community, with local authorities seen as 'enablers' rather than 'providers'. Means testing will increase with authorities 'assessing the client's ability to contribute to the full economic cost' (para 3.1.3). Victor suggests that the state is becoming 'a residual provider of social care' (1991 p.165).

These changes are likely to result in a reduction in state support services for many elderly people, including those unwilling or unable to meet the means-tested charges, a diminution in the perception of services as a right, and possibly a loss of control, as the 'case manager' designs 'packages of services tailored to meet the assessed needs of individuals and their carers' (DoH, 1989 para 3.13). If the outcome is more informal care falling on relatives and friends, this must be considered both in terms of the resultant burdens on the care-giver, and the disabled elderly person's feelings of dependence and self-esteem.

The chapters by Howarth and by Wilson show that elderly people are concerned not to be a burden on their relatives. Their acceptance of 'social care' involves a complex reckoning of reciprocity between themselves and the potential care provider, with less likelihood of accepting or asking for help if it is perceived as one-sided, or cannot be reciprocated in the foreseeable future. Thus, elderly people are actively constructing their lives and support arrangements, and these can only be understood by appreciating the meanings of their actions within a social and biographical context.

An individual's perceptions of the meaning and legitimacy of dependence will influence their actions in seeking assistance. Only in this way can we understand the refusal of elderly people to accept help or rehousing. Their refusal may be rational from their own point of view, even though defined as 'pig-headed' by service providers, or sometimes considered a symptom of their 'need' for institutional care. This is illustrated in the chapters by Wilson and by Gurney and Means.

Performance of the same personal care tasks by different relatives, a state-employee, or a private employee may have varying effects on the individual's perception of their own dependence and their self-esteem, depending on the cultural expectations of the elderly person. Among elderly married couples, when either partner is physically impaired it is not only seen as legitimate but expected that their partner, irrespective of gender, will provide the required support (Arber and Ginn, 1991a, 1992). In general, this support is less likely to be seen as dependence than if support were provided by the state or another relative, and is less likely to adversely affect their sense of autonomy and feelings of self-esteem.

Social, emotional and sexual interdependence

Research on dependence and independence is dominated by a concern with meeting the physical, domestic and personal care needs of elderly and disabled people (Oliver, 1990). This presents a one-dimensional view, which neglects the uniquely human elements of people. It is as if bathing, domestic work and the provision of hot meals is enough. Yet, in everyday life, the provision of such services is imbued with emotional significance. For example, meals and the provision and preparation of food are fundamentally social acts (Charles and Kerr, 1987, 1988; Murcott, 1983). To strip these acts of their emotional and social significance is in itself to devalue them (see Howarth chapter). Valued social and emotional relationships are prerequisites for the maintenance of quality of life (Jerrome, 1981, 1991).

Emotional and sexual relationships are valued because they involve interdependence and are freely entered into. Intimacy and sexuality in later life is still a taboo subject, characterised by myths, stereotypes and ignorance. Yet personal and intimate relationships are equally fundamental to a person's well-being whether they are seventeen or seventy. This is illustrated in Gibson's chapter where interpersonal relationships and sexual expression throughout later life are discussed using autobiographical accounts. He examines the experiences of older people embarking on new love-relations, and the responses they are confronted with from relatives and the wider society. Issues of conflict in relation to inheritance and sexual jealousy are considered. The chapter also challenges ageism in sexuality by examining literature, television programmes and popular humour.

Life course experiences and cultural stereotypes about appropriate behaviour of elderly women and men will impact on their ability to sustain and develop new friendships in later life. Loneliness in old age continues to be exaggerated in society reflecting not only stereotyping but also the difficulties it poses as a topic for investigation (Jerrome, 1991). This is because of its subjective dimensions, and because it relates to the individual's perception of the quality and meaning of personal relationships. Living alone and living in isolation from family and community does not necessarily mean that elderly people are lonely; isolation and loneliness are not coincidental (Townsend, 1973).

A key factor here is choice and autonomy; whether an elderly person has the financial independence, as well as the physical capacity, to maintain friendships in the way they wish. A housebound person maintained in the community through care assistants may be more socially isolated and lonely than a person with comparable functional abilities living in a residential setting (Gavilan, 1992). On the other hand, life in a residential setting, amidst others not of the elderly person's choosing may result in profound loneliness (Townsend, 1973).

Social interdependence is likely to be a key factor in the quality of life of elderly people. For elderly people who are married, their spouse may provide their primary social interaction. However, the demography of old age means that widows outnumber widowers by five to one and the gender differential increases with age, reaching three women for every man aged over 85 (Arber and Ginn, 1991a).

Gender is a fundamental distinguishing feature throughout the life course, influencing what is culturally considered as 'age-appropriate' behaviour, particularly for current cohorts of elderly people. Women, throughout their life course, have wider friendship networks than men, whereas the marital relationship has greater emotional salience for men. Thus, widowhood has different meanings for women and men, both because of gender differences in widowhood, and because men have less friends to fall back on and are less familiar with making and developing friendship relationships (Jerrome, 1981; 1986).

Conclusion: Continuity and Change

Life course events prior to retirement influence the socio- economic position of individuals following labour market withdrawal and into old age. The accumulation of state pension rights, access to and participation in private and occupational pension schemes, and the availability of housing wealth as a potential source of income in old age act to differentiate people at later stages of the life course. The acquisition of these resources is influenced by gender, experience of caring responsibilities and previous occupational group. Yet social policy in Britain largely fails to recognise the influence of the life course and does little to redress inequalities in old age. These issues are discussed in the final chapter by Evandrou and Falkingham, which examines the relationship between current policies and the changing pattern of resources in later life with respect to pensions and social care.

The movement away from the basic state pension and the changing mix between private and public provision of both income and social care, act to perpetuate and extend existing inequalities. The ability to pay for health and social care, and purchase long-term care insurance, is influenced by earlier life course experiences. Future policy proposals must acknowledge and tackle the heterogeneity in socio-economic positions of people in later life, if welfare policy is to be more effective in the future.

A life course perspective highlights the different ways in which elderly people make their transitions into new roles and statuses as they age. It emphasises the meanings which individuals use to make sense of their experiences, and shows that elderly people struggle to adapt and live their lives according to their own values. What is valued may vary according to the diverse biographical experiences of older men and women, their class and ethnic background, as well as varying between cohorts who lived through different historical periods. During the life course, people's values and attitudes crystallise and still affect the way they live and interpret their lives today.

We need to focus on the perspectives of elderly people themselves, rather than seeing elderly people primarily as passive objects of intervention, treatment and care. Their views should be central to the design and administration of services. We need to reassess the conventional problem-orientated approaches and consider elderly people as contributing to the well-being of society in a range of ways, providing services to other elderly people and to the younger generation.

Elderly people have shown that they value independent residence over at least the last two centuries, but they have used different ways to achieve and sustain that autonomy (Hareven, 1982b). In the nineteenth century, elderly people struggled to retain headship of their own households rather than move in with relatives or strangers, or into the workhouse. Today, elderly people may be involved in different struggles to retain their independence and autonomy and maintain their self-respect. A life course perspective which appreciates the interrelationships between generations and families, should also recognise that values may be in conflict. Independence and autonomy for an elderly person in the community may conflict with the values of independence and autonomy of their children's generation who prefer not to be hindered by providing informal care. These fundamental values of independence and autonomy remain, but the form of those struggles and the societal constraints within which they are played out differ.

Acknowledgements

We are very grateful to Jay Ginn, Jane Falkingham and Christina Victor for helpful comments on an earlier version of this chapter.

CHAPTER 2

'Forgotten But Not Gone'
The Experience of Ageing With a Disability

Gerry Zarb

The 'ageing population' is far from a homogeneous group; there are important differences between particular groups, sub-groups and age cohorts, which need to be identified and acknowledged. One particular sub-group which has been more or less completely overlooked are disabled people who are ageing. To be clear, this does not refer to people who may experience disability as a consequence of the ageing process, but to those who become disabled in child or adulthood and who are now beginning to age with their disabilities. Indeed, it is only within the last fifteen to twenty years that there has even been an identifiable cohort of ageing disabled adults; first, life expectancy for many types of disability prior to this was low; second, large numbers of people who became disabled as a result of injuries received during World War II are now entering older age; third, many children and young adults disabled as a result of the widespread polio epidemics of the late 1940s and early 1950s are now in their fifties or older. Added to this, there are an unknown number of people with various disabilities who have been disabled since as long ago as the 1920s.

Changing patterns of life expectancy brought about by advances in medical technology, treatment and rehabilitation also mean that the size of this sub-group of older disabled people is increasing. Whilst there are no completely accurate figures, we can get some idea of the numbers involved from the two national disability surveys carried out by the Office of Population Censuses and Surveys in the late 1960s and 1980s (Harris, 1971; Martin *et al.*, 1988). These surveys indicate that there are just under 100,000 people aged 50 plus who have been disabled for 20 or more years; it is estimated that this figure will reach 200,000 or more within the next 10 to 20 years (Zarb, 1992).

This increase in the numbers of people who are ageing with a disability is differentially distributed according to both gender and race. Although the prevalence of a few types of physical impairments is higher amongst males, many of the largest sub-groups of older disabled people contain more women than men. The most recent national survey estimates that there are a total of 3.6 million disabled women in Britain, compared with 2.5 million men. Amongst those aged 75 or more, disabled women outnumber men by a ratio of nearly 2.5 to 1 (Martin, Meltzer and Elliott, 1988).

The present population of Britain includes approximately 2.4 million people of minority ethnic origin. There are no national figures but a number of local studies indicate a high incidence of certain physical and sensory impairments amongst black and Asian communities; the high incidence of sickle cell anaemia and thalassaemia amongst people of Caribbean and Mediterranean origin is also well known (Keeble, 1984; Wandsworth CCR, 1978; DHSS, 1983; Cox, 1984; Begum, 1992). In addition, there are an unknown number of refugees from various countries, some of whom have impairments associated with war, torture and so on. Largely because of migration patterns, the minority ethnic population has a younger age structure than the indigenous population; for example, around 4 per cent (approximately 97,000) of the black and Asian populations had reached retirement age by 1986, compared with around 17 per cent of the white population (CRE, 1987). So, although it is not possible to state any overall figures, the prevalence of ageing with disability amongst minority ethnic communities is also likely to increase significantly over the next decade and beyond.

Little is known about the experience of ageing with a long-term disability and, while there may be some similarities with other groups in the ageing population, each group will bring its own perspective to the experience of ageing and disability. Virtually no policies or services aimed at responding to the needs of people who are ageing with a disability are being developed at present. Similarly, while academic study of ageing has addressed issues around disablement in old age (such as Townsend, 1981; Cameron et al., 1989; Bury and Holme, 1991), ageing with a disability remains a very under researched issue.

The Research Studies

It was against the background of these concerns that our three studies on the personal and social consequences of long-term disability, and on ageing with disability were initiated. The first two studies looked at the experiences of one particular sub-group – people who had been disabled as a consequence of spinal injury; the first (Creek et al., 1987; Oliver et al., 1988) included 77 men who had been disabled for up to 15 years and the second included 42 men and women who had been disabled for between 20 and 50 years (Zarb et al., 1990). The fieldwork for the first study was carried out between 1985 and 1986, and the second between 1987 and 1988. Both groups were selected from a random sample of patients and former patients at the National Spinal Injuries Centre at Stoke Mandeville Hospital. Respondents were resident throughout the U.K.

In the third study (Zarb and Oliver, 1993) the research was extended to cover the ageing experience amongst people with a wide variety of long-term physical disabilities or disabling illnesses. A total of 290 people have participated in the study by providing written or oral accounts of their own experiences, and 100 of these are being followed up with in-depth personal interviews; this group has been disabled for between 20 and 80 years and just over a third have been disabled since birth or early childhood.

Respondents for the follow-up interviews were selected by means of quota sampling from the membership of various national and local disability organisations, plus a small random sample of clients from two local Social Services Departments. The quotas were selected to reflect the main groups for whom ageing was known to be an issue. It is not possible to make any assessment of how far the participants are representative of all older disabled people, although it can be assumed they are representative of their own particular organisations. Most of the quantitative data presented in this chapter is based on 75 interviews which have been completed and analysed to date (mid 1992), 45 women and 30 men. Thirteen per cent of the sample were aged under 45, 35 per cent between 45 and 64, and 52 per cent over 65. Summary details of the survey samples for all three studies are shown in Table 2.1.

Ageing with Disability – The Forgotten Dimension

The research is tapping into widespread concern amongst many older disabled people who feel that their needs – and even their existence – has been overlooked; indeed, several describe themselves as being 'forgotten people' which – on the evidence of the research – is a fairly accurate assessment of the situation. This general problem is manifested in several ways:

- lack of understanding of the medical/physical consequences of long-term disability;
- lack of recognition of the needs of people who are ageing with long-term disabilities in policy debate and service provision;
- inappropriate services modelled on the assumed needs of older people experiencing disability as a consequence of the ageing process;
- lack of suitable/acceptable housing options;
- inadequate benefit and pension provision and lack of recognition of the extra financial costs associated with ageing with disability;
- lack of support for ageing carers.

There will often be considerable overlap between the concerns of older disabled people and of the ageing population in general. However, the main aims of this chapter are to highlight the important differences based on the dual experience of ageing and disability which cannot be adequately encompassed by our existing understanding of ageing; and to show that a biographical approach is essential to understanding this dual experience. We first outline a conceptual model for understanding the 'disability/ageing career' and then focus on four key issues:

1. The physical ageing process amongst people with long- term disabilities and 'premature' ageing.
2. Changing satisfaction with the quality of life over the disability/ageing career and the ways in which personal subjective responses to ageing are shaped by the prior experience of disability.
3. The perceived threat to independence associated with ageing and how this is often particularly acute for disabled people who have struggled to maintain their independence throughout their lives, and not just in older age.
4. The ways in which these life experiences are structured by race and gender.

Table 2.1 Details of research samples by disability group and gender

A. Long-term Effects of Spinal Cord Injury, 1985–86 (Oliver et al., 1988)			
	N	%	
Spinal Cord Injury (SCI)	77	100.0	(All males)

B. Ageing with Spinal Cord Injury, 1987–88 (Zarb et al., 1990)			
Spinal Cord Injury (SCI)	42	100.0	Males = 37 (88%)
			Females = 5 (12%)

C. *Ageing with Disability, 1990–92 (Zarb & Oliver, 1993)*

	(Full sample)		(Interviewed to mid 1992)	
	N	%	N	%
Polio	63	22	27	36
Multiple Sclerosis	37	13	7	9
Cerebral Palsy	6	2	4	5
Scoliosis	14	5	8	11
Arthritis	16	6	6	8
Limb Amputations	13	5	10	13
Diabetes	96	33	8	11
Parkinsons Disease	12	4	3	4
Multiple disabilities	6	2	2	3
Others	27	9	0	0
Totals	(290)	100	(75)	100
Male	119	41	30	40
Female	171	59	45	60

A Conceptual Model for Understanding the 'Disability/Ageing Career'

A common theme underlying the biographical approach to ageing is the conceptual distinction between chronological age as an explanatory variable, and ageing as a subjective life experience or career. In other words, between 'old age' as a category and 'ageing' as an experiential life process. Closely connected to this is the basic premise that, the present can only be fully understood in the context of past experience. This emphasis on subjective experience and the individual meanings attached to experience can help our understanding of ageing with a disability. However, the logic of the biographical approach dictates that, the personal biographies of people who are ageing with a long-term disability will incorporate both the 'ageing career' and the 'disability career'. While there will obviously be points of similarity, there are also important differences. In addition, there will be an interaction between the ageing and disability careers, such that similar objective circumstances and life events differ in the significance they have for the individuals concerned.

Our previous work on the long-term effects of spinal cord injury suggested that, the occurrence of a disability as a significant event in an individual's life is only a starting point for understanding the practical and personal consequences of living with disability (Oliver *et al.*, 1988). Also, that the social environment, material resources and the meanings which individuals attach to situations and events are the most important factors to be considered in developing our understanding of disability careers.

Since understanding the significance of ageing for older disabled people is a central concern, the concept of life events provides a very useful conceptual tool. However, just as the onset of disability cannot be seen as a one-off life event, neither can the intervening impact of ageing be considered as a self-contained life event, or even as a series of discrete life events. Consequently, the concept of career is a further essential component of the model as it allows consideration of people's experiences throughout their lives including, but not restricted to, their experiences of disability and, subsequently, ageing with a disability.

The specific questions addressed are: what changes in the 'disability career' (if any) are associated with ageing; when do these changes occur and why; and, how are such changes experienced subjectively by the individuals concerned?

We have constructed a conceptual framework which integrates the dual experience of disability and ageing in what we have termed the 'disability/ageing career' (see Figure 2.1). The 'disability/ageing career' is viewed as a series of physical, emotional and social processes punctuated by a variety of 'triggering events' which are likely to occur in older age. For example, periods of ill-health, retirement, changes in family circumstances, or bereavement are events which can trigger a range of personal, physical and social consequences, such as an increased need for social support. The

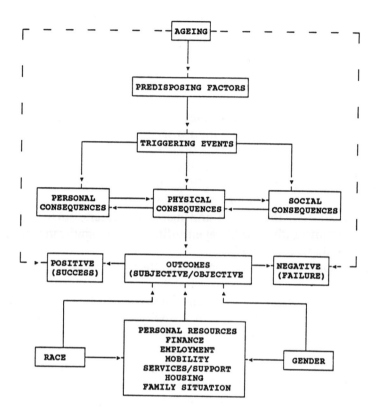

Figure 2.1 The disability/ageing career

consequences of such triggering events will usually be mediated by certain 'predisposing factors', which may themselves have personal or social consequences. For example, the reliance on an ageing carer as a source of informal support can lead to a crisis or potential crisis if such support comes under strain or breaks down.

The personal, social and physical consequences of ageing which may be experienced at any point along the disability/ageing career will, in turn, lead to both 'objective outcomes' (such as a move into sheltered accommodation), as well as 'subjective outcomes' relating to the 'meaning' of such experiences to the individual. These outcomes can be either positive or negative both objectively and subjectively. For most people, outcomes will be a combination of both. Also, it is not unusual for negative objective outcomes to be associated with more positive subjective outcomes as each individual will have their own perceptions of objectively similar events.

Further, these outcomes will be very much dependent on the personal, social and material resources available to the individual; in particular, the level of social support, as well as financial and housing resources. It is a central premise of this model, however, that such resources cannot be viewed separately from the meanings and values attached to them by the individual.

Both the objective and subjective dimensions of the 'disability/ageing career' will be shaped by race and gender. First, social and material resources are differentially distributed amongst the ageing population – differential access to pensions (for example, Arber and Ginn, 1991a). In addition, the ways in which disability is experienced subjectively throughout the disability career will be mediated by both race and gender. Such prior experience will influence the subjective experience of ageing, and the values, expectations and meanings people attach to any changes in their lives.

Physical Changes/Problems Associated with Ageing

Before considering the subjective experience of ageing with a disability, we examine the kinds of problems and changes typically associated with the physical ageing process. These two dimensions, the physical and the personal, are often inextricably linked in older disabled people's own descriptions of the significance of ageing, so both are essential to understanding the dual experience of ageing with disability.

There is a surprising degree of similarity in the kinds of physical problems/changes reported despite the broad range of disabilities covered. Two general themes have been consistently reported. First, many people's experiences are consistent with the notion of 'premature' physical ageing; the majority of people reported experiencing a process of 'general deterioration' which appears to be more closely associated with length of time since onset of disability than with age itself. Typically, there is a noticeable 'downturn' in physical well-being and health status around 20 to 30 years from onset of disability. This trend mostly appears to operate independently of chronological age.

Second, many of the physical problems/changes experienced are perceived as being long-term effects of people's original disabilities. The most common of these is the high incidence of arthritic and rheumatic problems. This is not restricted to wheelchair users however; for example, nearly all of the limb amputees in the study had experienced the same problem resulting from the extra strain on their remaining limbs; similarly, a high proportion of people with polio reported experiencing arthritic problems in limbs which were not originally affected by polio, while people with scoliosis often report that curvature had led to the same kind of problem.

For some groups, there are also common secondary impairments caused either by the original disability, or the long-term effects of medical or rehabilitation interventions and strategies. For example, blindness and neurological problems associated with long-term insulin dependence (diabetes); chronic pain resulting from building up immunity to certain drugs like morphine; chronic respiratory problems caused by spinal deformity (scoliosis); and a variety of physiological problems coming under the heading of 'post-polio syndrome'.

Different kinds of disabilities appear to have different 'trajectories' relating to the pattern of physical changes over time, although there is also a certain degree of overlap in this. Four main patterns or trajectories are indicated by the research:

1. *Progressive deterioration since onset.* This appears most characteristic of the process of 'burn out' reported by some people with Multiple Sclerosis and, to a lesser extent, the experiences reported by some people with long-term arthritis.

2. *Onset of gradual deterioration after 20 plus years of relative stability.* This pattern is characteristic of the experiences of many people with spinal injuries and also fits the experiences of people with polio, limb amputees, and people with long-term diabetes who also have physical impairments.

3. *Onset of increasingly progressive deterioration after either a period of relative stability or only gradual deterioration.* Although the numbers are too small to make any conclusive generalisation, this pattern seems to be characteristic of the experience of long-term scoliosis.

4. *Intermittent change with underlying pattern of gradually progressive deterioration.* This was most often reported by people with Parkinsons Disease and people with Multiple Sclerosis. While both groups typically experience intermittent 'remissions' and 'relapses', people have reported that they never quite regain the same levels of energy or strength after successive relapses.

Personal Responses to Ageing with a Disability

People's perceptions of, and attitudes to ageing cannot be understood without reference to previous life experiences. The experience of disability will have been a major feature of the lives of all long-term survivors so it is not surprising that this frames their personal responses to ageing.

As noted earlier, the process of physical ageing is more closely related to the length of time since the onset of disability, than to chronological age. Data collected on satisfaction with the quality of life shows a clear parallel 'downturn' in satisfaction levels at the same points along the disability/ageing career. Amongst those who become disabled when they are young adults or middle aged, the first 10 to 15 years are usually marked by a steady increase in satisfaction levels, followed by declining satisfaction after 20 to 30 years. The situation for people who became disabled during childhood, and those disabled from birth appears to be slightly different; we have observed the same pattern of increasing satisfaction preceding a downturn in later years, but the start of this upward trend in satisfaction often seems to be delayed until early adulthood. The interview data seem to indicate that negative (indeed often extremely distressing) early experiences in institutions play a major part in this. Also, women often describe these

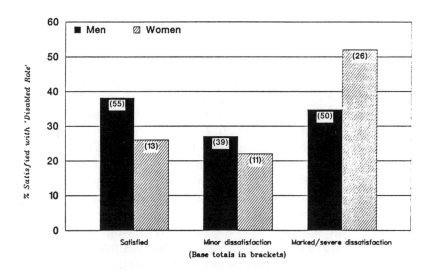

Sources: Creek *et al.*, (n=77); Zarb *et al.* 1990 (n=42);
                Zarb & Oliver, 1993 (n=75), Total = 194

Figures 2.2 Satisfaction with disabled role by gender

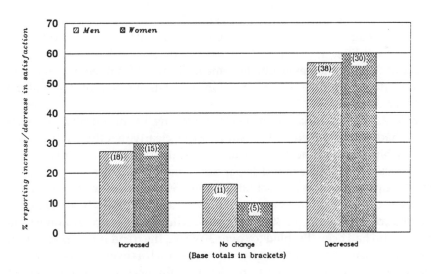

Sources: Zarb *et al.*, 1990 (n=42);
                Zarb & Oliver 1993 (n=75); Total = 117

Figure 2.3 Satisfaction with disabled role over time by gender

early experiences in noticeably more negative terms than men. Although the numbers are small, this appears to be related to women having been more likely to have lived in institutions during their childhood.

In addition to biographical interview data, quantitative satisfaction ratings were constructed in order to summarise these trends and make comparisons between groups who have been disabled for differing periods of time. The analysis focuses on people's responses to questions on how they perceive the impact of disability on their lives ('Satisfaction with the Disabled Role') and, retrospectively, whether their level of satisfaction has changed over the disability/ageing career.

Figure 2.2 shows data combined from the three studies. Nearly 70 per cent of the people interviewed were currently dissatisfied with the disabled role with over half of these expressing marked or severe dissatisfaction. Although the numbers are too small to make any definitive statements, the data also indicates that women are more dissatisfied than men.

For most of the older groups, the disability/ageing career involves changes in levels of satisfaction over time, in both a positive and a negative direction (see Figure 2.3). What we cannot tell from this data alone, however, is the pattern of such change. For example, did the individuals reporting an increase in satisfaction already have higher levels of satisfaction in the earlier part of the disability career? Or have some people who were previously dissatisfied found that their satisfaction has increased over time? Alternatively, have some people who were previously satisfied found that their satisfaction has decreased over time? Most importantly, we need to consider the impact of time and ageing on these trends.

Without comparable data on the same individuals collected at different times in their lives, it is not possible to provide clear cut answers to these questions. We can, however, obtain some indications from looking at cross-sectional data from different groups of individuals at different stages of the disability career.

Table 2.2 shows satisfaction levels, according to the number of years people had been disabled and illustrates quite clearly that there is a curved relationship with satisfaction over time; over the first 15 years or so, levels of satisfaction rise from around 25 per cent rating themselves as satisfied up to four years after onset of disability, to over 50 per cent after fifteen years. However, the proportion of people rated as satisfied when they have been disabled for between 20 to 30 years then declines noticeably. Amongst the groups who had been disabled for over 30 years, the trend is reversed – with satisfaction rising again, although not quite as much as over the first 15 years.

Although satisfaction levels are clearly influenced by the intervening impact of ageing. The data also suggests that this trend may not be entirely the same for men and women. Figure 2.3 seems to indicate that older women's satisfaction levels may be more prone to change than older men's – particularly in a downward or negative direction. As we shall see later in

**Table 2.2 Satisfaction with disabled role by
number of years disabled and gender**

(% Satisfied with Disabled Role)	Men	Women[ii]	All
0–4 years	26	-	26
5–9 years	29	-	29
10–15 years[i]	54	-	54
20–29 years	19	23	22
30–39 years	24	30	27
40+ years	50	42	46
All	30	40	33
N=	(144)	(50)	(194)

(i) The maximum length of disability in the first study was 15 years.
(ii) Women were included in the second and third studies only.

Source: Creek et al. (1987) (n=77); Zarb et al. (1990) (n=42); Zarb and Oliver (1993) (n=75).

this chapter, heightened anxiety about lack of appropriate support for older disabled women may be a crucial factor in explaining this difference.

The variations in levels of satisfaction were also found to be associated with age, although the trends were not as clear as with length of time since onset of disability. Chronological age does not seem to make very much difference up to the age of 50, with levels of satisfaction remaining fairly stable. Between the ages of 50 and 59, however, levels of satisfaction decline. As with the length of time since onset, this trend is partially reversed in the 60 plus age group.

While the general long term trend is for satisfaction to increase with length of time since onset and, to a lesser extent, with age, this trend is typically reversed between 20 and 30 years from onset of injury and between the ages of 50 and 60. This is also the same stage in the disability career when most of the physical consequences of the ageing process typically start to take effect. Thus, it seems that this 'downturn' in satisfaction is closely related to the onset of the ageing process.

Satisfaction tends to rise again after 30 years from onset and amongst the 60 plus age group, but this is certainly not universal among disabled people. Although the aggregate trends are useful as a guide to understanding changes associated with ageing, it is important to consider why satisfaction increases for some individuals and decreases for others.

Factors Influencing Changes in Levels of Satisfaction

There were numerous factors influencing levels of satisfaction – both with the 'disabled role' and the overall quality of life. First, several people perceived the intervening effects of ageing on the disability career as representing the onset of a 'second disability'. This was particularly likely amongst those who had experienced a sudden or accelerated downturn in their physical well-being. Often, this realisation would be quite sudden, being triggered by a particular problem or crisis.

Second, these triggering events were sometimes related to physical ageing, but were equally likely to be related to personal changes like a death in the family. Some people, for example, related how significant (negative) life events had seemed to trigger off a process of physical decline or a period of ill-health which, in turn, had often precipitated a decline in the overall quality of life. However, others who had experienced this kind of relatively sudden decline in their levels of satisfaction also pointed out that this is not necessarily permanent. Rather, while ageing was often experienced as a disruptive life event in itself, they were able to accommodate themselves to the practical and emotional changes in their lives. Consequently, their satisfaction subsequently improved again, although usually not to the same levels as before the effects of ageing had intervened in their lives.

Third, anxiety tended to continue to increase as people perceived their independence to be threatened either by further physical decline or, more often, by the lack of appropriate and acceptable support. Table 2.3, for example, shows that just under half of the people interviewed were dissatisfied with their overall support, with most of these expressing marked or severe dissatisfaction.

Table 2.3 Satisfaction with overall support by gender

	Men	Women	All
Satisfied	57%	42%	51%
N=	(38)	(22)	(60)
Minor dissatisfaction	12%	20%	15%
N=	(8)	(9)	(17)
Marked/Severe dissatisfaction	31%	38%	34%
N=	(21)	(19)	(40)
Base Totals	100%	100%	100%
	(67)	(50)	(117)

Source: Zarb et al. (1990) (n=42); Zarb and Oliver (1993) (n=75).

Further, anxiety about the lack of support appears to be heightened amongst older disabled women. Not only were women more likely to be dissatisfied with their overall support, but were also noticeably more likely to report increasing anxiety. Amongst those who were significantly dissatisfied with their support, for example, almost 70 per cent of women reported feeling anxious compared to under 50 per cent of men (see Figure 2.4). The factors taken into account when asking people about their overall support included

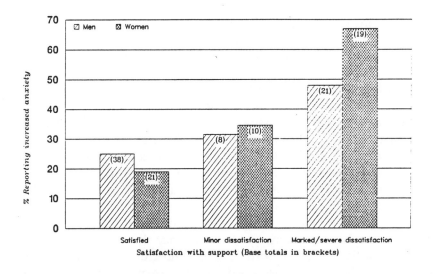

Sources: Zarb et al., 1990 (n=42); Zarb & Oliver, 1993 (n=75); Total = 117

Figure 2.4 Reported anxiety by satisfaction with overall support by gender

satisfaction with personal and domestic assistance, as well as material support in terms of housing and financial resources. It is likely, therefore, that structural gender inequalities in the distribution of such resources are reflected in older women being more anxious about the future. In the context of ageing with a disability, this manifests itself most strongly in perceptions of independence. This crucial dimension to the ageing experience is discussed in the next section of this chapter.

Fourth, several people emphasised that their physical and emotional well-being were inextricably linked, and that this had always been the case throughout their disability career. Consequently, one of the most common effects of physical decline experienced with ageing had been to reduce people's general levels of motivation. This can become a vicious circle; the drain on their emotional reserves meant that they felt less able to cope physically which, in turn, contributed to a further drain on both their emotional and physical resources.

On the other hand, some people reporting similar physical changes, did not necessarily view these in exclusively negative terms. In particular, changes like increased frustration, impatience or aggressiveness were sometimes seen as having positive benefits, particularly in avoiding depression or apathy. There were also a few people who felt that feeling apathetic had been a benefit to them in view of the problems they had experienced with ageing; the reasoning behind this view was that, developing a more 'resigned' attitude can help to avoid becoming over frustrated or anxious about problems which they felt were unavoidable in any case.

Fifth, many people felt that they were ageing faster than their able-bodied contemporaries. Others, who had not yet experienced this, nevertheless anticipated that they would be similarly effected in the future. In some cases, this knowledge had given rise to the feeling that 'time is running out'. On a practical level, this had also influenced people's plans for the future; for example, planning to retire early. Closely related to this aspect of the experience of ageing is the issue of people's perceptions of their own life expectancy. Some people anticipated, not only that they would age quicker, but also that they would die younger than their contemporaries. Interestingly, most people's attitude towards this was quite accepting; often, the anticipation of dying seemed to be less traumatic than dealing with the effects of the ageing process itself.

Finally, it is essential to locate people's attitudes to their own mortality in the context of perceptions of life expectancy throughout the disability career. In particular, it is important to remember that, at the time many of the people in these studies became disabled, life expectancy for people with various disabilities was low. Several people related how they had either been told, or simply assumed, that they would not survive adolescence, or would only live for maybe 20 or 30 years. This means they had had a heightened awareness of their own mortality more or less throughout their disability career. Clearly, this can have a significant influence on people's outlook on the future. At the same time, some people also said that, while they were aware that they may face an early death, they also felt fortunate that they had lived as long as they had. This reflects how perceptions from very early in the disability career had also influenced perceptions of the possible implications of ageing 30 or more years later.

Ageing and Independence

Many people in both of the ageing studies expressed significant concerns about independence, which they saw as being threatened by physical and/or personal changes they had experienced, or anticipated experiencing as they grew older. In some cases, this only extended to personal or physical independence, but for many people ageing represented a threat to their independence in the much wider sense of losing control over how they wished to live their lives. Several people were concerned about the possibility of having to make major changes in lifestyle, such as seeking more personal assistance or changing their living arrangements. Anxiety about the possibility of having to move into institutional care was a strong influence on these perceptions, particularly for women.

A small number of people stated that they would prefer to take the option of suicide or euthanasia rather than relying on support services or moving into institutional care. Such changes simply represented an unacceptable degree of compromise with how they wished to live their lives. There were others, however, who had a more philosophical view and felt that, having extra help was probably the best way of maintaining their independence, or at least avoiding any further loss of independence. At the same time, some people also stated that they would still resist such changes in their lives for as long as they possibly could.

A few people, on the other hand, had either never placed much emphasis on independence in their lives, or, had never felt they had that much independence in the first place. Consequently, they did not necessarily perceive ageing as representing such a potential disruption to their lives as some of the others.

The most important common denominator amongst these different perceptions is whether or not changes associated with ageing are compatible with how an individual wishes to live his or her life. It is very difficult to understand the significance and meaning of ageing without close appreciation of this crucial factor. It is also essential to place these perceptions of the possible impact of ageing on independence in the context of attitudes towards independence, autonomy and responsibility developed throughout the disability career. Many people described how, over the course of the disability career their independence had improved over time; usually, this paralleled a gradual increase in their levels of satisfaction with how they coped with disability.

Many people perceived the achievement of independence (however, they defined it) to be one of the most significant features of their lives throughout the disability career. This was particularly relevant in the early years, when there was often no support or guidance available. Achieving this independence had often taken many years and certainly involved a great deal of effort. 'Independence' is not a fixed state; many people also talked about the efforts involved in maintaining their independence and how this had become harder as they grew older. Consequently, it is easy to see how the possibility of having to give up some of their independence was a source of great anxiety. The fact that some felt that loss of independence would be totally unacceptable and that death would literally be a preferable option, shows just how important this can be.

Gender and Race Dimensions to Ageing with a Disability

Although practically all the issues discussed in this chapter are of universal concern, it would be mistaken to imply that the subjective experience of ageing is the same for men and women, or for people of different races and cultures.

Gender

Both old age and disability are dimensions of experience which are fundamentally linked to gender (Arber and Ginn, 1991a; Morris, 1991). Gender is also a particularly important factor in determining whether or not individuals are supported or prevented in their attempts to live independently. The chapter has demonstrated, for example, that older disabled women have noticeably higher levels of anxiety about the lack of appropriate support as they grow older.

Because women are generally expected to take a more dependent role in society than men, disabled women face a particularly acute struggle to overcome the obstacles against them controlling their own lives, or even defining their own identities. Indeed, other studies have clearly shown that disabled women are often treated as 'invisible', not only by society in general, but even within the disability and women's movements (Morris, 1989, 1992; Lonsdale, 1990). As suggested earlier, existing structural inequalities will also have an important influence on women's experience of ageing with disability (see also Wilson, and Higgs and Victor this volume). Amongst the women participating in our research, the issue of differential financial resources was a particular concern as this had often led to enforced dependency, either on inadequate pensions or on a spouse/partner. This had also been a factor in reducing satisfaction with their quality of life generally, as well as increasing anxiety about the possibility of institutionalisation.

It is not surprising, then, that many disabled women place an even stronger emphasis on maintaining their independence in later life than men. Further, many older women (disabled or not) are also supporting others, which can increase their anxiety about the future. For example, some of the men in the studies felt sure their partners would be both willing and able to continue supporting them indefinitely, so had not considered any other possibilities. Women were more likely to question whether their partners would do the same. This is not to say that older men do not take on the role of 'carers', nor that the perceived threat to independence is only an issue for women. However, both of these issues are likely to be particularly acute for women throughout the disability career and, consequently, crucial factors shaping their experience of ageing.

Race

Practically nothing is known about the race dimension to ageing with a disability. However, what evidence there is highlights the ways in which black and Asian elders are disadvantaged (in terms of income, housing, health, and access to services). As members of a minority group they also experience the added disadvantage of racial discrimination. There is considerable evidence of unmet support needs amongst disabled black and Asian people of all ages (GLAD, 1987; Ahmad, 1988; Begum, 1992; Askham et al., this volume). Our own research has been extended to look at the race dimension to ageing with disability. Although this is still at an early stage, it is clear that many older black and Asian disabled people live in extreme isolation, their existence often unrecognised even within their own communities. In this situation, the issue of independence tends to be secondary to concerns about basic survival.

Some writers have suggested that older people from minority ethnic communities are in 'double jeopardy' (Dowd and Bengtson, 1978). Class and gender, as well as race and age, are important dimensions of inequality; the cumulative effect of these factors has led to consideration of 'triple' or 'multiple' jeopardies in describing the experience of different sub-groups, particularly within the black population (Norman, 1985). More recently, however, black and Asian people themselves have argued that this kind of conceptualisation fails to speak to their own experience (Begum, 1992; Stuart, 1992). Rather, the emphasis should be on 'simultaneous oppression' as this avoids the marginalisation of their identities and focuses more clearly on the fact that the inequalities faced by black disabled are shaped by racist, disablist and patriarchal structures at the same time.

Placing Ageing with Disability on the Policy Agenda

This chapter has focused on the subjective dimensions of, and personal responses to, ageing with a disability. Many older disabled people feel that their needs – and even their existence – has been overlooked. It is useful, therefore, to consider how these problems might begin to be addressed through raising the profile of ageing with disability on the social policy agenda.

First, there is clearly a need to raise sensitivity and awareness amongst service professionals about both the objective needs and personal priorities of people who are ageing with a disability. Also, how these may differ from other older people whom they are more used to working with. This is particularly important in the context of attitudes towards independence. The struggle to maintain independence throughout their lives often makes the potential threat to independence associated with ageing even more acute for older disabled people than other groups in the ageing population (most of whom will not have to consider these issues until much later on).

Second, the experience of living with disability for most of their lives means that people in this sub-group of the ageing population are typically very self-reliant. Also, as a result of their experience, they are fairly expert in defining their own needs. Up to now, however, older disabled people's own expertise has not been utilised as a positive resource in the development of new models of service delivery. For example, older disabled people often find themselves in conflict with the medical profession over defining the nature of the physical problems and changes they experience with ageing (Zarb, 1992). Consequently, they face obstacles to obtaining the kind of health services they believe they need. These conflicts are largely due to the medical profession's lack of knowledge about the long-term effects of physical disability and, at the same time, their refusal to recognise the value of disabled people's own expertise. This problem is compounded by a very narrow view of rehabilitation which largely fails to take account of longer-term needs and, in particular, the fluctuating balance between health care and social support over the life course.

Third, people who are ageing with a disability often fall through the net of existing service provision. This is partly due to the inadequacy of disability services in general, but is also related to the way in which services are organised, that is, either services for 'younger disabled' or services for 'older people/over 65s'. As people who are ageing with disability do not fit neatly into either of these groups, their needs are often overlooked. This is reflected in the very low take-up of most community services by the people in our research. There is also the added dimension that, because of lack of knowledge and understanding about ageing with disability, existing services and welfare provision in general fail to meet the needs of this group even when an attempt is made to do so.

Fourth, the research also highlights that people's support needs do not remain constant over time. This not only has implications for strategic planning of services but also for the way in which individual assessments of need are made by service agencies (both health and social services). Existing models of assessment and case management do not address this crucial aspect of needs except in a very superficial way. Simply reviewing an individual's needs from time to time is unlikely to solve the problem. A much more effective approach would be for services to be organised in such a way as to provide continuity of support, whatever changes people may experience. Rather than waiting until an individual experiences a problem or crisis, possible problems and changes which may be experienced with ageing should be anticipated in advance and contingencies for dealing with these built into assessment procedures.

These general problems have implications for the full range of older disabled people's support needs. For example, there are very few living alternatives available apart from institutional care, which is totally unacceptable to many older disabled people. There are also obstacles to even the limited alternatives which are available (for example, sheltered accommodation) created by false assumptions about older disabled people's willingness or ability to live independently.

Another specific problem is that existing benefit and pension arrangements are too inflexible to take account of changing needs and circumstances. In particular, there is no recognition of the fact that, for many people, physical impairment itself is an increasingly changeable state. In conjunction with other personal and practical changes associated with ageing, this means that older disabled people will often incur additional expenses in order to maintain their independence. No extra provision is made for these expenses over and above existing disability related allowances. Consequently, most people either have to use their own financial reserves (if they have any), or go without essential supportive resources.

In conclusion, the experiences highlighted in this chapter clearly call for a more creative approach to developing services for older disabled people (Zarb, 1991). They also throw into sharp relief many of the problems faced by older people generally. As the population continues to age, the need to address these problems will become increasingly urgent. Older disabled people may have been forgotten, but their problems will not go away.

CHAPTER 3

Money and Independence in Old Age

Gail Wilson

This chapter concentrates on the material aspects of independence and autonomy in old age. It deals with exchanges and reciprocities as they relate to cash and to identifiable goods and services. The important part that emotional reciprocity, altruism and the need to serve play in the interdependencies of later life must be considered as a separate issue. Similarly a discussion focusing on independence and autonomy does not imply that interdependence is not equally important for the well being of elderly people (see McLaughlin, 1991; 1992). While *mutual* interdependence may carry no threat to individuality and self-respect, *one sided* or unreciprocated dependency very easily can. It follows that the ability to reciprocate help or assistance in old age is very important, but such reciprocity usually demands either material or emotional resources.

Access to resources in old age is pre-eminently a life course issue. The amount of money available to men and women after retirement is closely related to their income during the rest of their lives. While we may all expect to be poorer when we retire, old age is not the great financial leveller it is often assumed to be. Indeed to quote Stearns 'it would be tempting to see aging, like death, as one of those basic human phenomena which cut across class lines... But in modern society one of the main functions of social class has been to prepare a differential response to aging' (1977 p.42). The same could also be said of gender. Men in old age are less likely to have very low incomes than women.

The way elderly men and women use money, the way they think about it, and the meanings they attribute to it are influenced by past experience. Any consideration of the ways in which money is related to independence and autonomy in old age needs to consider the interactions of class and gender with other features of the life course. However, more research is needed on gender in old age (Arber and Ginn, 1991a) before clear gender distinctions can be drawn. One reason for this is that the views of women on money are rarely expressed. Married women's views tend to be subsumed under men's views and single women are rarely asked. Another reason is that gender distinctions alter in old age as men lose the gendered identity which comes from paid work and women (sometimes) gain financial and decision making power (see Bennett and Morgan, this volume).

Research is needed which is specifically directed at the hidden nature of women's experience and the ways in which it can be put into words.

Independence and Autonomy

The theory of structured dependency (Phillipson, 1982; Townsend, 1981; 1986; Walker, 1980) suggests that if we interpret independence as the ability to make and implement choices, there are many areas where older people in our society have very little independence. A relatively fixed retirement age, low incomes, fear of forced institutionalisation and the widespread stereotype of old age as a time of burdensome decrepitude all conspire to make ageing and dependency seem inseparable.

There are two main objections to seeing old age in such negative terms. First, structured dependency can be exaggerated (Johnson, 1988; Dant et al., 1988; Wilson, 1991a) and second, those old people whose incomes and savings put them significantly above the poverty line operate within different structures. Many aspects of structured dependency do not apply to them. However they are a limited group and likely to remain so. Although around half of all those reaching retirement age now have some occupational pension entitlement, Bosanquet et al. (1990) have calculated that the proportion of retired people with incomes above the national average is unlikely to rise above 20 per cent during the next twenty years. As at present, the best off will be concentrated among the newly retired young elderly who have good occupational pensions (Arber and Ginn, 1991a). Women and the very old will have lower incomes in the future, as they do today. However, even for the majority who have low incomes, structured dependency is not necessarily experienced as helplessness and incapacity.

An understanding of the ways in which money can reduce structured dependency needs a more exact definition of independence. The aims of this research were first, to distinguish between independence and autonomy, second, to relate independence to reciprocity and third, to relate independence and autonomy to quality of life. The data refers only to people over 75 – those for whom issues of independence and autonomy are most likely to be problematic.

Independence

Independence is seen in most Western societies as a major ingredient in the maintenance of self-identity and self-respect (Cicirelli, 1992). It commonly has positive and negative connotations. From a positive viewpoint independence can be defined as the ability to make choices and act on them without any extra assistance. For example, independence is associated with the ability to drive a car, to use public transport, to shop when and where one chooses, to decorate the house, or to visit friends whenever one wants. A degree of control over one's own life and an adequate income are important ingredients in determining levels of independence. Such a definition of independence is not in conflict with interdependence (McLaughlin, 1991; 1992; Howarth, this volume). Independence that enhances the quality of life almost always implies interdependencies of various kinds.

The negative use of the term independence often implies what relatives or professionals may feel is a 'pig-headed' refusal of 'necessary' services. This type of independence as Qureshi and Walker (1989) have pointed out relies on a restricted range of goals or a willingness to give up certain aspirations in exchange for remaining in control of some aspects of life. In most cases it also implies a reduction in interdependence. For example old people who have become isolated and housebound may have very little social contact indeed. A place in a day centre might, depending on the quality of the day centre, increase their chances of forming interdependent relationships. However it would also mean attendance at a fixed place at fixed hours and so a loss of control and may be refused in order to maintain independence.

It is therefore possible that a dislike of interference or control by social or health service staff or by relatives and neighbours, can result in a very restricted quality of life – something that looks to an outsider more like 'survival' than 'living'. It can be argued that independence which can only be maintained by accepting a poor quality of life (as judged by an outsider), is not a desirable goal. The corollary is not that services should be forced upon people. Service take up can be increased by well-motivated workers who respect the autonomy of their clients or patients, but there will always be some people who would rather refuse all help because they see it as of less value than their independence. A gendered manifestation of negative independence arises when frail or disabled married men, who are wholly dependent on their wives for care, refuse outside services because they wish to retain 'their independence'. In such cases the husband may feel he has retained his independence but his wife will have lost still more of her freedom of choice and capacity for independent action.

The phenomenon of willing acceptance of help which cannot be recipro-cated is most likely to occur in marriage. It is often assumed that emotional reciprocity is enough in marriage or that the duty to care over-rides normal conventions of reciprocity. Elderly married men, in particular, may take the care they receive from their wives more or less for granted and hence feel no need to reciprocate. Qureshi and Walker (1989) also found men who assumed their daughters would care for them if their wives could not. In these cases the patriarchal position of men obscures the issue of dependency and allows them to feel independent even though they receive assistance. Women on average receive less care from their husbands and it is not likely to give them the same feelings of 'independence' (Arber and Ginn, 1992).

In cases where older men or women willingly become dependent we may assume, though more research is needed, that they judge the improvement in the quality of life derived from their dependence on others to be worth any accompanying loss of independence. They willingly embrace the role of invalid or frail elder. Such people are rare – only three in the present sample.

Autonomy

Autonomy may either be treated as synonymous with independence (Cicirelli, 1992) or as a separate concept (Collopy, 1988). In the present context it is defined as different from independence and refers to the ability of older men and women to make independent choices when such choices can only be carried out with extra assistance. Autonomy, as used here, refers specifically to frail or disabled older people and is an indicator of their ability to live as they wish. It is dependent on an individual's ability to command sources of assistance which can be reciprocated as necessary and on the degree of respect which helpers accord to the wishes of the older person.

Autonomy is thus a vital concept when considering the quality of life of frail or disabled older people. First, as with independence, autonomy implies freedom from coercion by others. Second, the support needed to carry out decisions must be available as and when it is needed. Third, there must be some means of reciprocating help received. For example, people who for health reasons cannot drive a car may still be autonomous if they can afford to hire a reliable minicab or if they have a paid carer who will drive them as needed. Alternatively, they may be able to call on a relative, neighbour or volunteer to drive them, they may belong to a subsidised taxi scheme or they can ring the Dial-a-Ride service if one is provided by the local council. These options of paid help, a relative, a free or a subsidised service are not all equally conducive to autonomy. The differences between the categories of private, voluntary, informal and formal (state) aids to autonomy will be analysed below, focusing on the reciprocities they demand.

Research Methods

The research is based on interviews with old people living in 100 households in two different areas of a north London borough. People over 75 living either alone or in households with only other people over 75 were selected by the process of contacting every fifth household and asking if the residents were eligible for the study and if they would co-operate. Refusals were highest among low income households and people with very severe chronic health conditions and sensory deprivation. The resulting sample is therefore biased in favour of better off and fitter old people.

The only ethnic minorities represented were Jewish. This was first, because both areas were long established communities with little residential mobility among their older inhabitants, and second because the lower age limit of 75 excluded the great majority of ethnic elders who had not, in 1991, reached that age. The lack of ethnic elders was unfortunate because previous work has shown that different ethnic groups have different attitudes to money (Wilson, 1987a; 1987b; Thorogood, 1987), so the present analysis cannot be taken as relevant to all groups of the population.

The two areas sampled were chosen because they differed in home ownership and in social class, with the northern area being very much poorer than the southern area. This provided the opportunity to look at the impact of income levels over a wide range – from a single woman living on royalties who was able to pay £240 a week for a live in carer, to another who felt well off for the first time in her life because a volunteer community worker had encouraged her to claim income support on top of her very small pension.

Any enquiry into sources of reciprocity needs to consider income levels but researching money is not easy, especially among people of older generations. In the past money was rarely mentioned in polite conversation. Even now personal discussions of money, like sex, are still thought to be impolite by sections of the population. Old people are often very unwilling to talk about money for this reason. In addition to the general view of money as 'not quite nice' there is also the added influence of a morality which opposes the material to the spiritual and very much favours spiritual riches. This is illustrated not only in Christian teaching but also is such sayings as 'Money does not bring happiness', 'Money cannot buy love' or 'Better love in a garret than marry a millionaire'.

People over 75 belong to a generation when these attitudes were stronger than they are today. When asked what makes for a happy old age they rarely mention money directly and very few even mention it indirectly. The nearest direct mention in the conversations reported in this research came from a former banker who said 'if you've had a healthy upbringing then you stand a much better chance of living to a good age. Other people that live in bad conditions, the poor, they don't really stand a chance do they'. And yet money is clearly a key issue in the descriptions of daily life given by older people. It may even be freely discussed in relation to other areas of living, like rising prices, where there is less moral stigma attached to complaint.

Interviews were tape recorded and references to money and to material aspects of life, since such references were often a proxy for talking about money, were collated and analyzed. The aim of this chapter is to look in detail at different aspects of money in old age.

Autonomy in Relation to Sources of Assistance

The private market and autonomy

Private assistance in its simplest form is a matter of having the cash to buy an aid or a service which will increase independence or autonomy. In most cases old people do not mention the private sector as a source of help. When well off older women refer to 'my help', meaning their cleaner, they are not implying dependence. The goods and services bought are classified simply as another form of consumption and taken for granted. This is important because 'help' implies need and therefore possible dependence, whereas consumption does not. Consumption involves exchange of money for goods and services based on a known tariff. It is not normally conceptualised in terms of 'reciprocity'. The exchange is simple and unproblematic as long as the money and the service are available.

For some the ability to buy private services will be a way of remaining in control of certain areas of their lives and of guaranteeing their autonomy. For example one disabled elderly woman in the sample preferred to change her resident carer every fortnight because she felt that otherwise the carer would take her over. Others may find private services too impersonal.

The private market is not a panacea because, even assuming adequate income, a service or item may not be available. For example, some types of service may be unobtainable at almost any price (washer women, for example, no longer exist although a home help may do some washing and ironing). In areas where private services do not operate because they cannot at present make a profit, contracts from social service departments (Department of Health, 1989) are intended to help them set up after 1993. In theory this will increase choice for those well off older people who can afford to buy their own domiciliary care.

However private domiciliary care is also likely to lead to problems of abuse and exploitation, as have occurred in private residential care (Wagner, 1988). The risks will be greater if profits are squeezed and standards are driven down. A poorly regulated private sector can easily result in abuse. In the present survey there were three cases of very frail old people being cheated or frightened by private staff. The growth of such abuses will be hard to detect and very hard to prevent.

Other constraints on the use of private services may be cultural and the result of lifelong habits of economy. As one relatively well off widower said:

> When you've worked hard, I've worked hard all my life, you can't just, you know fritter it away. I mean I'd never think of getting a taxi if there's a bus. You know, things like that. Although I could if I wanted to, you know.

The majority of older men and women who are limited to a state pension or income support will not be able to afford more than the occasional private service. Vouchers given by central or local government to those who need them are the logical concomitant of an extension of private care. Any expansion of the private sector without a voucher system will increase the already great inequalities in old age.

Informal help and autonomy

Informal support systems are subject to different constraints from market transactions. Informal help may confer a degree of autonomy, but it is unlikely to be as effective as the ability to pay for a service. The taxi driver, or the launderette which delivers clean washing, are part of the economic system and are paid in money. However the services of family and friends must usually be repaid in different ways and feelings of obligation may build up if help cannot be reciprocated. Money can only be used in certain circumstances, such as to pay for petrol or phone calls. Emotional reciprocity, or the links of affection which bind families together, should, ideally, suffice in the family context, but they are likely to be replaced by duty if too much assistance is demanded (Ungerson, 1983).

Problems arise because most transactions in the informal care system are governed by a set of fully understood but highly negotiable rules. It is widely accepted that children should care for their parents (Finch, 1989; Qureshi and Walker, 1989). However, this duty is not all-pervading and does not necessarily take priority over other duties. Such caring is rarely something which an elderly parent can take for granted. It follows, first, that most children do have some choice over how much they will do for their parents and second, that what they do results in the build up of obligations which need to be reciprocated. The same is true for other relatives and friends, though as mentioned above, care by spouses is more likely to be taken for granted.

Children may think of themselves as reciprocating for care they have received in the past and may see no reason why their parents should worry about reciprocity (Qureshi and Walker, 1989; Finch, 1989). This view may occasionally be shared by elderly parents themselves, particularly if they are men who have been used to care by female relatives. However, such attitudes were very uncommon in North London, although Qureshi, working in Sheffield, did find people who took their children for granted (Qureshi and Walker, 1989). The difference may be regional or it may arise from the way the study populations were selected. The Sheffield sample was of old people with carers while the North London sample was of people over 75 living alone or with others in the same age group. It therefore seems likely that the great majority of old people do see the need to reciprocate informally provided help.

It is easier for active old people to provide reciprocal services like baby sitting, housework, DIY, or car driving for the younger generation. The problem for the very old who have functional disabilities is that their ability to reciprocate can be limited. This is another version of the inverse care law (Tudor-Hart, 1971): those who most need care are least likely to be able to get it in a way that enables them to increase their autonomy because of their limited ability to reciprocate.

The older people interviewed stated clearly that they did not like to impose on their relatives or burden them. As one older woman with a large and close family said:

I don't think I would want to go and live with a child. I don't think I would want that. I think that then you become a nuisance and a burden and you are not loved so much because you are just these things.

Some older people in the sample were dependent on their children, but it is important to understand that they felt the choice was not free and that in coming to rely on informal help they either had to ration the demands they made, or they were rationed by their informal helpers. The extreme position, those who live in the household of their informal helpers, has been found by Day (1985) in her Sydney study to leave old people with the least independence and the lowest morale.

Dependence on informal help may therefore reduce autonomy greatly if services cannot be reciprocated in some way. In the sample some of the better off had incomes which would have allowed them to pay their informal helpers. However, since these services are performed out of love or duty or neighbourliness, they are usually felt to be devalued if they are paid for (Ungerson, 1983). Long term reciprocity via inheritance has traditionally been one way in which those with property could repay their carers. The threat of disinheritance was also a way of constraining the younger generation to respect the dignity and wishes of the old. Such thoughts were not voiced by any of the present sample. In low income working class families payment was more acceptable, though certainly not the norm, but paying for services when income was already low could mean that expenditure on necessities had to be reduced.

State help and autonomy

Health and social services can be thought of as a just reward for a life time of citizenship, taxpaying and national insurance contributions. The state pension was almost always seen as a reward for a life time of work and contributions. However state services, which might contribute to independence and autonomy, are not usually viewed so unproblematically. The absence of stigma in consulting a general practitioner was the nearest that most old people approached to this view of the reciprocities involved in state provided services.

Services provided by the local authority were more likely to be seen as charity and demeaning. It is hard to tell how far this perception is a legacy from the past when the workhouse still existed and how far it is an accurate reflection of the way being a client is experienced by old people. The study population included only one person who appeared to be completely unambivalent about state services. She saw welfare in old age as a right. It is perhaps significant that she was an 85 year old Danish woman who felt that the Danish welfare state was much better than the English, which she saw as failing to provide adequately for her and all other old people. She hoped to move to Denmark and to benefit from the higher standards over there. Her complaint was about the poor quality of the British services and their inability to meet user needs for autonomy. Other respondents (particularly in the poorer area) felt the services had a duty to search out those in need and offer assistance, but that asking was demeaning.

It did appear that the local state-provided services had very little ability to increase either independence or autonomy. The inflexibilities associated with a rationed service were possibly responsible. One woman who had had a stroke mentioned that Dial-a-Ride had never been able to pick her up when she wanted and she had given up phoning. Similarly, community service staff who arrived without appointment or had to be waited in for all day long can only be seen as a restriction on independence not an aid to autonomy.

As Smith (1980) has pointed out, clients are assessed for a service and the next stage is that clients or patients have to fit in with that service. As a result their independence may be correspondingly limited. In these circumstances it is hardly surprising that many old people see becoming a client or a community health service patient as a signal that independence has been lost and dependency has set in (S. Sainsbury, personal communication). Badly managed and rigid state services have been rightly identified as a major component of structured dependency (Townsend, 1981).

The National Health and Community Care Act 1990 is intended to improve state services in ways that will increase client autonomy. Decisions about services will, in theory, be led by client needs not by service availability (Department of Health, 1989). However, as Osborne (1991) has pointed out, resource constraints, multiple aims and organisational imperatives will make such an outcome very difficult to achieve. If the intentions of the Act are fulfilled, there will be more private services available. Social Service Departments will contract with private care agencies to provide flexible, client-oriented services. However, the main weakness of this method of service delivery, in terms of client autonomy, is that the council is the customer and has the market power, not the client, who may well feel no more autonomous than at present.

Despite the limitations outlined above there is no reason in principle, why state provided services should not increase autonomy. The essential point is that they should be provided in ways that respect the autonomy of the users (clients or patients). Successfully provided state services are an example of third party reciprocity. Paid professionals are assumed to be doing a job and hence to be reciprocated via the market. Such services were often mentioned as being preferable to help from family if the burden of dependence grew too great.

Voluntary Sector Services

The activities of the voluntary sector are so varied that it is impossible to generalise about its ability to assist older men and women. In the present sample two cases of paid volunteers were particularly successful in providing acceptable additions to autonomy. They were seen as friends and neighbours but such emotional reciprocity was reinforced by Council payment to the volunteers.

The quality of life for many was improved by attendance at voluntary clubs. One in the prosperous southern area also provided a quick and relatively frequent chiropody service which was better than the local NHS provision. The cost of club subscriptions were low but reinforced feelings of self- help and independence. The clubs were not seen as charities.

Summary

It follows from this research that while autonomy is often best secured through the ability to pay for services, the services need to be available and of good quality. This is more likely to be the case in areas where there are large concentrations of relatively well off older people.

It is not possible to say whether informal services are more helpful in assuring autonomy that those provided by the state. In each case so much depends on the quality of the service, either in terms of the quality of the caring relationship or of the standard and variety of state services. In rare cases when it is possible for the very old to reciprocate informal services by indirect payment or in some other way, the advantages of flexibility and personal commitment will almost certainly outweigh the benefits offered by the private sector. On the other hand well managed state services, where staff morale is high, may reach more people in need than the private sector and increase autonomy by demanding less reciprocity than informal care. Voluntary services can have the same effect but their coverage is very limited compared to state health and social services.

Types of Payment

The way a service is paid for may be important in deciding how far it is an aid to autonomy and how far it builds up obligations which perhaps cannot be reciprocated. Types of payment can be divided into direct payment and indirect. Directly bought services are mostly available in the private sector but an increasing number of state and voluntary organisations charge for services and some transactions with neighbours or relatives can be directly paid for. The disadvantage of directly bought services is that a certain level of income is essential if they are to aid independence and particularly if they are to aid autonomy. At low income levels the use of one private service, such as chiropody, hairdressing or window cleaning, may mean that something else has to be foregone. Independence may be maintained but at the same time the quality of life may suffer.

Direct payments in the private sector are charged at the market rate. This is not necessarily so in the state sector and apparently unheard of in the informal sector. In the rare cases where relatives were paid directly, the price was unlikely to be anything near the market rate. For example the cost of the petrol might be the price of a lift to hospital. Council services may be free for those on state income support but increasingly all others will pay, though usually at less than the market price. Counties such as Kent bill service receivers indicating the proportion of the cost paid for by the council. This practice can be seen as a way of indicating to older people that they are still recipients of charity and should not think that because they pay a contribution they have any right to demand good service or challenge standards.

Indirectly bought services are characterised by the transfer of money but not for the specific service performed. The payment is nominally for another purpose. For example, one man had all his meals cooked by his next door neighbour. He made no payment for the meals but when the gas and electricity bills arrived he put both sets together and paid half. Since his bill was always smaller than his neighbour's he ended up paying a share of her costs (see Howarth, this volume). Similarly there were a number of elderly women who gave very large gifts at Christmas and other socially accepted occasions in return for a range of driving and cleaning jobs done by their relatives. In such circumstances neighbourliness or love can continue as moneyless transactions but indirect reciprocity via a cash transaction allows the service to be reciprocated and hence autonomy can be maintained. In other words any feelings of guilt or obligation are discharged and the person in need can continue to ask for help.

Money as a Resource

Money and day to day living

While it may be true that the quality of life in old age is closely related to the amount of money available, income in old age cannot be simply equated with a specific standard of living. There are often powerful normative or cultural constraints on spending by old people. Women who have brought up families on a low income often have a life-long habit of saving and find it hard to stop. Rather than spending on themselves they may give money to their children and grandchildren. Others in this sample, particularly men, may feel insecure if their savings begin to fall. They may fail to raise the housekeeping money they give to their wives to keep pace with growing needs. For example one wife with increasing mobility problems needed transport to and from the shops but was struggling to walk, partly because she did not want to hire a car for such a short distance, but mainly because she could not afford it on a housekeeping allowance that had not risen recently. Another husband did not increase the money he gave his wife although she had had to employ a cleaner since a recent accident. Such women do not like to ask their husbands for money and so their autonomy suffers, though their independence, negatively defined, is maintained.

In the same way, both men and women may pride themselves on having very simple needs, or refuse to spend on things they would once have bought because the prices are so high (see below). Others want to leave money and possessions to their children or other inheritors. Many, and particularly working class men and women, feel the need to leave at least £1,000 (in 1991) to pay for their funeral. On the supply side the things that old people would like to spend money on may no longer be available, or the shops that they can reach may not stock the things they want.

Spending less than current income and so having a lower standard of living than necessary is associated with income level. It is less common among working class elders who are often forced by state pension levels to live close to subsistence or even below. The decision to spend less and save more may be a manifestation of independence but in so far as money is needed to maintain autonomy, it is likely to indicate reduced autonomy and restricted goals.

Income level is also the main determinant of the ability to spend more than current income. Only the rich have large amounts of capital which they can run down on the assumption that they will die before it is exhausted. In the present sample those doing so were elderly women who had inherited capital from husbands or other relatives. Older people who are less well off can only spend more than their income if they have frequent presents of cash from family or friends. It seems very uncommon for old people to rely on such continuous financial assistance from family for their day to day living expenses and there were none reported in this sample, although many accepted occasional one-off gifts.

Income, quality of life, independence and autonomy are closely linked. The maintenance of autonomy for frail old people very often depends on how much they can spend. They may have to spend more than current income at certain times if they are to retain a measure of autonomy. For example, if a person with no available relatives is incapacitated by a fall the alternatives may be to enter a home (usually seen as a loss of autonomy if enforced by a physical condition), or to pay for a resident carer until mobility returns. In such conditions spending more than current income may be the only way to maintain autonomy.

Money and time

The passage of time is a key issue in relation to money in old age. A fixed pension or income from investments cannot give the same security to old people as earned income. Earnings usually keep pace with inflation. The long run trend over this century has been for earnings to rise faster than prices, so those in paid work become more prosperous and those outside the labour market fall behind. Until 1982 the British state retirement pension was linked to earnings and, although still low by European standards, it had risen faster than average wages as a result of a number of above average increments. As a result the old were to some extent able to take part in the general growth in national prosperity, despite starting from the very low base set by the Beveridge reforms in 1948. Since 1982 this process has been reversed because increases in state pensions are no longer linked to changes in average earnings, but now move with prices. The old have consequently become relatively poorer, even though in theory they can still maintain the same absolute standard of living. Time therefore means growing relative poverty for state pensioners.

In the occupational pension sector the situation is sometimes worse since very few private sector occupational pensions are inflation proofed. Their value therefore falls, faster or slower according to the rate of inflation. Another disadvantage of occupational pension schemes is that they do not always pay benefits to widows. The death of a husband could result in a sharp drop in income. However it is equally true that the transition from a small housekeeping allowance to income support can sometimes mean increased financial well- being for a widow.

The idea that money can bring security and independence in old age has a hollow ring for many elderly people who were encouraged to save or to rely on their husbands for a pension. Even those without substantial savings can find the effects of inflation on prices very disturbing and upsetting. Things that they could afford in mid-life become impossible to buy, for example, the price of tobacco is a common source of complaint. Women, who have usually spent a life time being more conscious of changes in day-to-day prices than men, are often protected from the worst feelings of insecurity related to price rises. They may however refuse to buy things which they consider have become too expensive. Old people who do not shop regularly – perhaps because they have been institutionalised – may be too shocked by changes in prices to spend what money they have (R. Bland, personal communication).

A final point about the changed relationship between money and time in old age arises out of the special needs of elderly people. 'Time is money' is a common statement and it is often assumed that elderly people have time on their hands. However by the age of 75 or 80, old people are often forced to do a wide range of things more slowly. Also the use of time to cut down on expenditure involves activities such as shopping around for bargains, buying fresh rather than processed food and going on holiday in cheap periods. Inability to use public transport, problems with cooking or with health can mean that these options are more limited than they appear to be. Very often time is not money in advanced old age and hence it can make no contribution to independence or autonomy.

Money and Property

Home ownership

Like income and savings in old age property ownership tends to be a legacy of working life. Widows may inherit but otherwise few people become home owners for the first time in old age, so housing tenure is a reflection of life long income. However tenure is not always a good indicator of current income. As Means (1988) has shown a house can become a burden to elderly owner occupiers. Many are 'housing rich and income poor'.

Although living at home is so closely associated in the popular mind with independence, caution is needed in equating the two. 'Staying put' may be an indication of independence, in the sense of reduced goals, but it may offer little in the way of autonomy. A poor quality of life may be the price of such independence unless income is adequate. Otherwise staying at home can reduce autonomy just because there is no money to make alterations to an unsuitable home or because the maintenance of home and garden mean that other activities have to be given up. Council and housing association tenants have the advantage that their internal decorating and external maintenance should at least be done regularly (though much depends on the housing authority).

The one person in the sample who had moved from being an owner occupier to a council tenant was very content with the change, and a disabled private tenant saw the advantages of her situation:

> You've got to be a good handyman to own, otherwise you're paying out all the time, while all I do is ring up the landlord. I can't do things. I find that my neighbours [owner occupiers] who can do things spend their time doing things.

These two cases indicate the importance of a good landlord in maintaining autonomy. Home ownership is not intrinsically an aid to independence or autonomy in old age. In the sample it was associated with greater independence but apparently only because homeowners in general had more money and better health than tenants.

In theory, owner occupiers have much greater flexibility than tenants because they can trade down to a smaller house and keep the difference in price, or they can use their property for a home and income scheme. Such schemes allow a person of a certain age (usually older for a women) to treat the value of their house either as capital or as security on a loan and to receive a monthly income from the interest. Even when interest rates and property values were high such schemes offered poor value for money unless a person could be sure to die within a few years. None were reported in the sample.

The move to a smaller house had usually occurred in early retirement, if at all, and it was not clear how far the benefits were still being felt by couples who were over 75. On the other hand widowed owner occupiers did appear to benefit from a move to smaller accommodation.

Car ownership

Car ownership in old age is strongly linked to current income. It was clear from the interviews that it is not possible to run a car on an income which is at or near state pension level. Cars that were acquired during years in paid work eventually cost too much to repair or replace, or simply became too expensive to run on a declining income. A part time job, a good occupational pension or substantial savings did make car ownership a possibility, particularly as running costs were relatively low when the car was only used for short journeys.

There was no doubt that, in the eyes of car owners and former owners, the car was the most important item contributing to their independence. Most were men and those who had given up the car regretted it intensely. Their ability to act autonomously in simple matters like going to the shops, helping others, or getting the washing done was dependent on the car. As one who was still in part time work said he 'would rather be dead than not have the car'.

Men who were less well off gave up their cars because of money problems. The rich were more likely to give up for health reasons. Women, who in the older generation were less likely to drive, were to some extent cushioned from this loss since most had always had less autonomy than men. Women whose husbands had been car owners did however feel the loss in material terms, as a drop in their standard of living, when spontaneous trips to the countryside or to visit friends and relatives were no longer possible. The few married women and single women who still drove were adamant that they would not give up until they were forced to. It is a paradox that when a car is most needed it is most likely to have to be given up.

There are no good substitutes for a car at present, which is the main reason why it is so crucial for the maintenance of independence and autonomy. Even the best bus service which is quite regular, stops anywhere on request and passes close to home, is of little use to those who cannot physically get on and off a bus. Cars were hired by men and women in all income groups but were expensive. Hiring was certainly no substitute for owning a car because drivers did not necessarily come on time and they were not there for the return journey. The exception was a woman who joined with her 70-year-old daughter to hire a car which waited for them while they went round the supermarket. Even she had had to change her car firm when one had proved unreliable.

Women, who were more likely to be physically disabled than men and less likely to have been drivers, appeared to be more likely to hire cars. In this sense their sources of autonomy were increased but they suffered from the poor reliability of car hire firms or taxis and, if their incomes were low, from the cost.

Consumer durables

Ownership of consumer durables was more common but showed a similar pattern to cars. Lack of money could mean that washing machines would not be replaced when they broke down, unless relatives could offer them as gifts. The more modern household appliances like microwave ovens and videos were also much more likely to be gifts than to have been bought, though the best off, who continued to consume almost as before they retired, did buy these things for themselves as and when they were needed. However many who had no income other than a state pension found it hard to raise lump sums from their own resources and did not wish to use hire purchase.

It is questionable how far modern consumer durables raise the standard of living of old people. Some, such as microwaves, can contribute directly to the autonomy of men and women who find it difficult to cook, but often only if they can afford to buy ready prepared meals as well. Men, having relatively higher incomes and less resistance to ready prepared food (see chapter by Howarth), appeared more likely to take full advantage of microwave technology. However it was not clear how far women, who often insisted that they kept to the old ways, were giving a publicly acceptable account (Cornwell, 1984) which played down their use of modern technologies in the home.

Many of the new aids to an autonomous life style are designed with younger age groups in mind and may be hard for older people to use. For example, washing machines speed up washing but assume that the user is capable of hanging out the clothes, ironing or simply folding sheets. A partially disabled person may be better served by a laundry, if they can afford it at £7 a week (in 1991) for linen only, or a launderette that delivers, than by the presumed autonomy that comes from a washing machine.

Money and power

Financial power, like home ownership, is something that most people acquire before retirement or not at all. It is also an attribute that is mainly associated with masculinity in our society. Older men whose life courses have given them that power may retain it even in later life. Some, however, lose it if their savings are not big enough or if their occupational pensions are not index linked.

In contrast, those widows who have combined a lifetime of limited spending on their personal needs with the inheritance of a good occupational pension or other source of income will find that they have more financial power in later life than at any other time. Sometimes, particularly if widowed early, they are able to take advantage of this accretion of power. Others, particularly if widowed in advanced old age, may find that long experience of economic dependency on their husbands, leaves them with little confidence in financial matters and no will to express their independence.

In lower income groups, married women may find that the real value of their income is higher than it was in earlier life. Their husbands continue to give them housekeeping but they are at the same time drawing a pension of their own, or their share of the state pension for a couple, and have reduced household responsibilities and so need to spend less on essentials. This phenomenon was first noted by Townsend (1962).

In this study there is evidence that a life time of financial power is advantageous because it builds up expectations of autonomy and the habit of buying goods and services as they are needed. This is undoubtedly important when services become necessary, for example, those who have always employed gardeners will go on doing so. Others, to whom the idea and the amount of money are unthinkable, may apply for residential care – often thought of as the end of all independence and autonomy – when their hedges and lawns become unmanageable.

The possession of money during the life course can therefore result in attitudes which increase autonomy in old age but such an outcome is not inevitable. The relative prices of goods and services have changed dramatically over the life times of people who are now over seventy five. Goods are now relatively cheap, whereas services have become very much more expensive as wages have risen. Someone to do the washing, a service that was common in the 1930s when labour was cheap but washing machines were an inefficient luxury, would do more for the autonomy of many old people than the most modern washing machine. A launderette that will deliver the washed and dried clothes might be the ideal solution for many older people.

Given these massive changes in the availability and prices of services, it is not surprising that some of the people who were interviewed expressed the view that a lifetime of having money left people ill-equipped to cope with the rigours of old age. A number of women pointed out that a life of hard work and self-reliance was useful in old age. Those who had always relied on servants, or delivery services were often seen as less able to cope.

Money and pride

Pride combined with the reluctance to talk about money, makes it very difficult to discuss poverty without giving offence in most interviews with old people. Elderly people who live on or near the state pension level, nearly always say that they can manage on what they have got. In cash value their pensions are very much higher than the money they earned or the pensions their parents had. While they are aware that inflation has reduced the real value of their pensions the money value may still seem high.

A life time of managing on a low income often leaves a legacy of unwillingness to ask for benefits, or to accept help that was formerly associated with pauperism or charity. Pride may therefore lead to pensioners saying they can manage on their incomes, but in this research there was no case of a low income respondent whose interview did not contain some instance of hardship or reduction in living standards. 'Managing' is therefore a very relative term in old age and it can conceal wide variations in degrees of poverty.

Unwillingness to acknowledge lack of money is often put down to independence, but it is a manifestation of independence that means accepting limited goals in place of asking for help. As a result autonomy is restricted because the standard of living is lower than if all benefits were claimed and all useful free or subsidised services accepted. It is unclear how far this type of independence is freely chosen and how far it is the result of the social structuring of preferences over the life course. It is certainly very common among people over 75 in Britain in the 1990s.

Conclusion

Money is of vital importance to successful ageing, even though few elders feel free to say so. In terms of maintaining independence and autonomy, the main contribution made by money is in giving access to a decent standard of living. This is true even though many old people are able to maintain their self-respect and independence on less money than younger generations might think necessary.

However if old people become disabled or frail the importance of money in maintaining autonomy becomes very much more salient. Autonomy can only be maintained if help is available and is offered in ways that respect the wishes of the recipient and do not create one sided obligations. Autonomy demands either that help is reciprocated in cash or in other material exchanges such as services, or that affective ties are strong enough for an imbalance in material reciprocities to be overlooked. The alternative is independence in the negative sense which means reducing goals and living standards so that help is no longer felt to be needed.

It is difficult to maintain autonomy if services cannot be obtained via the private market. Informal assistance is likely to build up obligations and in any case may well be rationed by the helpers. State services may be seen as charity and may be designed so that the client fits the service rather than as an aid to client autonomy.

When informal assistance can be fully reciprocated the quality of life obtained and the maintenance of autonomy are likely to be highest. This desirable outcome is usually only possible in exceptional circumstances when informal help can be paid for indirectly and is reciprocated emotionally.

Access to money, and the desirable attributes that go with it, such as car ownership and the power to buy services as they are needed, depends on life history rather than any special circumstances related to old age. All the older people interviewed could 'manage' on their incomes. However, the degree to which they could support their independence and autonomy if health failed or disabilities increased was affected by life time earnings, gender and class as well as individual preferences and capabilities.

Growing reliance on private services, which seems certain to occur following the implementation of the NHS and Community Care Act 1990, means that differentials in the ability to maintain independence and autonomy in old age between men and women and rich and poor will increase.

Acknowledgement

My thanks go to Hilary Gavilan and Glennys Howarth for comments and insights and to the Nuffield Foundation for financing the research on which this paper is based.

CHAPTER 4

Food Consumption, Social Roles and Personal Identity

Glennys Howarth

This chapter focuses on the patterns of food consumption of widowed people over 75 years old. Bereavement research has shown that death of a spouse is likely to have a profound effect on the survivor (Bowlby, 1981; Marris, 1986; Parkes, 1972; Stroebe and Stroebe, 1987). In old age the transformation from a two-person to a one-person household induces fundamental changes in domestic organisation. These are inevitably reflected in food related behaviour. Those who have always been single differ from the widowed in that, although ill-health may affect food related behaviour, there is usually no crisis (similar to loss of spouse) which forces them to question dietary behaviour in later life.

Food choice is a complex and multi-determined process influenced by culture and tradition, environment, gender, health, income, social relationships and stage in the life course. It is important for two reasons. First, research has shown that people believe diet to be a central factor in maintaining good health (Pill, 1983; Calnan, 1987). Second, and of greater concern here, the structure and content of meals and food preparation have symbolic significance (Twigg, 1983; Murcott, 1983). By examining the expressed food preferences of bereaved elderly people it is possible to discern something of the belief systems to which they adhere in respect of food. Exploring continuities and change reveals critical information about the strategies they employ as they strive to maintain familiar practices or venture into new ones.

Food consumption is a prerequisite for human existence and yet one which is subjected to a huge variety of cultural processes and meanings (Levi-Strauss, 1966). Food clearly has symbolic relevance and the way in which consumption is organised reveals much about social relations within the home (Charles and Kerr, 1988; Douglas and Nicod, 1974). Questions about who does the shopping; who prepares and cooks the food; which foodstuffs are highly valued; and how are meals structured, impart much information about social relationships, stage in the life course, power and autonomy within families, and the influence of tradition and culture in food related behaviour.

In order to understand the impact of bereavement on the eating habits of very old people it is first necessary to consider the importance of marriage and the effect of bereavement on personal identity and social meaning. An examination of some of the cultural influences on food choice will then serve as an introduction to the findings of this study.

The Effect of Bereavement in Later Life

There is a general lack of sociological research on widowhood and life course changes among elderly people. For the women and men in this study, all over the age of 75, the marital relationship has usually spanned the greater part of their lives, many had been married for over 50 years. For most, the relationship has been a central and purposeful feature of their life. Moreover, in retirement partners are commonly thrown together in an alliance of mutual dependence unlike any hitherto experienced. In some respects, the final years of married life are the most intense. Couples spend more time together and, having reduced the number of relationships outside the home, come to rely heavily upon one another for social, domestic, and leisure activities. If we accept that it is the intensity of the involvement in a partnership (rather than the love) that influences the extent of grief, then for older people the loss of their spouse can have a devastating effect.

Marris asserts that the 'fundamental crisis of bereavement arises, not from the loss of others, but the loss of self' (Marris, 1986 p.33). The process of grieving involves mourning for the lost partner, but a reappraisal of behaviour and meaning is also demanded if the survivor is to adjust to a solitary future. Bereavement necessitates a search for new purpose and a re-conceptualisation of social identity as the widowed are transformed from the role of husband to widower and wife to widow.

The nature of relationships with others and the ability to reciprocate or pay for the services required in old age are founded on past experiences and resources built up in earlier stages of the life course. Long standing beliefs and values are re-worked, and roles re-negotiated as the widowed struggle to make sense of their familiar surroundings from the unfamiliar viewpoint of their newly acquired, single status. Of central relevance to the task is the recognition of 'pathways' (Plath, 1980; Kaufman, 1986) or cultural expectations which provide models against which the appropriateness of role behaviour can be measured. A brief discussion of the relationship between class, gender and food preferences will reveal some of the cultural expectations which help to mould people's response to widowhood.

Class, Gender and Food Preferences

Studies of food preferences comparing working class and middle class groups (Calnan, 1987) demonstrate that although both valued fresh fruit and vegetables, middle class respondents stressed the importance of low fat and high fibre. Interviews with working class women emphasised the need to regularly provide their families with cooked meals of meat and two vegetables. The significance of cooked food for the working class was reiterated in the research of Charles and Kerr (1986) in which the Sunday roast, with 'high status meat' (Charles and Kerr, 1988) and two vegetables, was the epitome of the 'proper' meal (Murcott, 1983; Twigg, 1983).

Other research has highlighted the crucial role of gender in food choice and behaviour. Studies suggest that women, in their roles of wife and mother, prepare the family food in accordance with the preferences of their husbands and children (Murcott, 1983; Calnan, 1990; Charles and Kerr, 1985; Wilson, 1989). Furthermore, Charles and Kerr (1988) argue that if women were not compelled to cook for their families they would be unlikely to continue to prepare 'proper meals' and would be less conservative in their tastes.

For elderly people living alone the implications of gender as an organising factor are transformed. When children leave home and later their partner dies, food rituals take on new meanings. Women who lose their husbands are no longer obliged to cook meals which appeal to their family's tastes. Men, on the other hand, if they have no-one to cook for them, may have to learn a new set of skills – skills which have traditionally been seen as 'women's work'.

Food consumption and food preparation can be seen as ways of understanding life course continuities, especially the continuity of 'feminine' and 'masculine' social identities. In this respect food is a vehicle through which to explore and exemplify life course changes, as well as class and gender distinctions in later life. Cultural patterns, developed throughout the life course, influence the nature and extent of resources available to elderly people. For example, widows may be seen by their families as self-sufficient in terms of food requirements, whereas widowers may be offered assistance. Neighbours and friends may be regarded as a source of support by some elderly widowed individuals but rejected for this purpose by others. In this chapter these issues will be discussed and the social factors which influence people's choices considered.

The Research Study

The data collected for this chapter forms part of a wider project concerned with the maintenance of independence and autonomy among people over the age of 75. The study took a predominantly qualitative approach and in-depth interviews were conducted with members of 100 households in two districts of a North London Borough. A much higher proportion of elderly people lived alone than in households where both spouses were alive. Widowed people accounted for 62 per cent of the total sample. A detailed account of the sampling procedures is given in Gail Wilson's chapter in this volume.

To detect the impact of spouse loss, widowed respondents were asked about patterns of food consumption: shopping, choice of foodstuffs, favourite foods, cooking and use of domestic technology and convenience foods, timing and structure of meals, and any recent changes. They were also questioned as to whether, and in what way, their food behaviour had changed as a result of losing their partner.

The character of the two districts

The two districts differed in housing tenure and social class with the neighbourhoods roughly dividing into working class and middle class, north and south of the borough respectively. In the northern district, the majority of those interviewed had spent the greater part of their adult life in the area – some living in the same house. Many had moved from areas of central London during slum clearance programmes in the 1920s and 1930s and others were re-housed during the Second World War as a consequence of the blitz. A number of respondents remarked that when they had first arrived, the area was bordered by countryside and had the atmosphere of a rural village. Life was a very different experience from the one that they had left behind. The people who came to live in this area brought with them strong working class traditions. Born and raised in poverty, many had harrowing tales to tell of deprivation and misery. Equally most were proud of the lengths to which their parents (and more specifically their mothers) went to ensure their survival – terrible as life may have been in those days, it had equipped them with the skills to succeed in their own lives.[1]

By contrast, the southern area, was designed in the first decade of this century to house a complex mix of classes. In recent years it has become an attractive region for the London wealthy who wish to live within easy access of the metropolis. Consequently, elderly people remaining in this part of the borough are unquestionably more prosperous than those in the northern district. The majority, if not professionals themselves, were keen to recount the occupational successes of their children and grandchildren, for example, in the professions. These elderly middle class residents came from a variety of cultural backgrounds, and many expressed their enjoyment of activities requiring higher income levels, such as trips to the theatre, concerts and foreign travel.

Food Preferences

Significant differences emerged between the reported food choices of the widowed women and men in the study. This is to be expected given cultural traditions that define food preparation as women's work and the consequent dearth of cooking skills displayed by most men in our society. Furthermore,

---

1   See Ross (1983) for a discussion of working class mothers in inner London slums prior to the First World War.

it was noted that some respondents dealt with the problems of cooking for one by employing a form of neighbour support network built on reciprocity.

'Proper' meals

Most of the widowed women reported that they were still concerned with 'proper' meals. Mens' food preferences were largely motivated simply by the desire to 'get by'. The overwhelming majority of elderly widows declared that they continued to cook meals for themselves. Whether the main meal was taken at midday or in the evening it usually constituted a 'proper meal' in that it was either 'hot', 'cooked', or contained meat and two vegetables. 'I still do the old fashioned dinners' said an 83-year-old widow from the north of the district. Another woman talking of her diet said:

> I mean we were brought up meat, fish or eggs you should always have and I still keep to it.

Apart from minor modifications to the content of meals (for example, substituting side salads for peas) there was a notable insistence among the majority of women that cooking habits had changed little.

One woman placed the accent on continuity of meal content and eating rituals:

> We always had a roast on Sundays even when we was kiddies and we always laid the table up... Even now, on my own, I do love to sit at the table in my kitchen and have my main meal. I do. It's how we was fetched up I suppose.

The traditional Sunday roast was repeatedly described as a meal still eaten by elderly working class women. One widow with no local kin, described the content of her Sunday meal, cooked and eaten alone, as, '...a piece of roast chicken, roast potatoes, cabbage, sponge and custard afterwards'. A remarkably active 82-year-old woman in the north of the borough with a dense kin support network (Wenger, 1989) who took Sunday roast with her daughter and family, in addition cooked a roast meal each Saturday for her brother and son-in-law:

> Saturdays I cook a roast meal here because that brother of mine comes round and my daughter's husband come round to a meal because my daughter works on Saturdays so he comes to me and I cook a meal.

The lack of a Sunday 'joint' was used by a 76-year-old woman in the study, to mark the loss of social relationships. Recently widowed and severely disabled by a stroke, she relied on the local 'meals on wheels' service for her daily meal. This was supplemented by snacks prepared by her married daughter who visited every weekday but spent Sunday with her husband and children. Clearly 'in mourning' for her former lifestyle, she described her situation:

> We always had a house-full. It's not the same now. I get lonely and depressed. And Sundays are awful. There's no Sunday roast – so no-one comes and no-one goes.

Some of the men interviewed admitted to having few culinary skills when their wives were alive. These men appear to have experienced a high degree of gendered division of labour in all aspects of the domestic sphere. One isolated 84-year-old who had no outside help from family or formal support networks, struggled against a combination of poor health and lack of household competence to feed himself and keep his surroundings clean. He told of a diet of tinned soup and beef:

> I had beef and butter, £10 worth. You know, shove it in the fridge there and eat it as I go along, you know, everyday... I used to make the soup and all but I haven't done that. Don't know why I went off that, I love it, love it. I think the tinned food was the thing that put me off that... It was already cooked for me instead of me cooking it.

Convenience foods

There was a mixed response to the question of convenience foods, possibly due to the wide variety of foodstuffs which could be included under this heading. There were those women who were quite adamant in rejecting all but 'fresh' food. It was clear, however, that when referring to the concept of 'fresh food' respondents were employing a variety of criteria. For example, although pre-packed frozen foods were distrusted by many, food which was fresh when acquired (often home grown produce) and subsequently frozen, was still viewed as fresh. Some stated that all tinned or frozen produce was excluded from the diet. One woman explained that her disapproval stemmed from a lack of ingredients information:

> I like my own food because you know what's in it don't you. I know that now they put different chemicals on the food for it to grow fast, but, I still like to cook my own food.

Only a minority of women favoured convenience foods. They used the term to describe a variety of foodstuffs from packets of frozen vegetables, through 'boil-in-the-bag' meals, to the 'cook chill' range available in larger supermarkets. One widow, separated from her husband five years before his death, made great use of her freezer – a legacy from family days. A member of the local horticultural society, she preferred to spend time in the garden rather than in the kitchen.

> Sometimes if I've been a bit tired and doing about four hours out in the garden, I think, oh get something out of the freezer. And so I've been having the little dinners what you boil in the bag. The one's with the dumplings are very nice. I've tried a couple of those... Those little dinners they're marvellous, taste so lovely too.

For widowed men, experimentation, convenience foods and domestic technology often provided the solutions to lack of expertise. One widower, who throughout his married life had relied on his wife's cooking, said:

> I didn't know how to put a kettle of water on when the Mrs went. I was in queer street because I didn't know nothing because she done everything. Really, I was lord of the manor you know, clean shirt everyday and she done all that.

> I couldn't cook so I started to learn... And of course today you can go into Sainsbury's or Marks and Spencer and you can get meals if you got a microwave. And you can put it in there for four minutes and you've got a meal.

> I had to learn the hard way but I get by. I can do spaghetti bolognaise blinded, it's so easy... One of my favourites is sausage and chips. I love chips. I got an oil thing out there. When I first started I caught the place fire twice. So course then I got the proper thing. It's all exactly controlled.

Convenience foods did not appear to have the same negative connotations for men that they held for most of their female counterparts. Men who had never cooked tended to view food preparation as women's work. Resorting to pre-cooked foodstuffs therefore did not threaten the male's essential identity or traditional role. Not expected to possess cooking skills, there is no social pressure on him to learn. What stimulus there is derives from a personal need to survive. Elderly men are frequently assisted in this goal by female family members, especially daughters who live locally.

The meaning of cooking

The meaning of cooking appears to be different for men and women (Murcott, 1983). The elderly women interviewed saw cooking as a task which transformed items of purchased food into something quite different. This conversion was achieved through a variety of processes including washing, chopping, slicing, seasoning, applying heat and presentation. Using convenience foods was often not recognised by women as 'proper cooking'. Men, however, did not sustain the same moral associations with the need to cook food. If the food looked nourishing and tasted good, few were overconcerned with the process by which it arrived on the plate.

For the majority of women in the sample, 'sticking to the old ways'; continuing to prepare 'proper meals'; and refusing to use convenience food appeared to have moral connotations. Using pre-prepared or easy-cook food was not 'real' cooking. This threatened to betray either an inability to cook or a lack of care or concern for their own health. At this stage in the widows' life course – children having grown and moved away and partners' died – the social organisation of meals had changed dramatically. Preserving eating practices from the earlier 'family' stage may be simpler and more reassuring than changing them. Eating habits are retained but the meanings of the rituals are re-defined. Instead of cooking a meal to please or to care for a husband, these women justified their food consumption by defining it in terms of tradition, 'properness', or as being good for their own health.

Furthermore, children in close contact, particularly daughters, were able to exert a conservative influence on their parent's food choice. For some of the men this was a consequence of daughters' either preparing food for them or inviting them to the family home to share meals. This practice was far less common for elderly women but children were still able to influence food related behaviour. For example, widow's attempts to revise cooking and eating habits were sometimes met with disapproval as offspring feared that changes were stimulated by lack of money or poor physical or mental health. One woman who had decided to experiment with a vegetarian diet gave up when her daughter paid an unexpected visit one meal time:

> I thought to myself I won't have any meat, I'll just have vegetables. Course what happens? In walks one of the children. So there was a rumpus. The result was the next weekend my daughter turned up here with a chicken and a piece of pork.

This type of response has a bearing on the way in which the widow reformulates the meanings of everyday tasks. Children may reinforce the view that cooking is a means of maintaining good health. It then becomes a moral duty to one's family to continue to prepare food along familiar lines.

To understand continuities in food consumption there is also an element of personal identity and a sense of social identity which needs to be considered. For women, the legacy of pursuing the social roles of mother and wife throughout the life course may have become central characteristics of personal identity. Similarly for elderly men, the possession of, what are viewed as, traditional male skills retain their significance in the masculine identity. If this is so, the preparation of food facilitates the continuity of 'feminine' roles and detracts from 'masculine' ones.

Neighbourhood Reciprocity Among the Working Class

One of the most significant findings is an apparent need for the majority of the elderly bereaved, male or female, to maintain continuity in relation to food consumption. Perhaps the most unexpected feature of this endeavour was the extent of neighbour reciprocity practised in the working class district. Of the 29 widowed respondents interviewed in the northern area of the borough, ten (35%) were involved in intra-generational neighbour support networks in which cooked food was a key element of exchange.

Each of the ten networks in the northern area were mutually exclusive: six consisted of mixed gender and four of same gender neighbours. In the latter instances, the arrangement was described by respondents as a form of companionship. Eating was clearly regarded as a social activity. Regularly inviting elderly neighbours to share a meal combatted loneliness. Furthermore, it reduced the cost of food as neighbours took turns to prepare meals and thus saved money following the axiom that 'two can eat as cheaply as one'. In mixed gender cases the food was normally cooked by the female neighbour. The 'favour' was reciprocated by the male doing gardening, 'heavy' housework, odd jobs or, in one instance where the man was severely disabled, through a financial agreement.

In some cases the network was effectively a partnership between male and female neighbours. In other situations the support network clearly comprised a number of individuals. The extent of food exchange differed from one case to another and can be viewed as a continuum according to the amount or regularity of the transaction. The degree of cooking support ranged from an occasional bowl of soup, weekend meals or a main meal everyday, to the provision of all meals except breakfast. In return cooks might expect a variety of services from holding house keys in case of emergency, collecting pensions and doing supermarket shopping, to mowing the lawn, giving lifts in the car or contributing to the cost of food, electricity and gas bills.

In Chapter 3, Gail Wilson argues that receiving 'help' implies need and therefore possible dependence'. For these elderly neighbours the arrangement endured because it was founded on reciprocity and thus the relationship was transformed from one of dependence to inter-dependence. As one woman who cooked regularly for a male neighbour explained:

> The last couple of years it's handy 'cos he can go and get the shopping and he got me pension for me last week when I couldn't get out to get that myself. It is very handy but I'll do anything for him. If he wants any needlework I do it in return or give him plants for his garden. So its *vice-versa*. It's a, you know, two way thing…

Without the individual's willingness to reciprocate, it is unlikely that these networks, which are both socially and financially beneficial, would survive. As a respondent in Bulmer's (1986) work on neighbours suggests, 'Reciprocity occurs where it is needed… The more affluent a community, the less reciprocity is practised' (1986 p.85).

A multiplicity of considerations influence the development of food-based neighbour support networks. No single element can entirely explain the establishment and vitality of these reciprocal arrangements. The following discussion brings into focus some of the composite factors including: class – material and cultural resources, type of housing, length of residence, and the existence of other support networks.

Class – Material and Cultural Resources

Food-based neighbour support networks were less common in the middle class area. This may be partially accounted for by the relative affluence of the residents living in the south of the borough. Financial resources built up during the life course influence the way in which people respond to 'needs' in later life. As Wilson (this volume) points out, old age does not bring financial parity. Higher paid jobs in middle life and private and company pensions greatly increase the range of options available to elderly people. Although investment and pension income is higher for men than for women irrespective of class, there is disparity between the pensions of middle class and working class women due to differences in their own past employment and in their likelihood of receiving a survivor's pension (Arber and Ginn, 1991a). A 76-year-old widow in our study who lived in the middle class district described herself as 'very comfortably off'. Seeing no reason to continue to cook elaborate meals once her husband had died; she shopped in the more expensive food stores where she regularly bought 'cook-chill' ready meals. For women in the working class area such 'luxuries' (although never stated as desirable) were economically unrealistic.

Bulmer (1986) notes that sharing difficult circumstances may prompt people to support one another and he cites the potential for the elderly widowed to assist each other as an example. For many London-based working class people over the age of 75, sharing and neighbourliness is part of a cultural tradition (Ross, 1983). Helping others is to some extent an expectation and many of the respondents in the northern part of the borough remarked that they would be only too happy to help anyone in need. Others, in excusing a lack of communication with neighbours, employed phrases such as, 'I like to keep myself to myself'; 'I prefer to go to my family with problems'; 'I don't want everyone knowing my business'; 'I don't like to bother anyone'. These cultural and emotional attitudes, accumulated during the life course, are influential in regulating the individual's response to the problems of old age and widowhood.

Length of Residence and Type of Housing

Having lived in the area for some time, many naturally had long-term relationships with their neighbours. In at least two of the cases where individuals were involved in neighbour support networks there had been a friendly connection prior to both partners being widowed. One man explained that he and his late wife had spent the greater part of their leisure time socialising with his neighbour and her husband, now deceased. When their spouses died (her husband dying first) it seemed natural and sensible to combine resources. Another interviewee described her relationship with a neighbour for whom she regularly cooked food. The man had been a friend of her husband and had eaten meals with the couple for many years.

I should say I lost my husband three years ago. And he (the neighbour) used to have his meals with us for years and years and years and he

still has them with me. So he's kind of more than my neighbour he's
like a younger brother…

Previous research investigating the impact of housing type on the support
networks of elderly people has produced conflicting results. Some argue that
moving old people into purpose built accommodation may drastically
reduce their opportunities for support (Qureshi and Walker, 1989). By contrast, other research points to the importance of housing elderly people close
to each other. 'The elderly, too, more restricted in their mobility, tended to
develop close neighbourly ties particularly when living in housing occupied
by people of their own age' (Bulmer, 1986 p.84).

Evidence from the present study suggests that in working class areas,
proximity to other widowed elderly people is an important factor in establishing supportive relationships. Two contrasting cases illustrate this. An 81-
year-old man who was seriously disabled and living in a block of low rise
flats occupied predominantly by very old people, was able to secure a great
deal of assistance from an elderly widow. A similarly handicapped 84-year-
old, living in a comparable block but with much younger neighbours, was
thoroughly isolated. His predicament was compounded by the fact that he
had only recently moved from another part of the district and consequently
knew no elderly people in the immediate area. Recent migration alone,
however, was not a significant factor in the failure to encounter 'good'
neighbours. One man who had spent all his life in another distant locality
reported being looked after by the elderly widows in the flats above and on
either side.

Other Support Networks

Other forms of support available to elderly people in this sample were
formal organisations, such as social services, and informal help from relatives and friends. A combination of past experiences of hardship and recent
disappointment when one woman had asked for formal help, nurtured a
lack of trust and a resolve not to seek assistance from social services. Similar
experiences were related by others, many of whom recalled the humiliation
suffered by their mothers when applying for charitable help before the
Second World War. A tacit reciprocal understanding with a neighbour met
many of the requirements of these elderly widowed people without any loss
of dignity. One woman who prepared a daily meal for her male neighbour
commented that in return he had offered help with some of the jobs around
the home and garden which she now found difficult. The fact that she had
not requested assistance, enhanced the pleasure of receiving it.

It's like my neighbour next door but one, if he feels that he would like
to do something for me he does it but I don't ask him to do it. I don't
ask anybody to do anything for me if I can help it.

Studies of caring for elderly people have shown that it is relatives who tend to take on the role of principal carer (Wenger, 1989). Indeed, family contact may be greater once a spouse has died because kin can provide compensation in widowhood. Qureshi and Walker (1989) found evidence that neighbours and friends may also be involved in support networks in a back-up capacity to the primary caring relative. These friends and neighbours performed tasks such as heavy shopping, heavy housework, preparation and cooking of meals and gardening. Although it is unclear from the study, the emphasis on the heavy nature of the work points to the likelihood that these helpers of elderly people were not of the same generation.

The results of this research in North London suggest that the strength of working class elderly neighbour support networks may have been underestimated in other areas. In this study neighbours played a key role when other support networks were minimal or non-existent. The people who received and contributed the greatest amount of care to neighbours tended to be those with no family, or distant or estranged kin. Our findings imply that for these working class widowed individuals, if family ties are inadequate, neighbours may compensate for the loss of kin and partner.

Neighbour Support Networks and Social Roles

After losing a spouse, individuals tend to review their lifestyle and question the appropriateness of role identities and meanings. Widowhood usually divests very old women of the role of domestic carer. Unlike men who officially retire from paid employment at or before the age of 65, many women continue to perform their household duties until physically or mentally prevented from doing so. Bereavement for women, therefore, can engender a sense of loss of purpose similar to that experienced by men when giving up lifelong occupational careers. Hockey (1989), in a study of the experiences of elderly people in residential homes, reported that the persona of 'domestic carer' was one dearly missed by many of the women.

Cooking for men who are not part of the household enables elderly women to obtain companionship whilst retaining control over domestic activities. Furthermore, the reciprocal nature of the relationship results in the receipt of services in and around the home which may once have been the domain of the husband. Cooking for siblings or adult children also fulfilled these criteria and some women who were not involved in neighbour support networks reciprocated domestic services with relatives.

For men, their female neighbours may provide the ideal solution to the dilemma of food preparation. If they have no cooking or housework skills and no other form of support, neighbourly widows can become substitute wives and carers. This allows the men to continue with certain behaviours much as before in that they are not confronted with the need to learn new skills which may threaten their masculine identity. Furthermore, they can perform 'odd jobs', traditionally perceived as more suited to their abilities, around the widow's home.

The fact that similar intra-generation neighbour support networks have not been found in other studies may be attributable to our focus on food. Food preparation is traditionally regarded as women's work and is carried out in the private sphere of the home. It is therefore less valued than 'men's work' and to this extent less visible. A further factor is that many studies concerned with elderly lifestyles emphasise the caring relationship. The neighbour networks are not based on care or altruism but on interdependence. They are reciprocal agreements centred around people's ability to respond with material and emotional support. This may furnish another reason for their being overlooked. Although the working class community which forms part of the study is geographically specific, it is far from unique. Comparable networks may well thrive in other neighbourhoods providing elderly widowed people with a valuable source of continuity of purpose and physical and emotional security.

Conclusions

The domestic organisation of food may be transformed by loss of spouse. The findings of this study, however, suggest that many elderly widowed people attempt to maintain continuity of food consumption, both women and men strive to retain familiar practices. Women may persist in preparing and cooking food as they always had done. Some widows also stressed traditional meal structure, preferring to eat at the table as they would once have done with family and spouse. The men in the study also tended to strive for continuity but this was clearly more difficult than it was for the women as the former usually had no tradition of food preparation to fall back on. Hence most of the widowers expressed an inclination to use convenience foods and domestic technology which made the task of acquiring 'cooking' skills less foreboding. Some men reported being cooked for by daughters living locally, by lunch clubs, or in other cases as part of a reciprocal arrangement with neighbourly widows.

On an emotional rather than a simply problem solving basis, the arrangement between the widowed neighbours provided both men and women with companionship and an antidote to the loneliness which haunts so many elderly people. Eating, although essential for survival, is organised in our society as a social act. Meal-taking provides an opportunity for people to meet, talk, share problems and celebrate successes. All this is lost when people are widowed. Cooking for neighbours and sharing meals allows people to participate once again in the social activity that is an important element in the enjoyment of food.

Acknowledgements

I am grateful to the Nuffield Foundation who financed the study on which this research is based and also to Gail Wilson for comments on an earlier draft of this chapter.

CHAPTER 5

Ageing, Gender and the Organisation of Physical Activities

Kate Bennett and Kevin Morgan

Introduction

Physical activity has been associated with a variety of cognitive and behavioural changes which, collectively, allow the conclusion that regular exercise contributes to psychological as well as physical health. Considerable attention is now being paid to how these benefits are mediated, and at whom they might best be targetted. Retired and elderly people, in particular, are increasingly being seen as appropriate candidates for health promotion initiatives which, by increasing levels of physical activity (and, by implication, levels of physical fitness), aim to broadly improve quality of life. In this context, levels of customary or habitual activity (as distinct from formal exercise participation) are presumed to play an important role, and are now beginning to receive research attention.

At present, however, the empirical basis for activity-based health promotion initiatives owes much to information derived from younger age groups. As regards mental health, relatively little research has directly addressed the assumption that customary physical activity reliably contributes to psychological well being in later life. Indeed, the construct of customary (or habitual) physical activity itself, and its role in promoting and maintaining mental health in old age remains a neglected area of study. It is also methodologically problematic. In assessing relationships between mood and activity in elderly people, two problems in particular need to be overcome. First, numerous factors in the economic and social, and biological domains are known to exert a significant influence on well-being in later life. If the unique contributions of physical activity are to be isolated, the influence of these factors needs to be taken into consideration. Second, at the levels of both assessment and analysis, *social* activities (which may be accompanied by some degree of physical effort, and which are known to contribute significantly to morale and life satisfaction in older individuals) easily confound with *physical* activities (Larson, 1978). If the putative psychological benefits of customary physical activity are presumed to be mediated by training effects (i.e., the physiological consequences of training), then some attempt should be made to distinguish between activity as exercise, and activity as social engagement. This latter issue, of distinguishing between social and physical activities, provides the focus for this chapter.

The Nottingham Longitudinal Study of Activity and Ageing (NLSAA) was set up in 1983 specifically to assess the role of Lifestyle and Customary Physical Activity (referred to as CPA throughout this chapter) in promoting and maintaining psychological well-being in later life. However, while designed specifically to assess levels of activity relevant to physical fitness, the interview methodology also allows for analyses beyond these specific goals. This chapter examines the influence of gender on both the overall level, and the organisation of physical activity.

Method

The NLSAA was designed to assess levels of physical activity, mental and physical health, and psychological well-being in a representative sample of elderly people, and to monitor changes in these characteristics over time. In addition to providing detailed profiles of health, morale and activity the principal survey instrument, the Activity and Ageing Questionnaire also assessed socio-economic status, household structure, social support networks, lifestyle, attitudes to age and ageing, and service use. Anthropometric measurements of hand-grip strength, shoulder flexibility, stature and body weight were made on completion of each interview. Respondents were interviewed in their own homes.

Great care was taken in the selection of the sample to ensure its representativeness. Of 1599 elderly individuals randomly selected from the Nottinghamshire Family Practitioner Committee's records, 1299 were eligible for interview and, of these, 1042 agreed to participate in the survey (507 aged 65–74 and 535 aged 75 and over). The overall response rate was 80.2 per cent.

The survey was conducted in three geographically separate districts of Nottingham each within the psychogeriatric catchment area of the University Department of Health Care of the Elderly. Prior demographic analyses had established that the age, sex, social class structure and the proportion of elderly individuals living alone within the survey area showed no significant departure from the national pattern as described the 1981 census (OPCS, 1983).

With the consent and co-operation of general practitioners a register of elderly persons living within the survey area was compiled from patient records maintained by the Nottinghamshire Family Practitioners Committee. All general practitioners with surgeries in the three survey areas co-operated. In this way a total population of 8409 individuals aged 65 years and over was registered, representing the combined patients of 25 general practitioners in nine practices. While practice and census ward boundaries do not necessarily coincide, the number of elderly individuals identified in the survey area closely approximated the number provided by the 1981 census. Equal probability target samples were selected from the 'young elderly' (i.e. those aged 65–74 years) and the 'old elderly' (75 years and over) sub- populations. Those in institutional care were excluded from the target sample. As the intention was to interview approximately 500 individuals from both sub-populations, the samples drawn were large enough to accommodate losses due to deaths, migration and entry into residential care.

The first survey interviews were conducted in 1985 by ten interviewers who attended a two week training programme. This involved detailed discussion of the questionnaire, role playing, video-assisted practice in administering the questionnaire, and making anthropometric measurements on elderly volunteers.

The first complete follow-up of survivors, using identical methods and materials, was conducted between May and September 1989. All respondents who had participated in 1985, and who were still living in Nottingham, were invited to participate in the follow-up study. Information on respondents who had died, moved or migrated since 1985 was provided by the NHS central register, general practitioners' records and hospital case-notes. Principal causes of attrition were due to deaths (n=261), refusals (n=63), people who could not be traced (n=25) and emigrations (n=3). From an available sample of 781 individuals, 690 follow-up interviews were conducted, representing a follow-up response rate of 88.3 per cent.

Assessment of Customary Physical Activities (CPA)

The NLSAA is concerned with recording physical activities which contribute to physiological 'training', and the maintenance of physical capacities in later life. Since it is possible that fairly low levels of activity may supply sufficient stimulus for physiological training in later life, it was decided to assess (and define as 'customary') those activities with a probable energy cost of 2 kcal/min, performed continuously for a minimum of three minutes (at least weekly), for at least the previous six weeks.

These physical activities were divided into five functional and mutually exclusive categories: outdoor productive activities (e.g. gardening, house and car maintenance); indoor productive activities (e.g. housework, decorating and indoor maintenance); walking (i.e. purposeful walking outside the house or garden); shopping (i.e. continuous ambulatory behaviour associated with shopping); and leisure activities (e.g. cycling, swimming and calisthenics). In addition, a further two categories of non-continuous activities likely to contribute to either muscle strength (e.g. climbing high steps and dragging heavy loads) or joint flexibility (e.g. reaching for high shelves and bending for low shelves) were also assessed (Dallosso *et al.*, 1988). In total, therefore, CPA included *all* physiologically relevant activities.

In administering the questionnaire on outdoor, indoor and leisure activities the interviewer first determined whether the respondent's participation in the activity met the criteria for 'customary', and then asked in detail about the frequency and duration of participation. Each reported activity was scored as minutes per week. Non-participation was scored as zero. In the assessment of walking and shopping, the interviewer asked in detail about walking done on the day prior to the interview. If, however, this day had not been typical then another day was selected, going back up to a maximum of six days previously. Both walking and shopping were recorded as minutes per typical day. Non-participation was again scored as zero. Activities requiring strength or flexibility typically form discrete units of physical activity and so were recorded in terms of frequency of performance on a five-point scale; that is, never performed, occasionally performed, performed once or several times a week, performed daily, or performed several times a day. The validity and reliability of the CPA assessment have been described elsewhere (Dallosso *et al.*, 1988).

Gender Differences in Customary Physical Activity (CPA)

Since significant gender differences in activity patterns were found by Dallosso *et al.* (1988), the data for women and men are analysed separately throughout.

The mean period of time spent on the five continuous activities (walking, shopping, indoor and outdoor productive activities, and leisure) in 1985 and 1989 are shown for women and men in Table 5.1. These data are presented separately for older (75 and over in 1985) and younger (65–74 in 1985) respondents. The full information used to derive Table 5.1 is presented in the Appendix Table, which includes the ranges and skew values to illustrate the diverse nature of activity participation in later life.

Among women, an increase in mean participation was found for shopping and a decrease in mean participation was found for indoor productive activity. Participation in the other activities changed less or remained stable. For men, decreases in mean participation were found for outdoor productive activities and leisure, whilst changes in most other activities were small.

Gender differences were found for indoor and outdoor productive activities and leisure in both 1985 and 1989. Higher levels of participation were reported amongst women for indoor productive activity, whilst higher levels of participation in outdoor productive activity and leisure were found for men. These patterns of participation were not unexpected: women traditionally undertake those activities associated with the indoor domestic routine, whilst men participate more in outdoor productive activity and leisure. There were gender-related longitudinal changes in participation. Large decreases in participation for men in leisure and outdoor productive activity contrast with the relative stability of participation for women. Similarly women's indoor productive activity participation decreased somewhat more than for men. Thus, the greatest changes, for both women and men are in those activities where participation was highest in 1985.

Table 5.1 Time spent on customary physical activities[1] by age group, elderly men and women in 1985 and 1989

| | Men | | | | Women | | | |
| | Younger 65–74 in 1985 | | Older 75+ in 1985 | | Younger 65–74 in 1985 | | Older 75+ in 1985 | |
	1985	1989	1985	1989	1985	1989	1985	1989
Mean minutes per day								
Walking	37	40	25	22	28	33	15	20
Shopping	20	27	15	23	29	31	11	23
Mean hours per week								
Indoor Productive	4.8	4.3	4.1	3.7	10.1	9.6	8.0	6.7
Outdoor Productive	7.4	6.3	4.3	3.4	2.4	2.5	1.1	1.2
Leisure	3.6	2.4	4.8	1.7	1.8	1.6	1.0	0.3
Minimum N=	(206)	(160)	(164)	(80)	(238)	(205)	(319)	(148)

[1] Activities are only defined as Customary Physical Activities (CPA) if they involve the expenditure of 2kcal/min of energy for a minimum of 3 minutes (at least once a week) for the minimum of the previous 6 weeks. Full details for each activity, including the range and skew, are included in the Appendix Table.

Source: Nottingham Longitudinal Study of Activity and Ageing

Structure of Customary Physical Activities (CPA)

While it is often assumed that physical activity is a homogeneous construct (for example, we may classify, even informally, ourselves or others as 'active' or 'less active' individuals) there is little empirical evidence to support this assumption. The issue of whether older people are generally active or selectively active (or inactive) can be assessed directly by factor analysis, from which inter-correlated components – factors – are extracted. In this way it is possible to examine not only the structure of CPA, but also to extract for subsequent analyses different components of CPA. The former is particularly relevant to this chapter, that is, the study of the structure of CPA *per se*, since little is known about the organisation of CPA in later life.

The structure of the CPA in 1985 was analysed using a factor analysis of all seven activity categories (walking, shopping, indoor productive activity, outdoor productive activity, leisure, activities requiring strength, and activities requiring flexibility). Complete activity data sets were obtained from 914 respondents (238 women and 204 men aged 65–74; 312 women and 160 men aged 75 and over). The method of extraction was a principal components analysis, followed by a varimax rotation. Only those principal components with an eigenvalue greater than one were extracted (see Morgan *et al.*, 1991). Table 5.2 shows the factor structure and the loadings for the items in each principal component for women and men separately.

**Table 5.2 Factor (principal components) analysis
of customary physical activity (1985)**

(a) Women

Factor	Activities in Factor	Loading
1. Home Maintenance	Strength	0.81
	Flexibility	0.72
	Indoor Productive	0.71
	Outdoor Productive	0.47
	Shopping	0.42
2. Pleasure	Leisure	0.82
	Walking	0.80

(b) Men

Factor	Activities in Factor	Loading
1. Home Maintenance	Outdoor Productive	0.79
	Flexibility	0.78
	Strength	0.76
2. Pleasure	Leisure	0.83
	Walking	0.82
3. Home Management	Shopping	0.73
	Indoor Productive	0.66

For women, a two factor structure (which accounted for 52% of the variance) was extracted. The first component (accounting for 37% of the variance) comprised indoor and outdoor productive activities, shopping, and activities requiring strength and flexibility. As most of these categories involved some form of 'housework' or 'house-related' work, this factor was called 'home maintenance'. The second component accounted for much less of the variance (15%). This component was termed 'pleasure' since it comprised both leisure and walking activities.

For men, however, three factors were extracted which accounted for 64 per cent of the variance. Outdoor productive, strength and flexibility activities formed the first component, accounting for 31 per cent of the variance. The second principal component comprised, as with the women, walking and leisure (accounting for 18% of the variance). Since these components showed few gender differences the labels 'home maintenance' and 'pleasure' were retained. However, indoor productive activities and shopping formed a third unique (to the men) component which was labelled as 'home management' and accounted for 15 per cent of the variance.

As principal components analysis yields uncorrelated factors (or components), the pattern of loadings shown in Table 5.2 can be interpreted in terms of traditional gender roles for two reasons. First, and perhaps most obviously, the 'home maintenance' factor is the *dominant* source of activity for women. Second, levels of participation in domestic tasks like housework, shopping and reaching down to shelves tend to predict one another. Thus, a woman who shows high levels of participation in housework, is also likely to show high levels of shopping and report frequent stooping and reaching to access shelves etc. Nevertheless, *overall* high levels of activity within the 'home maintenance' factor do not predict high levels of participation in walking and leisure ('pleasure') activities. In other words, older women can be typified 'generally busy' as regards housework activities or pleasure activities, but levels of housework and pleasure activities are uncorrelated.

For men, the three components which were extracted in 1985 similarly reflect gender roles. Those activities which comprised 'home maintenance' – outdoor productive activity (typically gardening and DIY) and activities requiring flexibility and strength (typically reaching for high shelves and lifting heavy loads) – not only predict one another, but also represent the central feature of activity in men. In contrast, activities comprising 'home management' (shopping and indoor productive activities) form a separate component of activity and predicts little about men's overall activity levels.

Table 5.3 Factor (principal components) analysis of customary physical activity (1989)

(a) Women

Factor	Activities in Factor	Loading
1. Home Maintenance	Strength	0.75
	Flexibility	0.74
	Indoor Productive	0.72
	Outdoor Productive	0.53
2. Pleasure	Walking	0.80
	Leisure	0.57
	Shopping	0.49

(b) Men

Factor	Activities in Factor	Loading
1. Home Maintenance	Outdoor Productive	0.75
	Flexibility	0.73
	Strength	0.72
	Shopping	0.44
2. Pleasure	Leisure	0.78
	Walking	0.74
	Indoor Productive	0.54

Longitudinal Changes in Structure of CPA

In order to assess change in the structure of CPA over a four year period, responses from the five activity categories were examined for elderly survivors in 1989 using principal components analysis, see Table 5.3. For women there was little overall change in the structure of CPA. The first principal component resembles the factor 'home maintenance' extracted four years earlier (with the exception of shopping), and, therefore, the label was retained. The second principal component, similarly, approximated to the previously defined factor 'pleasure' (with the addition of shopping), so this label was also retained. The only notable difference in the structure was the loading of shopping. However, both in 1985 and 1989, the loading of this activity was fairly low, indicating that levels of shopping for women relate significantly though weakly to levels of other activities.

Table 5.4 Time spent on customary physical activities by marital status for elderly women and men in 1985 and 1989

		Married		Widowed		Single	
		1985	1989	1985	1989	1985	1989
Mean minutes per day							
Walking	Women	18	24	22	28	17	23
	Men	33	34	28	37	23	18
Shopping	Women	24	36	17	24	15	28
	Men	20	25	10	32	28	2
Mean hours per week							
Indoor Productive	Women	9.6	9.7	8.4	7.5	9.0	8.2
	Men	4.3	3.7	4.7	5.1	8.8	2.2
Outdoor Productive	Women	1.7	1.8	1.6	2.0	1.8	3.2
	Men	7.5	6.1	2.9	4.1	2.0	1.3
Leisure	Women	1.2	1.3	1.4	1.4	1.4	1.0
	Men	3.2	2.3	3.2	2.5	5.5	5.2
Minimum N=	Women	(182)	(114)	(320)	(210)	(39)	(21)
	Men	(257)	(162)	(85)	(60)	(17)	(11)

Source: Nottingham Longitudinal Study of Activity and Ageing

For men, however, the overall structure of CPA showed an interesting and more dramatic change. Unlike the three factor structure which was extracted in 1985, only two factors were extracted in 1989. The first factor resembled 'home maintenance', and although 'shopping' (previously loading under 'home management' in 1985) loaded on this factor, the name was retained. The second principal component now consisted of walking, shopping and indoor productive activity; since this factor too approximated to 'pleasure' the label was retained. The resulting 1989 structure, then, is similar to that found for women (though, in contrast to women, shopping loaded on the 'home maintenance' factor and indoor productive activity on the 'pleasure' factor.

Overall, it would appear that the longitudinal structure of CPA amongst elderly women is characterised by stability. The findings confirm the earlier, cross-sectional, suggestion that the organisation of physical activity reflects women's traditional, 'occupational' role in the home. In contrast, both the structure of CPA and the role of domestic activity for elderly men, change with increasing age, so that men come to adopt a pattern of interrelationships closer to that of elderly women (though differences between men and women do remain). Unlike women, indoor productive activity for men loads on 'pleasure' and shopping loads on 'home maintenance'. It could be that for men, indoor productive activity is in some way recreational. Shopping on the other hand is associated with other domestic activity. This is in contrast to the changes in CPA for women where shopping moves from the domestic to the recreational.

Marital Status and Gender Differences

We have shown that participation in CPA in later life appears to be delineated along traditional domestic lines – women doing housework and men doing more DIY. We expect that this gender differentiation will be less marked for elderly people who are not currently married. The longitudinal design of this study allows an examination of whether and how the gender-related nature of activities changes following bereavement. We therefore examined the pattern of CPA participation with respect to marital status for elderly women and men in Table 5.4. Data for the small number of elderly people who were divorced or separated have been omitted (13 women and 11 men in 1989).

Comparing women by marital status: married women participated most in indoor productive activity and single women participated most in outdoor productive activity. Examining change between 1985 and 1989 indicates that participation in most activities increased for most groups of women, but that there was a decrease in indoor productive activity for all groups of women.

Marital status for men had a greater impact on levels of physical activity than it did for women. Married men participated to a greater extent in walking, shopping and outdoor productive activity than widowed and single men. Single men were found to participate most in leisure, and widowed men most in indoor productive activity. Two patterns of change between 1985 and 1989, were generally found for men: participation in leisure and outdoor productive activity decreased (except for widowed men) and shopping increased (except for single men). It should be noted that the 1985 values presented in Table 5.4 are derived from the total sample.

Table 5.5 Customary levels of participation in selected
physical activities for recently widowed women and men
before and after the death of their spouse

	Women		Men	
	Before (1985)	After (1989)	Before (1985)	After (1989)
Mean minutes per day				
Walking	22	23	37	39
Shopping	24	29	21	13
Mean hours per week				
Indoor Productive	9.8	6.5	4.9	6.3
Outdoor Productive	2.5	2.7	8.4	4.7
Leisure	1.0	2.0	3.7	2.6
Minimum N=	(36)	(34)	(17)	(18)

Source: Nottingham Longitudinal Study of Activity and Ageing

Changes in mean values between 1985 and 1989, therefore, will to some extent reflect patterns of attrition as well as genuine changes in activity participation. Analyses to date, however, do show remarkably similar patterns of change when 1989 values are *paired* with 1985 values.

The results show that the traditional 'domestic' roles are common amongst elderly married men and women. However, amongst the single and widowed the traditional roles are less well defined, for example, single women participate in more outdoor productive activity and widowed men in more indoor productive activity. Among married elderly people the 'domestic' roles are most clearly maintained, while among other marital status groups patterns of activity participation are more diverse.

Respondents who were widowed in the 1985 survey are an especially heterogeneous group. For example, the length of time since the death of their spouse varied considerably (from less than 1 year to over 59 years), and consequently, patterns of activity may vary enormously within this group. However, we can examine patterns of change in activity participation in relation to the effects of recent widowhood by analysing the group of respondents who were married in 1985, but by 1989 had been widowed. These respondents are more likely than the other widowed respondents to illustrate changes in activity level which are primarily due to widowhood *per se*, especially when compared with the data for the whole sample. Data are presented for these recently widowed women and men in Table 5.5.

When compared to the whole sample of elderly women, recently widowed women (i.e. married in 1985 but widowed by 1989) were found to have increased (not decreased) their mean leisure participation and substantially decreased their indoor productive activity (Table 5.5). Their slight increases in outdoor productive activity and shopping, and unchanged level of walking activities were, however, similar to those reported by the wider sample of women.

For recently widowed men, there were decreases in shopping and outdoor productive activity but increases in indoor productive activity. The changes in shopping and indoor productive activity contrast with increases in shopping and decreases in indoor productive activity reported by the wider sample of men (Table 5.1). Outdoor productive activity was almost halved for recently widowed men compared with a much smaller decline for all elderly men.

Thus, levels of participation of elderly people in leisure, indoor and outdoor productive activity and shopping are influenced both by gender and recent widowhood. There appears to be a direct exchange of responsibility between men and women following recent widowhood for indoor and outdoor productive activity. Women do less indoor productive activity and men, probably from necessity, do more. Recently widowed women increase their participation in the other four areas of physical activity. For example, they may now have to take responsibility for more outdoor productive activity, since the death of their husband, but they also have more 'freed up' time from traditional domestic role responsibilities to participate in more leisure activities. The increase in leisure activities may reflect a re-structuring of their use of time compared with when they were part of a couple. There are parallels between these findings and those of Howarth (in the previous chapter).

Recently widowed men, on the other hand, participate less in outdoor productive activity and do less shopping following bereavement. There are several reasons for these changes, including decreased necessity and decreased opportunity, since indoor productive activity is more important. There may also be more complex factors, such as poorer morale, poorer health, and changes in social support, which may affect CPA following bereavement.

Conclusions

Both the levels of participation in, and the organisation of Customary Physical Activities (CPA) is influenced by gender. Patterns of participation in CPA differ between elderly women and men with CPA organised in a gender specific manner. Longitudinal changes in its organisation reflect gender differences.

Levels of participation are shown to change between 1985 and 1989 in a gender-related manner. Essentially, decreases, by 1989, are found for those activities where participation is highest for men in 1989, whilst women's participation increases. For women, activity decreases in 1989 for those activities where their participation was highest in 1985, and men's participation increases. This indicates either a change in responsibility or, a levelling out in participation and a breaking down of gender divisions.

The organisation of CPA in women emphasises the dichotomy between domestic responsibilities and recreational activities. Over time this structure shows stability of the factors. In contrast the structure of CPA in men changes from a three factor structure with increasing age to a two factor structure which resembles that found for women. This suggests an increasing feminisation in the structure of CPA for men. There is also evidence to suggest, tentatively, a future gender 'convergence' in the structure of CPA.

Marital status is associated with CPA participation, and changes in marital status influence levels of participation in different activities (Table 5.4). There appears to be an exchange of participation in those activities which best illustrate the gender influence: widowed and married men participate more in shopping activities, while widowed and single women reduce the time they spend on indoor productive activities, and single and widowed women undertake more outdoor productive activity. The 'gender exchange' is most marked amongst those who have recently been widowed (Table 5.5). Recently widowed women substantially reduce their indoor productive activities and increase their leisure participation, whilst recently widowed men increase their level of participation in indoor productive activity.

To summarise, CPA among elderly people is organised in a manner which reflects gender divisions in domestic and leisure activities. In general levels of activity decrease for men and women over a four year period, particularly in those activities where participation is high. Patterns of participation are dependent on marital status: the traditional division of activity is represented most clearly by married men and women. The effects of recent widowhood exemplifies the potential for change, in relationship to gender, within CPA in later life. There are indications of a levelling out of gender differences in old age, characterised both by increased feminisation amongst men and elderly women taking on hitherto more masculine roles.

Table 5A.1 Customary levels of participation in selected physical activities by age for 1985 and 1989

Activity		Year	Age Group	N*	Range	Mean	Skew
Walking	Men	1985	Younger	206	0 - 250	37.1	1.8
Minutes/day			Older	164	0 - 200	24.7	1.9
		1989	Younger	161	0 - 220	40.2	1.7
			Older	84	0 - 150	21.6	1.7
	Women	1985	Younger	238	0 - 195	28.3	1.9
			Older	319	0 - 245	15.2	3.5
		1989	Younger	205	0 - 315	33.4	2.9
			Older	158	0 - 200	19.5	2.6
Shopping	Men	1985	Younger	219	0 - 240	20.3	2.8
Minutes/day			Older	180	0 - 240	14.9	3.3
			Younger	160	0 - 210	26.9	2
		1989	Older	84	0 - 180	22.9	1.7
	Women	1985	Younger	282	0 - 310	29.4	2.3
			Older	337	0 - 180	11.2	3
		1989	Younger	205	0 - 240	31.3	1.7
			Older	154	0 - 330	23.2	3.4
Indoor	Men	1985	Younger	217	0 - 3240	290	3.6
Minutes/week			Older	180	0 - 1500	248	1.7
		1989	Younger	162	0 - 1500	254.8	1.7
			Older	82	0 - 1500	226.9	2.3
	Women	1985	Younger	282	0 - 2100	606.8	1.0
			Older	337	0 - 1958	481.2	0.92
		1989	Younger	216	0 - 1940	569.7	0.95
			Older	177	0 - 1690	398.4	1.6
Outdoor	Men	1985	Younger	219	0 - 2850	446.6	1.8
Minutes/week			Older	180	0 - 2640	260	3
		1989	Younger	160	0 - 2160	379.4	1.6
			Older	82	0 - 1701	201.3	2.3
	Women	1985	Younger	282	0 - 1680	141.8	2.6
			Older	337	0 - 1680	65	4.6
		1989	Younger	204	0 - 2400	148.5	3.7
			Older	148	0 - 1680	69.9	4.8
Leisure	Men	1985	Younger	218	0 - 1710	215.9	2.0
Minutes/week			Older	180	0 - 1560	167.3	2.2
		1989	Younger	162	0 - 1980	169.3	2.8
			Older	82	0 - 900	120.4	2.1
	Women	1985	Younger	282	0 - 1740	105.8	3.6
			Older	337	0 - 1500	57.3	5.6
		1989	Younger	205	0 - 1996	105	4.3
			Older	152	0 - 510	42.9	2.8

*N of complete data sets for each activity

CHAPTER 6

Lifestyles and Perceptions of Elderly People and Old Age in Bosnia and Hercegovina

John Vincent and Željka Mudrovčić

This chapter examines the lifestyles of elderly people and their perceptions of old age in the Republic of Bosnia and Hercegovina in the former Yugoslavia and provides comparisons with the United Kingdom.[1] The term lifestyle is used in order to emphasise the active choice of 'how to live' made by elderly people. Giddens states:

> lifestyle can be defined as a more or less integrated set of practices which an individual embraces, not only because such practices fulfill utilitarian needs, but because they give material form to a particular narrative of self-identity...Overall lifestyle patterns, of course, are less diverse than the plurality of choices available in day-to-day and even in the longer term strategic decisions. A lifestyle involves a cluster of habits and orientations, and hence has a certain unity...that connects options in a more or less ordered pattern. (Giddens, 1991:81–82)

The concept 'lifestyle' implicitly contrasts with 'way of life' which suggests, through the use of the singular, a degree of cultural homogeneity and determinism which is inappropriate. 'Ways of life' would be one alternative possible conceptual formulation. However, the established literature on the 'life course' has proved very insightful for the study of elderly people, in that it emphasises historically developing patterns of behaviour as people progress through their lives.

Our research has been framed around the idea that old age is not simply a role adopted at a certain chronological age – an experience which can be considered in isolation from the rest of the life course, but that the 'lifestyle' of an elderly person is profoundly influenced by the life that went before. Thus the use of the term 'lifestyles' reflects a desire to examine a range of

---

1   The fieldwork on which this chapter is based took place between January and June 1991. Many of the elderly people interviewed remembered the Second World War vividly and said 'please God don't let it happen again'. We do not know how many of our interviewees have survived the shelling and 'ethnic cleansing' which has occurred since that time.

elderly peoples life experiences, and indeed to avoid making the assumption that old age is necessarily a meaningful category in people's understanding of the way they live. The purpose of this chapter is to look at the background cultural constructions of old age taken from interviews in Bosnia and Hercegovina.

In all societies age is recognised as being of social significance, but the expectations of age based statuses vary from culture to culture and over history. In each society there is some degree of phasing of the life course; whereby it is taken for granted that you have to 'act your age' because some ways of behaving are more or less appropriate depending on a progression through a series of age related roles. However, the meanings that are attributed to old age and other roles which are allocated, or which are permissible, on the basis of age, vary enormously. Not only does the social significance attributed to old age vary but the social cues which are taken to mark out those who are 'old' also varies across cultures.

It is a common view that the contemporary life course is more tightly scheduled and interlocked than in the past (Musgrove and Middleton, 1981 p.42) and that there is now more regulation of life according to specific age norms (Hareven, 1982a p.15). Martin Kohli has used the term 'chronologization' to describe the process by which the life course has become standardised across class, ethnic and gender boundaries (Kohli, 1986). Grillis, however, suggests that theories which propose an unilinear process of 'chronologization' oversimplify the past. In addition, they falsely subsume the experience of women under that of men, and ignore class and ethnic differences. An important critique of Kohli's approach is that it 'reifies the life cycle in such a way the individuals are denied a role in defining the meaning of their own lives' (Grillis, 1987 p.98).

Some writers like Arthur Imhof argue for the importance of demographic changes in producing 'chronologization' and suggest that increasing certainty of living the full life-span made it possible to think in 'life career' terms (Imhof, 1987). Kohli, on the other hand, argues that it comes largely from the state, particularly through state welfare activities, which set life course stages. These in turn derive from the organisation of production, in particular the divorce of the labour process from the family and the creation of labour markets with the subsequent need for the state to intervene in setting the conditions for stable control of the labour process. Hence he suggests a powerful three fold chronology of pre-work, work, and post-work. Schooling and retirement are key transitions, largely set by the state but around which people organise their lives.

In contrast, post-modern writers have identified a destructuring of the life course (Featherstone and Hepworth, 1989), and raised the question as to whether there is a reversal of this 'chronologization'. For example, marriage is becoming a less key transition as couples not only live together but many have children without marriage, and divorce and separation are increasingly frequent. However, the transition from work to retirement in capitalist society is structured by the labour market. Therefore it is an inevitable transition, although the age of the transition is not necessarily fixed but related to contingent features such as an ageing society and the supply of labour (Kohli *et al.*, 1992; Guillemard, 1990).

It is possible to identify a process by which the criterion of age comes to structure society and relations within it as a self re-inforcing process, with the pattern reproduced in a stronger form over time by the specific circumstances of contemporary industrial capitalist society. Old age is becoming more socially salient, in other words old age is more likely to be used by social actors in defining the situation and through that process it becomes increasingly institutionalised. Thus old age becomes a structured part of systematic power relations in society which constrain and condition people's opportunities and the ways in which they live, and which in turn they do not simply passively receive but think, re-evaluate, act and organise around. The argument, therefore, is that in industrial society in the last part of the 20th century, age is becoming much more important in relation to people's experience and is becoming a criterion which more people use to interpret and understand their experience of society and structure their own consciousness and action.

A problem with current literature on the life course is that it tends to be very Western in its orientation. It is based on the assumption of the patterns of industrial and social development in dominant economies and cultures of Western Europe and North America. The discussion is about the nature of, and changes to, the life course in the 'West', while the 'Rest' are seldom considered. Even the post-modern emphasis on the range of lifestyles available to elderly people is essentially euro-centric because it is driven by the concerns of understanding contemporary social and cultural change in a limited and affluent section of world society. A robust theory of the 'life course' should be genuinely comprehensive and encompass a global perspective, which will require comparative study.

Comparative Research

Making sense of lifestyles in 'other' cultures necessitates being specific about 'our' society. Studies based in a single research are sited frequently and allow too many questions to go unanswered and too many assumptions to be left unchallenged. The Republic of Bosnia and Hercegovina and Britain contrast in significant ways which can further an understanding of elderly peoples' lifestyles. The principle social contrasts relate to three factors: economic, familial, and demographic.

In terms of industrialisation and urbanisation, Britain was the first industrialised country but in the last forty years its economy and employment structure has shown a decline in industrial occupations, growth in tertiary, professional and service occupations, and de-urbanisation as people move from older industrial cities to suburban and rural commuter locations. In contrast, the Republics of Yugoslavia are still industrialising and urbanising in that the dominant movement in the last thirty years has been from agriculture to industry and from village to town. British people have a significantly higher standard of living than those in Yugoslavia. In 1986 the annual gross domestic product (GDP) per capita was 9,651 US$ in England and Wales, while it was 1,913 US$ in 1985 in Yugoslavia (OECD, 1988a; 1988b). Other indicators of living standards illustrate this difference; in 1986 England and Wales had 312 cars per 1000 inhabitants and Yugoslavia had 121 per 1000; in the same year England and Wales had 336 and Yugoslavia 175 telephones per 1000 population; and infant mortality was almost three times higher in Yugoslavia (31.7 per 1000) than it was in England and Wales (10.6 per 1000) in 1984 (OECD, 1988a; 1988b).

In terms of family structure British families have never been characterised by extended households (Anderson, 1971; Watcher et al., 1978). Evidence suggests that at least from the fourteenth century it was normal to establish a new household on marriage (Macfarlane, 1978; 1986). There was an expectation that children should support aged parents, and to live with a daughter was not uncommon. However, unlike in Bosnia, to reside with daughters-in-law was very rare indeed. In Bosnia the historical institution of the zadruga (Hammel, 1972; Halpern and Wagner, 1984) has meant that large households with father and married sons living together are frequent. In Britain in 1985–7, 15 per cent of men and 12 per cent of women sixty-five and over lived in a household which included an adult child, while 4 per cent of men and 8 per cent of women lived only with adult children (Arber and Ginn, 1991a). This contrasts with Bosnia where Stojak (1990) reports, that 48 per cent of elderly people live with a child (21% of whom do not also have a spouse in the household).

A comparative study of elderly people in five countries in the late sixties, suggested that in Britain 19 per cent lived with a married child compared with 44 per cent in Yugoslavia (Nedeljkovic, 1970). The different expectations between sons and daughters in the two countries was further reflected in the reported 42 per cent of unmarried elderly men living with married sons in Yugoslavia compared to 8 per cent in Britain. The equivalent figure for unmarried elderly women was reported as 35 per cent in Yugoslavia and 4 per cent in Britain (Nedeljkovic, 1970). The tradition of nuclear families and the avoidance of living with in-laws has meant many elderly people in Britain live on their own. Twenty per cent of British men and 48 per cent of women over 65 years old live on their own (Arber and Ginn, 1991a), while in Bosnia only 18 per cent of over sixty-five year olds live alone (Stojak, 1990). This familial difference leads to differing family development cycles and differing lifestyles for elderly people.

The demographic differences relate to the age structure of the population and patterns of migration. Yugoslavia has a much younger age profile than the United Kingdom. Bosnia has a higher birth rate than most of the rest of Yugoslavia (Republicki zavod za statistiku Bosne i Hercegovine, 1987), while

Britain has a significantly lower birth rate than both. In 1988 the expectation of life at birth in England and Wales was 71.2 years for males and 77.5 years for females, and 68.1 years for males and 73.6 years for females in Yugoslavia (UN Statistical Yearbook, 1987 p.72).

Patterns of migration affect elderly people's lifestyles. In Bosnia the dominant pattern is migration from rural to urban areas which leaves elderly people in the most poor and remote villages. There are considerable differences in wealth between the rural and urban elderly in Bosnia, with urban workers having greater access to retirement pensions. In Britain migration is to commuter suburbs which leave the elderly in inner city areas, and retirement migration which creates, in resort locations like the Devon coast, very dense concentrations of elderly people. In some places in Devon over 50 per cent of the population is over 65 (Phillips *et al.*, 1987). In both Devon and Bosnia the migrant elderly appear on average to be more wealthy but less well supported by kin and neighbours (Vincent and Mudrovčić, 1992).

Data and Methods

In order to obtain material on elderly people's lifestyles, interviews were conducted with 36 people selected by a stratified random sample method to be representative of the over sixty-five-year-old population of Bosnia and Hercegovina (Finsterbusch, 1976a; 1976b). The interviewing method which was that of the life history (Dex, 1991; Samuel and Thompson, 1990), has the advantages of having a degree of structure, in that it covers the events and progression of the subject's life, but is also not so tightly structured that the subjects cannot volunteer their own perceptions of old age and its significance. Elderly people were asked to recount their personal histories – to set out their life time's experience in a way which would illuminate and explain their current life situation. The interviews were conducted in Serbo-Croatian by the second author with the first author also present. This technique permitted the use of the 'stranger' role whereby respondents could be asked to elaborate the most basic and taken for granted ideas for the 'stranger' who could not be expected to necessarily understand them, but also made use of the necessary language competence to understand a range of rural dialects.

Recent debates have pointed to the need to combine quantitative and qualitative methods in comparative research (Bengston, 1986; Bertaux, 1991; Ragin, 1991a; 1991b). Qualitative analyses are not less 'rigorous' than those using numbers (Turner and Gherardi, 1987). The method utilised here attempts to combine an essentially qualitative analysis of life histories as discourses constructed by informants (Coleman, 1991) with an attempt to ensure that the respondents collectively have some degree of typicality of the research locality, and that the contextual data on the communities in which the elderly respondents are living is systematically derived.

As part of the sampling process, all the 109 communities (opcina) in Bosnia and Hercegovina were, on the basis of data from the 1981 census, classified into twelve groups. The variables used for the stratification were (a) the largest nationality in the opcina, (b) the proportion of over sixty-five-year-olds in the population in the opcina, and (c) a rural/urban index based on occupation patterns. A sample was then selected using computerised random numbers in proportion to the numbers of elderly people in each category of *opcina*, such that each elderly person had a 1 in 10,000 chance of being in the sample. Thus 36 of the 360,000 over sixty-five-year-olds in the population of Bosnia were selected on an equal probability basis. They were located in 31 *opcine* in such a way that they have a reasonable spread of the different kinds of communities found in Bosnia.

In each of the 31 opcine key people (the President or Secretary) in the administration were interviewed in order to obtain a better understanding of the area in which the interviews were conducted and the public services available. This was part of establishing a context for the life of the old person whose personal story was to be recounted. Information was sought on the economic, political and social life of the area. This contextual information was further augmented by discussion with key individuals from voluntary organisations such as the Red Cross, and religious, professional and cultural organisations.

Thirty-six interviews were successfully completed. The characteristics of the sample can briefly be described as follows. Twenty-five were women (69%) and 11 were men. Only eight individuals (22%) lived on their own, while 28 (78%) were part of larger households. By nationality there were 19 (53%) Serbs, 9 (25%) were Croatian and 8 (22%) Moslem.[2] Half were married, 17 were widowed (15 women and 2 men) and one was never married. In terms of accommodation, 3 people were living in urban flats, 14 in new houses with 'modern conveniences' and 19 in older houses. By age, the oldest was 94 or 96, nobody was quite sure which; the mean age was 72, and the median age was 69. Three individuals were confined to bed.

Rural and Urban Perceptions

The major differences within Bosnia in terms of lifestyles of elderly people were between the conditions of urban and rural life and not between members of different ethnic groups. Those in rural areas continue to live on farms and have poor access to pensions, health care, and public amenities compared to those in towns.

There were differences of opinion between the Bosnians we interviewed (both lay and medical personel) as to whether rural or urban people had

---

2   The age profile of each of these national groups are not the same. The Moslem
     population having the youngest age profile, and the Croatian and Serbs the oldest
     profiles. Thus, although the Moslems are the largest single group in Bosnia, with
     just under fifty per cent of the population, and the Croatian the smallest, with less
     than one fifth of the population, the sample represents an approximation of the
     ethnic distribution of the elderly population.

more health problems. One local government representative, who thought that health was the biggest problem for rural elderly people, said 'after they reach about fifty they get ill. This is because of poverty and hard work'. However, others thought that the clean air and water, and unpolluted food meant that rural people were fitter and lived longer, and in contrast the industrial workers in the grossly polluting steel and chemical factories of central Bosnia did not survive long. One version of this point of view suggested that those who managed to survive the hard rural life were tough enough to live to an old age.

Poor transport communications to rural villages meant it was difficult physically for elderly people to get medical care and access to doctors and clinics. Those who have never worked for an institution or enterprise, frequently do not get a pension and have limited entitlement to the full range of health and social security benefits.

Economic, demographic and familial processes come together to structure different possible lifestyles for rural and urban elderly people in Bosnia. In the countryside the problems for old people are not seen as different to those of other rural people. They consist of how to raise enough food from the family land to sustain a basic standard of living, and to obtain enough income to provide for ones family. The economic problems for people in town are rather different. They are usually in receipt of better pensions, and those that do get a good pension are clearly substantially better off than those living in the countryside. However, the problems associated with the structuring of elderly people's lives by the state and welfare institutions are reflected in the situation of the urban Bosnian elderly. Pensions in Bosnia, because of the economic collapse, are unreliable, paid only intermittently, and not cushioned against inflation. In 1990–91 people who might have anticipated a good standard of living from their pension found that in some months they were receiving little or nothing. Although at a basic poverty level, rural people had more control of their economic resources than did the potentially richer but more financially dependent elderly people in the towns (Phillipson, 1982; Phillipson et al., 1986).

Social expectations, geographical and occupational mobility, and urban living in flats, mean that it is difficult to sustain an extended family living in urban industrial communities. However, this continuity is much more easily maintained in the rural areas. Even if a joint household is not preserved, it is possible in rural areas to build new houses on family land or adapt existing farmhouses. Thus many rural elderly people have their children in adjacent houses or construct separate apartments in different parts of the same house. Thus the possibilities of family support are likely to be greater in rural areas provided that other factors such as out-migration do not intervene.

This rural-urban difference can produce varying experiences of loneliness. It is possible to distinguish three kinds of family situation. First, where the extended household is still intact. Second, where at least one child, usually a son and a daughter-in-law, live either in a separate section of the same house or in a neighbouring house. Third, in villages which have seen a massive out-migration (Mudrovčić, 1990), much of which has been abroad,[3] and only the old couple are left with occasional visits from their children. Loneliness in this last circumstance can be the result of physical isolation, and this is where the greatest social care problems for elderly people can occur.

There are different kinds of problems relating to loneliness in the first and second types of household. The elderly people in the second household type, whose children live immediately next to but not actually in the same household, can feel lonely. They can still feel that their expectations of joint living have been let down. Even as part of an extended family elderly people experience grief at loss of their spouse, kin, and friends and neighbours of the same generation and thus a feeling of loneliness. It is wrong to over idealise extended family living for elderly people. Extended families, like other family forms, have their tensions and, although daughters-in-law may do their duty, it is not necessarily the case that these relationships are without conflicts.

Concepts of Old Age and the Idea of 'Snaga'

The elderly in Bosnia are considered by many people not to constitute a meaningful social category. There is a simple absence of such a cognitive category in many Bosnian people's understanding of their society. This is mainly because they do not separate elderly people from their household and think in terms of family problems rather than old people's problems. Those who do utilise such a concept tend to consider old age to be a problem characterised by ill health and decline.

When the Bosnian community leaders were asked about 'what kinds of problems elderly people had' in their area, the most usual type of response was that they had the same problems as other people – material problems (by which they meant poverty and lack of money) and health problems. A number of respondents said that current unemployment was a problem for elderly people because their children could not get work or money which necessarily affected them. There was also an alternative conflictual view presented by a few respondents which saw the elderly and the young in economic competition because of the collapse of the economy and state finances. This latter conflictual position contrasts with a majority of people who did not naturally think in terms of age at all.

If the concept of old age is not significant in this society, how is the inevitable progress through the life course conceptualised? The theme which

---

3   Of the foreign population living in West Germany in 1981, 637,300 (13.8%) were Yugoslavs. These people came primarily for work and then stayed to live there (Mudrovčić, 1990).

kept repeating itself in our discussions of old age in Bosnia was that of *snaga*. It was widely stated that ageing involved and could be detected by loss of *snaga*. *Snaga* is a difficult word to translate. It means 'power' or 'force', but has a positive connotation such that perhaps 'vigour' might be appropriate in English. Yet in the Serbo-Croatian language political parties or military hit squads can be denoted with this same term. The dictionary translation of *snaga* is:

> *Snaga:*   1. power, strength, energy, force; physical strength, will power, will all one's strength, legal force, moral (spiritual) force, to be in one's prime.
> 2. power; horsepower, capacity (as of pipeline), electrical power.
> 3. forces; military forces; progressive forces.

(Benson, 1980 p.580)

Towards the end of each interview with an elderly person in Bosnia, questions were asked about their personal feelings towards their age. They were asked whether they were 'old' and to those who answered the question positively, further questions were asked such as – 'in what way are you old?' or 'why do you think that you are old?' or 'what makes you feel old?' In other words, respondents were asked to elaborate those clues which identified for themselves their status as 'old'. The most common reply was the short answer 'I have loss my *snaga*' – 'I have lost my strength'. This response would be elaborated with comments such as 'I can't do things like I did them before' or sometimes 'I feel weak, slow'. For example, one very elderly lady who was effectively housebound and very poor said that it is not easy to be old and that if someone were to kill her she wouldn't mind. She went on to explain she doesn't have any *snaga* ('power') any more. She said she was most happy when it was good weather and she could work outside. In other words she did not have the 'force' to work outside in bad weather like she used to. Like many rural people work and life to her were synonymous, work is not merely something one is paid for. Work in this sense is not the British concept of paid employment but rather the activities in the house, on the land, in the factory or workshop necessary for survival (Vincent, 1987).

This idea of *snaga* is not limited to rural or non-professional people. A medical doctor attending a seminar given on the social definitions of old age in Serbo-Croatian advanced his hypothesis of ageing – that it involved loss of *snaga* ('power') and felt that this was due to the wearing out of the digestive system which prevented old people getting the energy they needed. *Snaga* can be distinguished from a similar term *moc*. *Moc* connotes a more physical condition than snaga which refers to both a mental and physical state. The distinction suggests that in the use of *snaga* people are not merely referring to ill health.

The following two interview extracts illustrates how the concept is used in discourse. A sixty-nine-year-old woman with a heart condition, living on a farm in the north of Bosnia, discussed the subject in the following terms:

Željka: You know we have been talking with many elderly and all of them have used the term *snaga* like you did, and John would like you to explain to him what do you mean by that, what is *snaga*? He doesn't understand.

Respondent: I don't know how to explain that to you. For example, I just said '*snaga*'. I get tired. I am going along and 'huh','huh' [breathes heavily] I can't breath...[aside to grandson] to say that I am ill, I am not. I am not that. I just don't have strength. I don't have strength to like huh [breaths], to move and to be mobile. I used, when I walked, really to walk and not to [*meljati*] amble along like now. That's that what I think is *snaga*. I don't know how to explain that, was that clear?

Another sixty-nine-year-old woman from Bosanska Krupa responded to the question what makes you feel old:

Željka: Will you describe it [feelings of old age] for me, I don't understand that.

Respondent: Weakness, weakness...sometimes you can get to your feet easily sometimes not. Yes...Yes. It is the years that are pulling you down...

Željka: Does that affect your work?

Respondent: Oh course, some time ago I could work easily without problems and now I simply can't; sometimes I still can, but...*godine pretezu* [the years take their toll], old age, suffering, there is all of that in life.

The nearest equivalent in Britain is perhaps the perception of one of Thompson *et al.'s* (1990 p.109) respondents who is quoted as describing herself as 'slowing down'. Although this phrase is instantly recognisable as a meaningful conceptualisation of old age, in Britain it was, however, the only occurrence in their sample. We suggest that, the concept of *snaga* is a distinctive cultural way of conceptualising the ageing process, and in the absence of distinctive status changes, like retirement in rural Bosnia, probably the only one.

Feelings of Loss

In the introduction of his book *Anthropology and the Riddle of the Sphinx*, Spencer (1990) asks the very complex question about what it is that is lost through ageing? He identifies a universal problem of loss through ageing and says that the universality is not based simply on biological processes but cultural, environmental, and psychological ones. Thus despite its universality the process is experienced as a personal one by each individual.

The peak of physical condition, the so called 'prime of life', is often characterised as lasting from about eighteen to thirty years. Biologically ageing is probably associated with a cumulative inability of cells to reproduce themselves. The process is a long one during which initially speed declines, while 'strength and endurance might still remain'. Subsequently, there is a change in the metabolic process and through the fifties the organism starts to lose adaptive capacity. Spenser sees a 'natural life span', thus there is a subsequent period in human life when the organism is not what it used to be. There comes a time when feelings of weakness and of 'slowing down' occur in contrast to one's former condition. Hence, not the particular physical or social condition but the feeling of loss, it is argued, is universal.

If the problem of 'loss' through ageing appears as an universal attribute of ageing, the culturally specific manifestation of those feelings in Bosnia are expressed through the phrase loss of *snaga*. This chapter has explored how elderly people in Bosnia conceptualise the ageing process that they have experienced, including those aspects which might be understood as diminishing feelings of mental and physical strength. This idea of old age, as loss of power, is more appropriate for a society without institutionalised age based roles, such as that of pensioner. In these circumstances concepts elaborated around an individual's subjective feelings are more likely to become meaningful for defining old age rather than other criteria such as chronological age, or even external appearance.

An individual's feelings about their age have to reconcile the status of adulthood and their experience of physical changes associated with advancing years. It may be further argued that this reconciliation is universally required in all cultures even although concepts of old-age, adulthood, and even of physical condition and bodily appearance, are themselves culturally constructed and very varied. Thompson *et al.* (1990) discuss these issues in a British context. It is clear from their work that elderly people in Britain have to manage a discrepancy between the cultural expectations of elderly people and their own feelings about themselves.

> You can feel old at any point in adulthood. Men and women in their twenties or thirties or forties can feel they have failed to find the right person to marry, or have made the wrong career choice, and that they are 'too old' to start again. Feeling old is feeling exhausted in spirit, lacking the energy to find new responses as life changes. It is giving up. Feeling ourselves means feeling the inner energy which has carried us thus far in life. (Thompson *et.al.*, 1990 p.250)

Dragadze (1990) discusses the unusually late attribution of adulthood in Soviet (now independent) Georgia. Here maintaining the social statuses and cultural expectations of adulthood in old age combined with declining physical condition is a problem for some elderly people. In this society adult status is acquired in their late thirties and forties when people are considered to have acquired the level of self restraint and wisdom to be regarded as responsible for their actions. Few words and much wisdom is what is expected. Elderly people who still retain good eyesight or hearing are likely to retain their full authority. Those people who are physically unable to fully compete in the economic and social life of the community, respond by withdrawal into more limited and isolated activities often outside the house, so that they can maintain the socially expected demonstration of self-control and carefully controlled comment and thus their adult status. Dragadze says of the situation in Georgia:

> Diminishing strength, however, accompanies advancing age. Old people, in order to retain some measure of 'respect', will avoid risking a rebuff from their juniors. They tend to anticipate this increasing loss of powers by participating even less in the day to day running of the home. They spend, for example, more time at the private plots than before on tasks such as weeding that are considered light but boring. They do similar work on the collective farm. (Dragadze, 1990 p.97)

Similarly in the Alpine villages of the Val d'Aosta the social expectation of social equality leads to strict rules of social reciprocity, whereby favours are always asked for but not offered. Thus elderly people who are, because of increasing infirmity, unable to offer reciprocal services and labour, increasingly isolate themselves socially (Vincent, 1973a; 1973b).

The strategy of social withdrawal by elderly people does not appear to be common in Bosnia. The strong expectations both of family solidarity involving, if not joint living, continual mutual visiting, and the expectations of *pomoc*, neighbours help, which involves mutual exchange of visits for coffee, have a strong socially integrating effect for elderly people. In these circumstances of family sociability, if not extended family living, physical ability to maintain social activity and social status are related. Loss of 'power' has linked psychological and social status implications and are experienced as the same, and expressed with the idea of loss of *snaga*.

The onset of physical dependency leads to a psychological sense of loss of energy as the elderly person takes less responsibility for family decisions. This further leads to a diminished ability to take the initiative in determining collective behaviour. The accompanying loss of fully adult status, means loss of social power. This analysis can be linked to the frequent association of inability to work and of ill health with the idea of old age in Bosnia, whereas the association of old age with a yearly chronology is seldom made.

Conclusion

There is not a simple mechanism of attribution by which physical disability leads to lowering of social status in Bosnia. The obedience, respect and care due from children and daughters-in-law is widely acknowledged as a normative expectation. In reality the development of economic and physical dependency leads to changes in social relationships, internal to the family which are experienced by the elderly person as 'loss'. This 'loss' is of course a relative concept, people may still be relatively fit, but experience loss of *snaga* when compared to their previous position, when they were 'in their prime' at the peak of the family cycle.

In the rural extended family situation while fit and able to work, at whatever age, the senior generation still keeps control and has the highest status in the household. Physical impairment which leads to dependency, whatever the age, leads to loss of status and 'power' (Elias, 1985). The concept of *snaga* identifies the interconnected loss of health and loss of social status and the feelings associated with that experience within a single concept. People are able to 'explain' old age in Bosnia by this one notion which identifies the point at which full adult status starts to be lost.

This chapter suggests that the subjective experience of ageing in Bosnia contrasts with that in Britain because differences in labour processes, migration patterns and differences in households structures, lead to different life course patterns and differences in the way that elderly people construe the physical and social changes that happen to them.

CHAPTER 7

Emotional and Sexual Adjustment in Later Life

H.B. Gibson

This chapter challenges the general stereotype that society has of the emotional and sexual lives of older people, a perception that owes much to outmoded Victorian standards which are greatly at variance with modern social reality. It is exemplified, with reference to both ancient and modern literature, how older characters are mocked if they aspire to achieve an active love-life, and demonstrates that within the Western Christian tradition, older men and women are expected to be celibate if they are rendered single in later life. Popular culture, as expressed in television programmes and in demotic jokes, also serves to perpetuate a stereotype of elderly people that is both false and demeaning. Some signs of change are noted in all these expressions of the *zeitgeist* of the modern age.

Later in the chapter, it is shown how the stereotypes we have inherited produce a confusion over roles in men and women in the period of their lives after child-rearing and retirement from full-time work. This confusion may lead to conflicts within families when parents challenge the prevailing stereotypes while children try to maintain them. Finally, some empirical evidence from the author's on-going research is presented concerning people who have formed new love-relationships in later life. This is discussed with relation to the growing numerical imbalance between the sexes in the older age cohorts, a disparity that has important implications for the institution of marriage and heterosexual relationships in later life.

Not only do younger people have a somewhat distorted view of what their elders do and feel emotionally, but older people in the Western world – now characterized as being in the 'Third Age' (Laslett, 1989) – have an unrealistic view of what is 'seemly' for their age-group. David Clark, who ran a series of seminars for the University of the Third Age in Cambridge, reported that:

> We sometimes discussed things that it was not appropriate for us to do... It was certainly clear that we should not be irritable, cantankerous or drunken in public and we had the impression that sexual activity or interest on our parts was usually regarded with dismay when it was brought to the attention of the younger generation. (Clark, 1989 p.36)

Here we have the paradox that while in the Victorian era it was politic for younger people to conceal much of their sexual interest and behaviour from the censorial eyes of their elders, in this modern age many of the older generation deem it proper to conceal even their *sexual* interest from the younger generation, and equate it with public drunken-ness.

The present generation of people who were born in the first third of the twentieth century experienced in their younger years the formative influences of a society that was very different from that which developed after the Second World War. They were brought up by parents and parental figures who were themselves strongly influenced by an ethos that is generally characterized as 'Victorian'.

The Victorian Heritage

In the Victorian ethos the frank expression of sexuality was taboo, and while some latitude might be extended to young males, the taboo was especially strong for women. The ethos also decreed that when people reached a certain age they should behave, and indeed dress, quite differently from younger adults, so that 'the elderly' – that is, at that time people a little older than 50 years – wore distinctively sober clothes, the contrast being most noticeable in female dress. Expressions of sexuality in older people were regarded as pathological, and the medical profession in general gave its authority to the perpetuation of a great deal of mythology that had no basis in scientific research or empirical observation.

Havelock Ellis, a late Victorian writer whose *Studies in the Psychology of Sex* was first published in 1897, and who continued to write in the present century, accepted that normal women had sexual feelings, in contrast to many of his medical colleagues such as William Acton (1862) who maintained that such an idea cast 'vile aspersions' on female nature. Nevertheless, Havelock Ellis later proclaimed that, 'There is a frequent well-marked tendency in women at the menopause to an eruption of sexual desire, the last flaring up of a dying fire, which may easily take a morbid form' (1933 p.181).

Modern authorities such as Butler and Lewis (1988), Alex Comfort (1990) and Paula Weideger (1975) would dismiss this as one of the many menopausal myths, and observe that as post-menopausal women are normally quite active sexually for the ensuing decades if they have a suitable partner, it is absurd to refer to 'the last flaring up of a dying fire'.

Havelock Ellis was equally mistaken about the effect of ageing on men. He believed that age-related changes in the prostate produced a 'physical irritation' that led to a flaring up of sexuality in elderly men which caused them to molest children: 'The average age of the victim regularly decreases as the average age of the perpetrator increases...It is in this way sometimes that senile dementia begins to declare itself before intellectual failure is obvious' (Havelock Ellis, 1933 p.182). In fact, later research has shown that elderly men as a group are the *least* likely to engage in child molesting (Rubin, 1977).

The Portrayal of Sexuality Among Elderly People

Literature and popular writing

Although it is easy to use the appellation 'Victorian' as a convenient shorthand describing public attitudes that are no longer taken for granted today, we should not forget that what has come down to us is largely a record that was *published* in the days when there was a considerable censorship of printed matter, a restriction that lasted until the 1950s. We know little about the actualities of prevalent attitudes in a society that was considerably more pluralistic than we may be apt to imagine. We do not know whether Victorian men and women were really more prudish than their counterparts in Regency and earlier times; what we do know is that they were considerably more hypocritical and concerned to present standards that they considered ideal, as though they really believed in them. In literature they simply tended to perpetuate age-old stereotypes of elderly people, and because of the different age-structure of the population, there were rather fewer elders around to give the lie to the stereotype.

Similarly, we may make the mistake of thinking that what we have discovered about the sexuality of elderly people by painstaking research in the present century was quite unknown to the Victorians. Although research such as that by Raymond Pearl (1930), the Kinsey studies (*Kinsey et al.* 1948; 1953), Masters and Johnson (1966; 1970), and Pfeiffer *et al.* (1968; 1983), have greatly added to our detailed knowledge of sexuality in later life, we do not know how much this was known in a general way in Victorian times, although not published. Above I have cited Havelock Ellis' absurd picture of the a sexuality of post-menopausal women, but we may question how widely this myth was believed. Brok (1992) quotes an anonymous and bawdy verse that sets out facts about human sexuality that are now accepted through the research of those cited above. This verse describes, with a fair degree of accuracy, how the potency and frequency of intercourse declines with age in men, and it describes how, with women, there is no such marked decline, and how they may retain their capacity and enjoyment of intercourse and other forms of love- making for their whole lives. It is remarkable that this verse originated at the end of the nineteenth century when, in the eyes of many respectable authorities, 'a modest woman seldom desires any sexual gratification for herself. She submits to her husband, but only to please him; and but for the desire for maternity, would far rather be relieved of his attentions' (Acton, 1862 p.102).

In the *Ecclesiazusae*, a comedy by Aristophanes (450 – 388 BC), there is a clear recognition of the fact that many women have a need for erotic love when they are old, just as they have when they are young. The play is a brutal satire but it recognizes the facts which were acknowledged in ancient Greece, as they are not generally acknowledged today – that age makes very little difference to a woman's sexual appetites. The theme is that the women of Athens have taken over the government, and recognizing the need of elderly women for a sex-life, enact a law that no young man may have his girl friend without first giving sexual service to any elderly woman who desires him.

A more humane view is taken by the Greek lyric poets like Philodemus, who celebrates the erotic capacity of older women:

> Charito is more than sixty...
> Lovers, if you do not run from hot desire, Enjoy Charito
> And forget her many decades. (Quoted by Barnstone, 1962 p.211)

But Philodemus displays a macho male's attitude to female sexuality, for he praises this courtesan simply because she *resembles* a younger woman, and misses the point that attractiveness in older women depends upon such things as the character of the face, which can still be striking and charming despite many wrinkles, and an attractive personality that is conveyed by the whole demeanour.

The idea that later life should be a time of renunciation of sexuality finds some expression in the ancient world, but their attitudes were ambiguous. The Christian tradition is less equivocal in this matter: Chaucer, following Boccaccio, generally adheres to the convention of condemning erotic love in later life. In his 'Merchant's Tale' the 'old' knight January marries the young woman May, and is cuckolded and made a fool of accordingly. Shakespeare is often negative in his attitude to the loves of older people: there is the well-known scene in which Hamlet denounces the sexuality of his mother in the crudest of terms; Falstaff is mocked and pilloried because, *at his age*, he responds to the flirtatious invitations of the Merry Wives who lead him on. The same theme is repeated in Restoration comedy, as in Congreve's Lady Wishfort, who is ridiculed because she loves Mirabell.

In the novels of Charles Dickens there are several examples. When he introduces older women contemplating a love-affair he becomes positively vitriolic, and cruelly pillories such figures as Mrs Nickleby, Madame La Creevy and Flora Finching because, despite their age, they are attracted to a man. It may be remarked that in earlier literature it was generally ageing men who were mocked because they aspired to love young women, but in later literature ridicule was more often directed against ageing women who had erotic aspirations.

More modern writers who have written a good deal about the theme of love and sex, such as Colette, Thomas Hardy, Henry James, D.H. Lawrence, Somerset Maugham, Proust, and Shaw, largely ignore the fact that people can fall in love in later life, and that such love can be as great and as meaningful as love in youth and middle-age. Bashevis Singer, the famous Yiddish writer, dealt with 'old love' in his stories, and he wrote:

> The love of the old and middle-aged is a theme that is recurring more and more in my works of fiction. Literature has neglected the old and their emotions. The novelists never told us that in love, as in other matters, the young are just beginners, and that the art of love matures with age and experience. (Singer, 1982 p.7)

This emphasis may be related to the fact that, being Jewish, he is not writing in the Western Christian tradition which has perpetuated certain assumptions about elderly people.

Another modern author in the Jewish tradition who writes realistically about older people is Saul Bellow. In his *Mr Sammler's Planet* Artur Sammler, aged 72, is the central character, and he brings out very effectively the association between sexuality and power in later life. When Mr Sammler attempts to lecture to young students and presents a politically unwelcome message, he gets a noisy response and one of them presents their objection to his views and age thus:

> Orwell was a fink. He was a sick counter-revolutionary. It's good he died when he did. And what you are saying is shit... Why do you listen to this effete old shit? What has he got to tell you? His balls are dry. He's dead. He can't come. (Bellow, 1970 p.42)

Thus the young objector to Sammler's lecture and Orwell's ideas, expresses his ageism in sexual terms, wishfully attributing sexual impotence to the elderly lecturer.

Outside the Christian tradition also, we must consider Japanese writers. Mary Sohngen lists 87 novels published between 1950 and 1975 in America or the UK which are written from the perspective of a protagonist over the age of sixty. She comments that among these novels written 'During this period when sexual frankness was an accepted element in fiction, only a few include the sexual activity – or the sexual fantasies – of the protagonist' (Sohngen 1977 p.72). There are, in fact, seven novels in this category, and two of them are translations from the Japanese. The Japanese have their own traditional attitudes towards the elderly, to whom they display a certain ambivalence. The Confucian teachings enjoin a somewhat excessive respect, which is countered by an opposing tradition embodying a wish to dispose of the burden of the elderly quite ruthlessly which goes by the name of *obasute* (literally, 'discarding granny'). But like the ancient Greeks, and the Jews, the Japanese do not overlook the fact that erotic interest and need do not disappear with age.

A notable exception to the writers in the Christian tradition was Graham Greene, who, after a series of gloomy novels presenting the Roman Catholic point of view, went into a period of non-productive depression, and then recovered to produce a hilarious novel, *Travels With My Aunt*. This is the tale of a woman in her seventies, who after a lifetime of affairs and actual prostitution, retains her sexual appetite unabated, and as part of her generally joyous life-style continues to take new lovers, and ends up happily with one of her old lovers. Among other writers who take a more positive approach, is Eudora Welty. Her 'Old Mr Marblehall' is a humorous story of how an old man, married for the first time at the age of sixty, manages to retain the sexual habits of his youth in discreet secrecy, despite the stifling atmosphere of a life-denying society around him that would relegate him to the scrap-heap of the old and used-up if they could (Welty, 1941).

In his later years, V.S. Pritchett wrote about older people defying the stereotype of 'the old', and used the theme of the erotic impulse to remind people that they should try to live in the present. The idea that some elderly single people need sex, as an immediate concern, more than companionship or love, as maintained by Pritchett, may seem shocking to those who are conditioned to accept the Darby and Joan stereotype of elderly people.

Of course older people want love, companionship and secure relationships, but so do people of all ages. Most men are less likely in their later years, to have the compulsive need to 'prove themselves' sexually to demonstrate their masculinity, although some may do so just to show that they are not senile. However, it is probably better that they should try to keep the life force alive, and heed Dylan Thomas:

Do not go gentle into that good night,
Old age should burn and rave at close of day;
Rage, rage against the dying of the light. (Thomas, 1988 p.148)

There are many elderly people who are so conditioned by the assumptions of the society in which they grew up, that they are, sadly, prepared to 'go gentle into that good night', living on a pittance and willing to give up many of their rights as citizens. The examples of the resignation and humility of many of the poorer section of retired people today illustrated by Henwood (1990) in matters of health care, and by Walker (1990a) concerning social security, make dismal reading.

As well as Eudora Welty and V.S. Pritchett, there are many younger post-war writers who are trying to give a more accurate picture of how elderly people try to express themselves emotionally and erotically. Celeste Loughman (1983) discusses their work and comments that their stories extend to elderly people the liberal sexual attitudes which other segments of the population have been experiencing, and challenge long-standing myths that have effectively severed old age from other stages of life. They confirm that life is a continuum, and urge that behaviour in the sexual sphere which is tolerated in the young should not be censored in the old.

Television

In the 1970s there were various studies in the USA which showed that older people were almost invisible on television, as summarized by Davis and Davis (1985). When they did appear in programmes it was either in the role of dear old sweeties mouthing platitudes in the background, or horrible old figures of fun acting as an occasional foil for the real characters, the young. Pressure was brought to bear on television companies by groups like the Grey Panthers who insisted that people over the age of sixty did exist in society, and that their lives were as important as those of younger people. Changes began to occur in the programmes showing that it pays to make a fuss, and of course television companies are sensitive to the complaints of consumers of the products they advertise.

A research project in the UK in 1984 was designed to study how the four British television channels represented elderly people (Lambert, Laslett and Clay, 1984). While all types of programme had instances of elderly people being totally absent, their absence was particularly noticeable in some. Older people appeared more frequently in programmes concerned with the news, current affairs and documentaries, which was to be expected, as many prominent people in the world are elderly; in fact if you are rich enough and powerful enough your age does not seem to matter.

As 18 per cent of the population of the UK can now be classed as elderly (Arber and Ginn, 1991a), representative group or crowd scenes should naturally present them in this proportion, or a little less, as perhaps they are less publically visible. They were found to be between 10 and 20 per cent present in scenes where groups were shown.

One striking feature of this inquiry relates to the sex of the elderly figures shown. Although there are a lot more women among the elderly population, they were grossly under-represented in television programmes, and were seldom in central roles. As for the class structure, over four fifths of those appearing belonged to the managerial and professional classes. This bias was less pronounced in fictional programmes where older working-class women had some significant roles in popular soap operas such as Coronation Street. Taking into account both the sex and class distortions of the presentations, the authors of the research say:

> The result can only be called a caricature of the real social world of the British elderly...an important reason why the elderly as we know them are negligible in television appearance is *because* the successful elderly people who do figure there are not regarded as elderly in society. Thus, even when they are themselves biologically elderly, politicians and leaders do not represent the elderly as a social category. (Lambert *et al.*, 1984 p.7)

If we inquire how the sexuality of older people was portrayed, it is notable that although an attempt was made to rate elderly people shown in the programmes on various characteristics, such as 'wise/foolish', 'active/passive', 'fit/infirm', the one characteristic that proved to be very obviously different from the others was 'sexually active/inactive', because it applied in so few cases and so was not rateable. This was even true bearing in mind that it was not an average section of the population who are shown, but a rather superior class of people in socio-economic terms, and over-whelmingly male.

The portrayal of elderly people on television programmes improved during the 1980s (Mullen and Zwanenberg 1988; Swayne and Greco 1987), partly due to agitation from pressure groups, but also because many older people are now significant consumers, and have changed their attitude towards spending: they are less likely to hoard their capital and live penuri-ously for the sake of their descendants (Batty 1989). They are now beginning to spend more freely in order to live more comfortable lives, thus forming an important new market. Purchasing power counts with television adver-tisers, and they have been making some attempt to woo the older consumer, as discussed by Minkler (1989). Thus there are new programmes like 'Tea and Sympathy' where three sets of lovers appear – young, middle-aged, and elderly. More recently, programmes such as 'One Foot in the Grave', and 'Waiting for God', portray sexuality in old age in a very positive light.

Popular humour

Popular humour is an excellent indicator of issues about which people feel strongly, hence the popularity of sex jokes and lavatory humour in the aftermath of Victorian prudishness. There have been a number of studies of how the perceived ridiculousness and nastiness of growing old is reflected in popular humour, particularly with regard to sexual matters. One review of jokes about old people revealed that over half of them showed a highly negative attitude, and *ageing women* were the especial butt of aggressive humour (Palmore, 1971). As Itzin (1984) has pointed out, attitudes of sexism and ageism combine to make the lot of elderly women especially difficult. Another review (Richman, 1977) compared jokes concerning elderly people with those about children, and found that whereas most of those about children were appreciative, viewing them in a positive if 'quaint' light, most of the jokes about old people were definitely derogatory, ridiculing the decline of their sexual powers, among other things. A few jokes were more complex, however, turning upon those who denigrate elderly people be-cause their turn to be ridiculous would be coming in due course. A number of jokes affirmed that some old people have a lot more life in them than is generally supposed, old men being shown as being absurd whatever they do, as they are seen either as sexless wrecks or over-sexed lechers (Fry, 1976).

There are two main theories of the meaning and function of jokes that are worth considering, the disparagement theory and the incongruity model (Suls, 1976). It is easy to interpret jokes about old people in terms of disparagement theory, but unlike racist and sexist jokes, the younger people who make them know that they themselves will eventually be joining the group that is the butt of their humour. In the incongruity model, there is a necessary paradox to be perceived – that the crowing young man taking pride in his strength and virility, will one day have to accept the decline that is in store for him. This is the riddle of the Sphinx that was posed to Oedipus – he who walks on two legs at noon, will hobble along on three in the evening – that is, he will have to use a walking stick when he is old.

That ageist jokes are particularly derogatory about women, is an example of the tragedy of the approach of many men to sex, for if he loves a woman simply for her blooming, youthful charm, she will be taken from him inevitably when she changes with age into someone he cannot approach in the same way.

In studying popular humour, we may look at greeting cards of various sorts. Birthday-card humour displays examples of aggressive ageism, often combined with sexism. There is, of course, the traditional mother-in-law joke; this aged female figure, ugly, stupid and domineering, has no counterpart in a father-in-law figure. A demotic joke runs as follows:

A. I've formed quite an attachment for my mother-in-law.
B. How strange!
A. Yes, it fits over her mouth.

The older woman represents what the young wife *will become* in the course of years. Birthday cards are particularly significant, as they remind people of the passing years and of the spectre of old age that looms ahead. Those designed to be sent to older relatives are typically sentimental and cheerful, reassuring the recipients that they don't look their age; it is those designed to be sent to contemporaries that contain crude jokes about the coming of old age with all its supposed horrors.

In summary, all ageist jokes display just what racist and sexist jokes display – fear. Jokes against black people display the fear of the dominant white man that those he exploits will rise up against him; sexist jokes against women betoken that the exploited female will likewise emancipate herself from male dominance, and ageist jokes show a fear that old people will no longer accept their status of pathetic nonentities, fit only to poke the fire and look after the grandchildren.

Emotional Fulfilment in Later Life

Confusion in roles

It has been pointed out that as they age, people are treated in accordance with derogatory stereotypes of 'the elderly', and they are apt to accept such stereotypes for themselves and their age-peers. According to Alex Comfort:

> Modern research indicates that a high proportion of the mental and attitudinal changes seen in 'old' people are not biological effects of ageing. They are the results of role-playing. When women were expected to faint at the sight of blood, or working folk to touch their forelocks to squire; some of them did so. Now that these roles are seen to be demeaning or ridiculous, they don't and won't. (1990 p.12)

Elsewhere, I have referred to 'Older people as gaolers of "the old"' (Gibson, 1991 p.218) and in no aspect of life is this more evident than in the expression of sexuality. Many professional people would agree with Rasjit Skinner, a clinical psychologist, that: 'it is important to be aware that a satisfactory sexual relationship is important for most people's well-being at any age. In the elderly the increased needs for love, self-esteem and for close human contact give sexuality an enhanced value' (1988, p.25). But, as mentioned earlier, Clark (1989) found in his seminars with older people, a distinct reluctance to acknowledge anything but an a-sexual role for themselves and their age-peers.

Rosow (1985) points out that as people age, they face roles that are increasingly ill-structured. They are faced with 'dilemmas', that is, problems that have no clearly defined solutions, so it is natural that they should cling to traditional roles, even if they become increasingly uncomfortable in them. Where the role is grossly at odds with an individual's life situation, considerable stress may be suffered. Thus, if an ageing woman tries to cling on to the role of a nurturant grandmother, and no-one in the family continues to need or want such a figure to be around, her life will indeed be unhappy.

Retirement from work obviously entails some re-adjustment of role. There has been research and related controversy as to whether men and women exchange their sex roles to some extent, the men becoming more androgynous (Belsky, 1992; Guttmann, 1987; Bennett and Morgan, this volume). If a man has had a strongly 'masculine' role that was expressed in his work, and bound up in his interaction with male work-mates, he will inevitably relinquish at least some aspects of it on retirement. Troll (1971) points out that retirement for many working-class men may bring a sense of humiliation because their wives expect them now to engage in household tasks that they have previously regarded as 'women's work'. Such men may wonder, after retirement how they can continue to express their masculine role: in masculine sports? But they have lost their former physical vigour. In bed? But their potency has declined and they may blame sexual failures on the decreased attractiveness of their wives. Such role re-adjustments may be very difficult for some men, and lead to marital conflicts that ostensibly have a purely sexual basis, but which are really due to complex psycho-social factors. This finding about the discomfort of retired males was probably truer twenty years ago at the time that Troll was writing. The general opinion then appeared to be that post-retirement alterations in roles were more stressful for men than women, but Brecher (1984) found comparing 803 retired husbands with 386 retired wives, there was no significant difference. Belsky points out that much of the earlier research on retirement created a depressing picture which is no longer true for the present cohorts of people who are now retiring, and 'retirement is far from the emotional trauma it is supposed to be' (Belsky, 1992 p.164). This view accords with the findings of Palmore et al. (1985).

Conflict with younger members of the family

A recent anonymous writer to The Lancet comments: 'the younger gener-ation, so liberal, so free, so uninhibited by old- fashioned conventions according to themselves, are often rigid, narrow, puritanical, and censorious when it comes to the behaviour of older citizens' (Anon, 1986). Disapproval of the behaviour of parental figures, particularly when they form relation-ships with new partners in later life, has two main roots: an irrational emotional reaction, and practical or economic objection. Some writers have stressed the jealousy aspect of the emotional reaction; according to Butler and Lewis 'The thought of a parent becoming involved with a new partner can provoke anxiety, threat, jealousy, hurt, anger, or grief' (1988 p.140). The so-called 'oedipal' reaction has been referred to by Pfeiffer: 'Our denial of sexuality among the elderly may result, in part, from feelings which all of us harbour regarding sexual expression in our parents' generation, and more specifically, in our own parents' (1983 p.68).

Some writers have stressed the rivalry motive as well as the 'Oedipal' distress:

> Among the younger age groups, the negative attitude to sexuality in the elderly stems from unconscious factors; an extension of the incest taboo, (i.e., a continuation of the children's discomfort about regarding their parents as sexual beings); and a rivalry motive (i.e., by portraying the elderly as asexual, the young can eliminate them from competition as sexual objects). (Thienhaus, Conter and Bosmann, 1986 p.47)

The economic objection has several obvious reasons. If a parent forms a new attachment in later life there is the danger that the inheritance will be divided, and in the case of a man, he may even father additional children. Elderly parents, especially grandmothers, are less easily exploited by the younger generation if they have a new partner to occupy their time and interest, instead of devoting their energies to looking after the grandchildren and acting as general 'dogsbodies' on demand. There is also the fact that, as pointed out by Byers (1983), a lone parent is easier to *manage;* a new spouse or lover will be an ally and protector, and the whole future power-relation-ship will be altered.

Where the parent is bereaved, attempts to begin a new domestic and sexual life with a new partner may be opposed by middle aged children on the grounds that such action would be 'disloyal'. This powerful though irrational argument may serve to compel a bereaved person to reject, through guilt, the promise of future happiness, and to 'enshrine' the memory of the dead spouse (Lewis, 1989).

Fear of sexual incompetence

People may be deterred from forming new erotic relationships in later life because they fear facing sexual demands that they cannot meet. This may apply specially to men, because they are generally expected to take the initiative, and after a period of celibacy after divorce or bereavement, they may wonder if they are impotent. As pointed out by Masters and Johnson (1966), what constitutes 'impotence' is rather vague; most men, even in their younger years, experience occasions on which they are unable to perform normally in lovemaking. What is regrettably common is that an ageing man will experience one or two such incidents, and then conclude that he will be 'impotent' for the rest of his life, and withdraw from all sexual contacts even to the extent of withdrawing socially from the company of women who may find him attractive. Sexual counselling may be needed to restore his self-confidence and to rid him of the many false beliefs about sexuality that are still current (see Gibson, 1991).

Women are less likely to be deterred from forming new erotic relationships for fear of sexual incompetence, because by tradition they take a passive role. They are more likely to be deterred because they falsely believe that no man will ever find them attractive again. In more recent years there have been a number of publications designed to give both women and men more confidence in their potential for forming and maintaining new loving relationships in later life, such as Greengross and Greengross (1989).

The Formation of New Sexual Relationships in Later Life

The statistics of the population structure show that with increasing age, there is a greater numerical predominance of women over men (Arber and Ginn, 1991a). Far more women than men are living singly in the older cohorts, and the possibility of forming a one-to-one relationship with a man becomes more and more remote for women as they age. In a recent issue of the paper Reporter (Issue 15, Summer 1992), which caters for people over 50, there were 165 advertisements for partners. Of these only 29 (18%) were inserted by men. Some marital introduction agencies now refuse to take women over 60 on their books.

Illustrations from on-going research

Gibson (1992) advertised widely for autobiographical accounts from people who had formed new love-relationships in later life, and the preliminary results illustrate some interesting points relating to the numerical imbalance between the sexes, and changing attitudes among elderly people.

One woman reported that after a lifetime of normal marriage and rearing children, she fell in love with another woman while living apart from her husband. Her love was reciprocated quite passionately, and they have formed a stable lesbian relationship that is very satisfying. As the old taboos on sexuality and homosexual relationships recede, it seems likely that more and more women who have previously been entirely heterosexual over their previous life course, will form lesbian relationships in later life.

Among the interesting things shown by these autobiographical accounts, is the notable feature that patterns of falling in love, or of selecting new partners, seem to differ very little from what is experienced in other periods during the life course. Often elderly people are amazed at their own emotional reactions. It seems that while our bodies decline in vigour and robustness in later life, our emotional drives stay very much the same.

Although most of the relationships reported by both men and women have led to marriage, six reveal women who have taken new male lovers on a stable basis in their sixties, but have not wished to confirm the relationship by marriage. Although there is still some prejudice against older people, and in particular, older women, embarking upon a sex-life, these unmarried relationships have not caused any significant social inconvenience even among quite conventional people who might have some qualms about the propriety of living in an unmarried union themselves. The point that these women make is that in their earlier years they worked hard as mothers and housewives, sometimes in addition to having a demanding job, and now they are in the Third Age they do not want to drop back into the habit of being housekeeper to a man as well as his friend, bed-mate and companion. This tendency is in accordance with Lopata's (1973) study of Chicago widows, four-fifths of whom said that they had no wish to re-marry, and gave practical reasons for preferring to live alone.

In the great majority of cases which have been collected so far, the newly formed relationships have been between people of much the same age. Obviously this reflects the opportunities that are present in the Third Age, but it also reflects deliberate choice, and confirms the finding of Brecher (1984). In his survey of 4,246 older people, when men and women were asked to describe the characteristics of the 'ideal lover' they would like to have, the great majority described someone who was about their own age. In the on-going research there is only one case of a man who formed a relationship with a woman much younger than himself, and it illustrates an important weakness in such relationships. Mr S was sixty and had been divorced for some years when he took a woman aged thirty to live with him. She was a widow with two young children. All went well for about eight years; their relationship was a strongly erotic one, and she reported:

> He was a vibrant and considerate lover, and took great pleasure in giving pleasure. He had the gift of making me feel glamourous and feel proud of my body, and he obviously loved my ample build which had always been an embarrassment to me. For the first time I became confident and adventurous in bed.

When Mr S's health and sexual potency began to fail prematurely, partly because he was a very heavy drinker, he was conscious that he was no longer satisfying his partner in the way they usually made love, and he even urged her to take other lovers, although she knew that this would have been impossible as he was a very proud and jealous man. Eventually she left him, although she still loved him, and sought sexual satisfaction elsewhere. This instance highlights an objection that is seldom discussed: that men's sexual powers decline in later life far more rapidly than is the case with women (see Gibson 1991, Chapter 1 and 2). This situation also has a bearing on the proposal that the numerical imbalance between the sexes in later life could be compensated for by the formation of polygamous relationships, as suggested by Kassel (1975). While a vigorous man in his prime might be an adequate lover, at least in a physical sense, for a group of women, such would not be the case in later life. As our society tries to give equal status to both men and women, it is doubtful whether any such polygamous relationship would be successful in an emotional and social sense either.

Gibson's research refers only to that minority of women in the Third Age who wish, and are able to, form new heterosexual relationships in later life, because of the numerical shortage of male partners. So far, only one account of a lesbian relationship has been volunteered, as mentioned above, but as the research population are self-selected there are likely to be biasses associated with its composition. In Brecher's (1984) study, the question 'Have you ever felt sexually attracted to a person of your own gender?' was responded to positively by 11 per cent (196) of the women, and 8 per cent (184) of the men. Yet of these respondents, 56 per cent of the men, but only 23 per cent of the women had actually formed a same-sex relationship after the age of 50. Brecher relates this difference to two factors: first, the stricter upbringing in relation to sex that the females of this generation had experienced; and second, that the men had been conditioned by the mores of a society in which males actively sought sex, but women were expected to wait until they were sought after. It may be that this difference will no longer exist when the cohorts who were brought up in more liberal circumstances, and who were significantly affected by the feminist movement of the late 1960s enter the Third Age.

Mrs N, an elderly respondent in the Gibson survey (1992), does not report having formed a new love-relationship herself, but her views are worth quoting. She writes:

> Over three million of us are widows. I feel that most of us have spent most of our lives in a close relationship and would prefer to live this way. Sometimes a feeling of loyalty to our lost partners, or lack of confidence in ourselves, leads to a withdrawal from society, and I am all in favour of any measure that helps to bring us back to life...

> Of course there are some men around, even after eliminating those who are already married or seriously unfit. But there are still problems ahead. Gold diggers and con-men have a field day, but can usually be spotted in time. More tricky is the 'hot meals and slippers' syndrome; those men who are really looking for an unpaid nurse/housekeeper for their 'old age'. Fortunately for them, there are many women who relish such a role, but at least both sides should know where they stand.

I am in favour of a realistic approach. Of course one can fall in love at any age and have that love reciprocated. Such people are extremely fortunate and I wish them all the best. But surely it is a waste of the precious days left to us not to realise the odds against finding another partner, and face up to life alone. The greatest advantage is freedom; freedom to come and go as you choose, freedom from domestic routine, freedom to experiment and try out new lifestyles, perhaps discover new aspects of yourself you never knew existed. The greatest disadvantage is loneliness. No-one to talk things over with, to give encouragement when the going is tough. If you have been used to life in couples, it is hard to find you no longer fit in.

This elderly lady appears to take for granted the conventions of the society in which she grew up. She does not appear to realize that there are a certain number of women who are now in the Third Age who enjoy all the freedoms mentioned in her last paragraph, but who have a lover living in a separate abode – who likewise enjoys all these freedoms. She also takes it for granted that 'another partner' for a widow must necessarily be male. Only time will show how attitudes will change as new cohorts of people who have developed in a changing society enter the Third Age. Some of these respondents illustrate less conventional life styles that are beginning to develop among older people.

CHAPTER 8

The Meaning of Home in Later Life

Craig Gurney and Robin Means

Few social gerontologists would doubt the importance of housing and the home to older people. Indeed, early social gerontological work in Britain such as *The Family Life of Old People* by Peter Townsend (1957) was centrally concerned with home life. Since then there has been surprisingly little research in Britain on the meaning of home in later life. This is despite the fact that community care policy in this country is predicated upon the belief that nearly all elderly people prefer to live in ordinary housing rather than institutions, because institutions lack the capacity to be a home. In summarising the limited literature on elderly people and the meaning of home, Wilson makes two critical comments. First, that theoretical models are weak, and based upon stereotypical assumptions about old age. Second, that, 'old people themselves have rarely been asked for their views' (1991 p.263).

This chapter attempts partially to redress this situation. It firstly considers debates surrounding the meaning of the home within urban sociology during the early 1990s. The impetus for this debate came with the publication of Peter Saunders's research on owner occupation and 'ontological security' (Saunders and Williams, 1988; Saunders 1986b, 1990) which has proved to be highly influential yet very controversial (Madigan *et al.*, 1990; Somerville, 1989). The second section argues the need for an experiential perspective on the meaning of the home. The third part of the chapter outlines research carried out by one of us on the repair needs of elderly owner occupiers and the relationship of this to community care policies (Harrison and Means, 1990). As part of this research, respondents were asked to express their general feelings about their house as a home. The fourth part of the chapter considers an hierarchical approach to understanding the meaning of home which distinguishes between cultural, intermediate and personal levels of meaning. The final section considers the implications of this framework for understanding the meaning of home to older people. Key issues for further investigation, some of which are addressed in Chapter 9, are drawn out.

Urban Sociology and the Meaning of Home

By the start of the 1990s a fierce debate had emerged in urban sociology about the meaning of home, although little of this debate focused on older people.

This interest in the home emerged out of the analysis of the changing class structure in Britain.

It was argued that during the 1980s a convergence in goals and aspirations created a new 'middle mass' in British society (Pahl, 1984 p.319–320). The significance of home ownership was continually stressed in this debate. Peter Saunders, in particular, argued that England has become *A Nation of Home Owners* (1990). He claims that the rapid growth of home ownership (which in England rose from 56.6 per cent in December 1979 to 68.1 per cent a decade later), at the expense of public and private renting, is one part of the emergence of a new class cleavage based upon access to the means of consumption. His argument rests upon the claim that:

> The divisions between the public and private sectors in state-capitalist societies are...a new and crucial aspect of stratification...and as such they generate real crucially important effects. These effects will most certainly be found in the patterns of political alignment which emerge,...but...will also become manifest in patterns of economic privilege and cultural advantage. (Saunders, 1986a p.162, emphasis added)

These three differences – political, economic, and cultural – were identified by Saunders and lead him to argue that consumption sector cleavages are neither secondary to production-determined class inequalities, nor merely a product of ideology. Thus he argues that 'nineteenth-century' Marxist explanations of social stratification are no longer able to account for contemporary inequalities (1986b Chapter 8). The growth of home ownership, is, he contends, the best example of this transformation in contemporary British society taking place. Specifically, he argues that the extent to which home ownership serves to encourage social stability, to generate and transmit capital amongst home owners, and to enable a greater potential for personal control and autonomy are all inherent advantages in the tenure, 'which are grounded in the rights of private property and cannot therefore be extended' (1990 p.119) to private, or to public sector tenants.

The main empirical work carried out by Saunders involved interviews with 522 individuals, from 450 households in Burnley, Derby and Slough. Only owner occupiers and council tenants were interviewed. At the end of a lengthy interview questionnaire each respondent was asked the following question:

> People often distinguish between 'house' and 'home'. What does the home mean to you?

In all three towns, home was widely associated with family life and children, with images of comfort and relaxation and with the idea of a personal space over which one enjoys some degree of proprietorship or control. But he did find key differences between the tenures. Owners seemed more likely to identify their house as home, while tenants placed greater emphasis on the people around them. As Saunders put it:

> Home for many council tenants has to do with family and neighbours. Home for many owner occupiers has to do with a place where they feel relaxed and where they can surround themselves with familiar and personal possessions (Saunders, 1990 p.272).

Saunders goes on to discuss whether this means that private ownership generates a greater scope than council renting for the expression of self and identity in a private realm, with the private realm being defined as freedom from surveillance. At this point in his argument, Saunders introduces the term 'ontological security'. R.D. Laing first used the phrase in a study of existential psychology 30 years ago, commenting:

> The individual may experience his own being as real alive, as differentiated from the rest of the world so clearly in ordinary circumstances that his identity and autonomy are never in question... He thus has a firm core of ontological security. (Laing, 1960 p.43, gender in original)

Giddens (1984) reinterprets Laing's definition of the concept as:

> Confidence or trust that the natural and social worlds are as they appear to be, including the basic existential parameters of self, and social identity. (1984 p.375)

He argues that in the advanced stages of capitalism the organisation of social, political and economic life have undergone profound changes. These changes, it is argued, have 'stretched' social relations over time and space with the result that everyday life is no longer a product of people's everyday experience. His thesis contends that people are neither in control nor can understand their localised everyday existence. Instead, the decisions of multinational companies and globally organised money markets shape peoples lives. Giddens' argument is that this stretching of social relations over space and time has prevented people from making sense of their lives, thus eroding any feelings of ontological security.

Saunders claims that his data suggests owner occupiers, but, crucially, not council tenants, can achieve ontological security through their home based life. This, he suggests, can reduce the feelings of alienation described by Giddens. Evidence presented to support Saunders' claim includes the high levels of emotional attachment felt by owners, their sense of relaxation at home and their positive enthusiasm for self provisioning. Since these attitudes were held equally by male and female respondents, Saunders goes on to make one final contentious claim: that private ownership has the capacity to deliver ontological security irrespective of gender.

There has been no shortage of critics to attack Saunders' theoretical and methodological assumptions (see, for example, Franklin, 1986; Somerville, 1989; Gurney, 1990, 1991, 1992; Madigan, Munro and Smith, 1990; Forrest and Murie, 1990a, 1990b; Darke and Furbey, 1991). Their criticisms have included the argument that Saunders persistently minimises the anxieties and difficulties associated with owner occupation especially for those on low incomes, a point less easy to forget since the house price slump and high interest rates of the early 1990s. He also seems willfully blind to the attempts of central government to make council housing stigmatising, expensive and uncomfortable. The interviewing of couples together may not have predisposed female respondents to express their true feelings about the home. While the question 'what does your home mean to you?' may be too complex to slot into the end of a very lengthy questionnaire. Interviewers might have found it very difficult to fully write down the complexity and ambiguity of comments from respondents. A simple postal survey by Gurney generated a far wider and more ambiguous range of responses to this single question than that uncovered by Saunders' three town survey (Gurney 1991).

This last methodological point is part of Gurney's general critique of the work of Saunders, and has led him to propose an alternative framework for studying the meaning of home (Gurney, 1990). He argues that a much greater emphasis needs to be placed on the experiences of home and the emotions of home than suggested by Saunders, and indeed by many of his critics.

An Experiential Perspective

Home is a complex concept. Its very complexity is grounded in the wealth of personal experiences which structure its meaning. Elsewhere, one of us has argued that the wide variety of meanings attached to the home cannot adequately be explained by generalisations around class, income or tenure (Gurney, 1990). An experiential perspective (which is neither wholly sociological nor wholly psychological) to study the home is suggested. This is essential if the significance of home is to be comprehended and its complexity unraveled.

The emotions of home are a central concern. Domestic violence, child sexual abuse and elder abuse take place in the domestic sphere, and yet for many home is a happy place. It is in the home that supportive and loving relationships between kin and non-kin relations most often take place. It can, therefore, be argued that the positive feelings of niche and belonging to be found at home seem most likely to stem from an emotional (not ontological) security. In other words, security comes from something less tangible than control over the home environment.

Home for a couple will hold less positive meanings and significance to them if they are going through a relationship breakdown. Anthony (1989) provides empirical evidence to show that the perceptions of 'broken homes' amongst heterosexual couples who have parted is charged with bitterness and negative feelings. Evidence of this kind illustrates one way in which personal experiences are far more salient in shaping the meaning of home than the sociologist's taxonomies.

Perceptions of home vary over time in response to life cycle changes. In a study of 'favourite homes', Anthony (1984) illustrates that recollections of housing histories are closely linked to important personal events or stages in the life cycle (childhood home, first home away from parents, child rearing home, retirement home etc.). Steinfield (1981) has pointed out that for younger people, moving house often confirms a positive status passage, because moves are associated with marriage, new employment or increased affluence. In later life, accommodation change is more likely to signify a negative status passage and so many old people may be keen to retain their present accommodation to minimise the impact of loss of income, bereavement or increased disability (see also Means, 1987).

Equally, the emotional intensity and familiarity found at home can be seen clearly in the desire of terminally ill people to die there, rather than in the confusing and impersonal atmosphere of a hospital. Claudia Melnyk nursed her husband through the final stages of a terminal illness at home. Her moving account of this experience illustrates the importance of the emotional intensity of home. She describes her feelings after his death.

> The hours after his death were totally private. We could each say goodbye in our own way. There was no one to pull curtains around his bed, send his body to mortuary or hand me a bundle of his clothes. We all look back on Andy's final illness as a positive time of immense tenderness which we were privileged to share...With his passing went all our fear of death. (Melnyk, 1990)

For this woman and her family this experience of home will undoubtedly colour the meaning of home in the present and the future.

It is crucial to recognise that the meanings of home are specific to the experiences of certain moments in time and are constantly changing. Emotions are inextricable parts of such experiences. The next section illustrates the importance of the use, experience and emotions of home by drawing on research on elderly owner occupiers.

Housing: The Essential Element of Community Care

Research was conducted in early 1990 on the potential contribution of Care and Repair and Staying Put projects to community care (Harrison and Means, 1990; Means and Harrison, 1992). Such projects typically provide assistance to elderly and disabled owner occupiers who would otherwise be unable to keep their houses in good repair or who need adaptations to enhance mobility. The main focus of the research was upon the detailed advice work of project staff and the key finding was that housing is an essential element of community care. As part of the research, we carried out 29 exploratory taped interviews with clients from three such projects, all of whom had extensive repair work carried out. Each interview probed in detail the client's feelings, expectations, fears and worries before the work, during the work and after the work.

Respondents were also encouraged to discuss more generally how long they had lived in the house and their general attitudes to moving and 'staying put' options. The significance of each particular house in the life of each respondent seemed an important influence upon the decisions of this small group to seek repair options which would facilitate staying put. Two elements appeared to contribute to the importance of the house. One was symbolic, reflecting the role the house had played in key events and relationships in the respondent's life. The other was practical and reflected how the house and location enabled them to engage in or with key networks and activities.

The deep attachment some clients felt towards their houses was associated with the length of time they had lived there. Of the 29 clients interviewed, 21 had lived in their homes for over 20 years. It was perhaps not surprising that 'I've been here so long' was often offered as an explanation and sometimes almost as an excuse for not moving, even when the repair and maintenance of the house had become a major problem.

The responses to our question 'could you tell me a little bit about how long you have lived in this house and this neighbourhood' often illustrated the interweaving of people's life history with their houses. The house, for some, was still 'the place they had come as a bride', 'their mother's house', 'their husband's family home'. People could recall specific days and dates when important events took place in the house, the day they moved in, the day and circumstances of a partner's death, even though this was many years ago, for example, 'Our roots are really in the house' (Mr. and Mrs. L., 76 and 71 years), and 'I couldn't leave because of his memories' (Mrs. P., 85 years).

The house was either symbolically, and for some actually, an indication of the effort they had put into a life together with their partners. Some clients talked of the steady way they had kept the house in good repair and in some cases transformed it over the years, adding amenities or shaping the garden. Some expressed pride in what they had achieved, others tolerated the house, like an eccentric relative, not expecting great things from something of such an age.

For the clients who had spent many years in the house, their accounts gave the impression of it being a fixed spot from which they had observed, with varying degrees of pleasure or anxiety, the changing scene of the street or neighbourhood. The more housebound respondents derived confidence from having a very vivid mental map of their location. While alternative houses and locations may offer better day-to-day circumstances, for some it is easy to imagine the sense of loss and confusion which may arise from moving from their homes. Their houses are an anchor orienting them both in time and place.

Mrs. P. had lived in her house since she was married, at the age of 21 years. She was now 85-years-old and her husband had died 19 years ago. The house had been her husband's family house and during their married life he had done a great deal of work on it. Originally it had only a pump outside for water and a toilet at the bottom of the garden. The house, however, had fallen in rather a bad state of repair, as Mrs. P. observed:

I know it's old, it's damp and my roof wants doing – it leaks. It is in a mess. I can't afford to pay for it, but I'm not going to leave it...I've always lived in it. They reckoned it was cold and that to live in, but if you've always lived in it, you don't bother do you? They keep telling me it's old fashioned – but it's an old house. The children all have been down from the school with the teacher...they are looking at these old houses...and they are going to make a model of them... I said, what, this old place!

Her grandson replied:

Yes Gran, it's perhaps one of the oldest houses in the town, so we're making a survey of them.

Inextricably bound up with the more abstract and emotional attachments of elderly people with their home is a bundle of more pragmatic issues. Individuals who have lived in one place for most of their lives tend to have friends, neighbours and quite often family nearby who may offer a variety of support. Others identified the proximity of the house to shops, buses etc., which was important in managing their day-to-day activities.

On a more material level, it was suggested or hinted that the financial investment they had made in the home gave it importance in their lives. Several clearly gained a sense of satisfaction in that the repair work had put up the value of the house and a few were pleased to note that even the neighbours had commented on this too. This small study of elderly owner occupiers underlines the importance of developing an understanding of the meaning of home to older people, and illustrates the importance of the emotions and experience of home.

The rest of this chapter draws together the theoretical and empirical material discussed above by outlining a framework and an agenda for further research into the meaning of home for older people.

Towards a Methodological Framework

The methodological implications of an experiential approach to studying the meaning of home have been outlined elsewhere in relation to the social significance of owner occupation (Gurney, 1990). Here we outline the implications of this approach to a study of the meaning of home in later life.

In attempting to construct a theoretically robust model to study the meaning of home, we will draw on the experience of researchers outside the urban sociology tradition outlined earlier in this chapter. Clinical psychology, environmental psychology, social psychology and phenomenology have all expressed interest in the meaning of home to the individual (see Hayward, 1975, 1977; Altman and Werner, 1985; Sixsmith, 1986; and Despres, 1989). In the vast majority of these studies the approach is micro-psychological with the emphasis upon the 'person-home' or 'person-environment' relationship. Such approaches have their own weaknesses (Gurney, 1990 p.34–35). They often display a selective and interpretive bias. The focus is frequently on the meaning of home to the middle class nuclear family who own their own house. The typical approach emphasises the individual, ignoring structural forces and influences. Individual action and choice is assumed to be free and unconstrained.

An experiential methodology has the promise of drawing on the strengths of sociological and psychological traditions. It should be sensitive

Table 8.1 Home: a hierarchy of meanings

Level of experience	Nature of issues	Appropriate research tools
1. Cultural	Everyday use and understanding of the word 'home', response structured by peer group, gender, media etc.	*Discourse/ etymological analysis, self-completion surveys.*
2. Intermediate	Experience of the state, lending institutions and local housing market. Tenure and class relations. Contradictions between this level of meaning and cultural understanding and expectations emerge.	*Social survey with closed and open-ended questions, construction of housing histories.*
3. Personal	Important decisions and events in biography which colour experience of home in particular ways at different times in the life course.	*Respondent-led, in depth interviews.*

Based on Gurney, 1990 p.41.

to the intimate relationship between the individual and the home on a day-to-day basis, and responsive to changing roles in this relationship, and the inter-relationships of the household members over a period of months or years. Abstract micro-psychological issues of emotional security, identity, and privacy must be explored. We know surprisingly little about these issues in relation to older people. Such an approach does not necessarily imply that the individual within her or his home must be elevated to the primary level of explanation. The intimate relationship between the individual and the home must be firmly placed in a political, social and historical context. An analysis of housing histories and careers must be part of a study which aims to discover the changing nature of the relationship between the home and the individual (see Chapter 9 for an example). Research of this kind must be both historicised and politicised.

This experiential perspective is based on the belief that there is no single meaning of home. Rather, there is a three-tiered hierarchy, based on the cultural, the intermediate and the personal meanings attached to home. A hierarchy exists because the meaning of home is derived from the interplay of a variety of levels of experience. The home is the subject of political rhetoric, popular adages, myths and aspirations at the cultural level. It is a commodity which is consumed and produced at the intermediate level. It is also an intensely personal sphere where personal biographies are formed at the personal level (see Table 8.1).

The cultural level

The cultural level is the most fundamental level of enquiry in any research into the meaning of home. It is concerned with the everyday use of the word 'home' and the uncertainties surrounding its definition. These uncertainties are perpetuated by cliches, adages and myth. 'A woman's place is in the home', 'keep the home fires burning', and the dream of an 'ideal home' are all examples of how this uncertainty has hardened into homilies and dogmas. The Thatcher government's 'Right to Buy' policy for council tenants displayed explicit and implicit assumptions based upon 'conversational utterances' (Forrest, 1983 p.205) which state that home ownership is 'natural', or at the very least the most favoured tenure. Staying Put takes its name from the belief that elderly people have a desire to stay in their home rather than in institutions. Both these assumptions should be questioned. Where do they come from? How accurate are they? How desirable are they?

These common ideologies and images of home must be examined to assess the extent to which they are shared by older people. Do older people think of their homes as happy and secure places where a sense of meaning and belonging can be sustained? If not, what are the policy implications?

To examine these issues, the notorious inflexibility and simplicity of self-completion questionnaires would be a strength. Because the data generated by these types of surveys are 'instant' and based upon little inconvenience, effort or thought on the part of the respondent they would reflect the most superficial understanding of home perpetuated by cultural influences. The extent to which the responses of elderly people differ from the dominant ideas of 'what home is' forms an interesting and valuable research question in its own right.

The intermediate level

Contradictions and conflicts emerge at this level as older people's aspirations and expectations differ from their real-life situation. To measure just how much the meaning of home is an ideological construct or reflects lived experience, a different set of questions must be addressed. Why had Mrs P. and her late husband (see above) stayed at one address for so long? Were local labour and housing markets important, was it the birth of children, or was the fact that the house had been in the family for several generations more important? Why do other people move much more frequently? What influences people's decisions about whether to move or stay put?

Housing histories provide answers to these and other questions. This flexible research tool is, at the time of writing, enjoying some popularity in British housing studies (Forrest and Murie, 1987; Gurney, 1992), and is discussed in relation to the life course in the following chapter. When carried out as part of a semi-structured interview, the act of constructing housing histories with respondents enables households to reflect upon what their home may have meant to them in the past and what it means now. In doing this, links with important events such as retirement, or the death of a partner, can be explicitly made. Such an approach can reveal much about the timing and context of decisions to move. Jones's (1987) research concerning the timing of the move from the parental home, and Ineichen's (1981) and Savage et al.,'s (1992) studies of mobility between housing tenures illustrate the importance of context and timing in the housing market.

The personal level

We have already seen how the homes of people in later life assume a profound symbolic and personal significance. It is at the personal level of the hierarchy that the emotional intensity of home life can be assessed. It is widely recognised that a 'respondent-led' approach is best suited to this level of enquiry. A respondent-led interview creates a situation where the role of the researcher is primarily to ask questions, summarise what the respondent has said and tape record the interview. Full textual analyses of interview transcripts used in conjunction with follow up interviews are time consuming, but provide very rich data (Miles and Huberman, 1984). Respondents might be asked to recall their memories of 'favourite homes' or 'favourite times' and then to link them back to specific events and choices sketched out at the cultural and intermediate level. Important personal events like changes in a relationship, the birth of a child, bereavement or the onset of a disability can then be viewed alongside the crucial decisions like moving house or changing jobs. It is only when such personal milestones are understood in relation to the changing meanings of home in later life that a full picture emerges. This picture can be used as a measuring rod against which to judge respondents' assessments of their present and likely future experiences. These may or may not come into conflict with the choices and decisions people may have to make in later life.

Key Issues About Home in Later Life

The discussion above provides an illustration of the complexities in the meaning of home together with a methodological framework for further research. We conclude this attempt to develop a research agenda by reflecting on four key issues which are of particular relevance to a consideration of the meaning of home in later life.

Age versus length of residence

The 29 respondents expressed strong attachments to their present home and a great reluctance to consider any housing options which involved moving (Harrison and Means, 1990). Why? Was this mainly a factor of old age or a reflection of their long length of residence? The assumption is often that older people dislike change and that their ability to adapt reduces with age. But it could be that length of residence in a single house is the more potent factor in encouraging people to stay put. Linked to this is the issue of whether chronological age is an important variable which distinguishes attitudes to the home (that is, older people are more reluctant to move) or does an emphasis upon old age as a key variable cover up the enormous differences amongst older people in terms of their personal experiences of housing and home? How many elderly people have a genuine attachment to a particular house rather than a more generalised fear that the need to move represents a failure to cope with old age.

Tenure in later life

Since Saunders (1990) claims that the home is only a source of ontological security for the owner occupier, his findings can be used to justify local authority housing policies which encourage elderly tenants in 'family' accommodation to move to smaller property (often sheltered housing) in order to create a re-let for a family on the waiting list. Two points need to be borne in mind here. First, his own evidence suggests home has to do with neighbours for many council tenants. A move to alternative accommodation may destroy these relationships. Second, Saunders may have underestimated the importance of the home as a source of essential security for many people who rent. Elderly people who have seen their children grow up in a house, and perhaps their partner die there, may have very powerful attachments which they are reluctant to break. Does a house lose its symbolic importance to its occupant if it is not owned?; especially if that occupant grew up without any cultural expectation that 'owning' was for people like them.

Is ontological or emotional security transportable?

Irrespective of whether we accept the view of Saunders that it is only owner-occupiers who experience ontological security or the view of Gurney that emotional security is experienced in the home by many irrespective of housing tenure, the question remains as to how easy it is to transport ontological security and/or emotional security from one house to another. And does transportation get more difficult as individuals get older, and if so, why? Certainly, there is considerable evidence that accommodation moves in later life can be successful with high levels of satisfaction often found in those who have moved into private residential care, sheltered housing or bungalows by the sea (Means, 1987). Do movers miss their old houses more than their old neighbourhoods or their old friends, and how does this vary by age, disability and tenure?

Memories or money?

Increasingly, people enter retirement having experienced several house moves previously as owner-occupiers. In the 1980s, many people became used to moving house on a regular basis as a mechanism for accumulating wealth during the house price boom. Elderly people in high price housing are increasingly taking the option to trade down as a mechanism for releasing equity (Mackintosh, Means and Leather, 1990). In other words, many middle aged and elderly middle class people are perhaps becoming used to treating their houses as part of their investment 'nest egg' for retaining living standards in later life. One possibility is that they perceive ontological security and emotional security as transportable items and that wealth creation is more important than the memories and emotional attachments associated with a specific house.

Conclusion

This chapter has drawn on an established literature in branches of sociology, psychology and social policy to illustrate the significance of home in later life. Additionally, we have outlined a methodological framework for future research on this aspect of elderly peoples' lives.

Far too often, research agendas are overlooked because they do not fit into the dominant epistemological tradition of the discipline in which they are set. By drawing on links with a variety of disciplines and through illustrating how such research might be carried out, we hope that this chapter goes some way towards stimulating the interest of a wider audience.

The population structures of advanced industrial societies are ageing rapidly. That there is an urgent need for more interdisciplinary research on the meaning of home in later life is self-evident. There is little hope of developing appropriate and sensitive policy responses without such a research effort.

CHAPTER 9

Housing, The Life Course and Older People

David Clapham, Robin Means and Moira Munro

The home is central to the lives of most older people as it is a place where many spend a large proportion of their time. The condition of the property, the facilities available and the capacity to live an independent life in that home are, therefore, of vital importance. To an older person a house may be a source of comfort and security or a source of anxiety if, for example, essential repairs cannot be carried out. Housing can have an important impact on the lives of older people both for its own sake, but also through access to wealth stored as equity. It can be a crucial factor in determining access to care and to desired lifestyles. With the growing numbers of older people, their problems, including housing, have been given a high profile in political debates. Housing has (at least in principle) been recognised by the government as the cornerstone of community care (Department of Health, 1989) and a number of specific programmes such as those focused on house repairs and improvements for older owner-occupiers have been pushed forward.

The increasing visibility of housing in old age has resulted in a growing level of interest and activity in this area from housing researchers. At first there was a narrow focus on the pros and cons of sheltered housing, and there is still a tendency to focus on particular forms of 'special' provision or programmes (Clapham and Smith, 1990). Nevertheless, there has been a gradual movement towards the integration of older people into mainstream housing research with at least some consideration of the housing circumstances of older people in many large-scale studies or surveys. For example, the housing finance programme funded by the Joseph Rowntree Foundation (Maclennan, Gibb and More, 1991a; 1991b) drew attention to the housing problems experienced by some older people as well as providing good information on their diversity of experience.

The major problem with such research is that it has invariably provided a snapshot picture at one point in time. We know more about the circumstances currently facing older people, but we know little about how they reached their present position. Why do some older people live in poor conditions whereas others with similar characteristics reach very different housing destinations? Cross-sectional research also tells us little about the possible housing circumstances of future cohorts of older people. What impact will their different housing and life experiences have on their housing destinations in old age?

Our contention in this chapter is that a more dynamic or longitudinal approach to housing research is needed if these questions are to be answered. In the first section we review existing dynamic approaches in housing studies, focusing on the work on mobility and life-cycles, while the second section looks at the concepts of housing careers and housing histories. Our conclusion is that the concept of housing history in particular offers a useful starting point for further development. To start this process we need to look outside current housing perspectives and examine the life course perspective in social gerontology which is reviewed in the third section. Through a biographical approach and to a lesser extent through the political economy tradition, insights can be gained which, when applied to housing, can offer a way to tackle the gaps in our current knowledge of how and why older people have reached their different housing destinations. These approaches emphasise the need to see old age, and housing in old age, as stages in the life course which can only be understood by reference to previous experience and the attitudes and choices of people and the opportunities open to them during the whole life course. An attempt is made in the fourth section to sketch out what a life course approach in housing would look like both in terms of the concepts used and the research methods which are most applicable and, finally, comments are made about the priorities for further research.

Mobility, Life-Cycles and Housing Careers

There is relatively little work in the housing field that takes an explicitly longitudinal focus, and which can help us to understand housing destinations in old age. However, there has been a great deal of attention given to mobility within the housing market and associated questions about access to particular tenures. Moving house is an important element of what might be understood as a housing career. Indeed, at one level, the progress of households from one dwelling to another or one tenure to another is often taken to be the housing career of that household.

Two broad questions have been investigated in empirical work on residential mobility. The first has analysed what causes households to move: such work has focused on comparing movers and non-movers to analyse the characteristics that pre-dispose households to move (see Greenwood, 1985; Cadwallader, 1986; Munro, 1987 for a review). A second strand of analysis has focused more on the spatial patterns and determinants of where households choose to relocate. This has been the particular focus of geographer's interest in mobility (arising from early analysis of 'place-utility' and 'mental maps' of urban space (Wolpert, 1965)) as well as an expanding economics-based literature on search within the housing market (Clark, 1982; Smith and Clark, 1982a; 1982b). The links between these two research questions are immediately apparent: to move in the housing market is costly, time-consuming and stressful and hence the decision to move is inevitably linked to perceptions about possible housing conditions after the move as well as a reaction to current conditions. Moving house is not typically undertaken lightly or frequently in response to minor dissatisfactions. This has led to a perception of the mobility process as one in which a disequilibrium between the household's preferred and their present circumstances gradually widen, until a point is reached at which the improvement in housing conditions is worth the expected costs of the move (Goodman, 1976).

A considerable amount of work has been undertaken which analyses the determinants of tenure choice among households. Typically, such choices are bound up with decisions to move house. The decision has been modelled in economic terms as a utility maximising problem subject to the constraints of wealth and income and the dictates of preferences and prevailing market conditions (Fallis, 1985). The importance of income and wealth emerge strongly as predictors of access to owner-occupation as do the relative price and tax advantages of the two tenures. This is an important issue because access to owner-occupation is usually determined early in a housing career and can crucially influence the opportunities and constraints experienced throughout the life course.

Calendar age has a well-established effect on propensity to move. Generally, holding other factors constant, young people are the most mobile while increasing age is associated with declining mobility. This is considered to reflect the increasing costs of disruption (in psychological and social terms) as the length of stay (and consequently strength of ties to the area) increases.

However, overlaid on this relationship with age is argued to be a 'life-cycle' effect, which is usually an event-based description of a supposedly typical life-cycle (Speare, 1970; Mincer, 1978). Thus, marriage, the arrival and departure of children and retirement are common points in the life-cycle which precipitate moves. Divorce, separation and widowhood are also precursors to mobility. These events are related to, but not directly collinear with, calendar age and the close relationship makes disentangling the causal mechanisms problematic (Thorns, 1985). These difficulties are compounded by the relatively simple way in which life-cycles are conceptualised and operationalised in much empirical work (see for instance, McAuley and Nutty, 1982; Coupe and Morgan, 1981). In general, the 'life-cycle' approach implicitly assumes a straightforward, linear progression through life as a nuclear family. Indeed, the use of the term 'family' in the categorisation emphasises this assumption. As Forrest and Kemeny (1984) point out, this type of progression does not apply to a great many households, including the never-married and those without children as well as the growing number of divorced and separated people, for whom there will be a more disrupted career, perhaps including time as a single person, a single parent or in less conventional households. It is now well known that only a minority of households are two parent families with dependent children (Watson, 1988).

While these categories may be useful in a purely predictive sense (the early stage of family building is associated with more mobility than later stages), they do little to explain the underlying motivations for moving. There is some evidence that households respond more readily to sudden changes (for example, separation, loss of employment) than to gradual changes in household circumstances. Yet it has become clear that moves are not caused by such factors in the sense that not all who have another child, or whose children reach adulthood, or who retire choose to move.

The problems in identifying the motives for moving are exacerbated by the essentially cross-sectional nature of most of the research. For instance, a couple may buy a large house in the expectation that they will have children in the future. At the time that such a move takes place the researchers will most likely record a demand for extra space, apparently unrelated to any change in household circumstances. Similarly, older households may move into a smaller house long after their children have left home. Again, researchers may pick up on the most proximate reasons, which may be to move nearer some amenities or simply to meet demands for a smaller house without identifying the longer run changes in household circumstances.

These problems are evident in research on older people entering sheltered or specially adapted accommodation or residential care (Oldman, 1991a; Butler et al., 1983; Clapham and Munro, 1988). What is lacking from these investigations is an understanding of how people have arrived at the point of making such decisions. Families and professional advisers play an important role in making many people in sheltered housing aware of the option (Clapham and Munro, 1988). There can be assumed to be many who have adopted alternative strategies, rather than seeking special accommodation: either because their needs were different, or because they took earlier decisions to find accommodation suitable for their changing future needs. The constraints that people faced at the point of making such decisions must also be fundamentally conditioned by previous paths taken through the housing market and these are unlikely to be adequately captured by a cross-sectional investigation.

One lesson which can be drawn from the mobility literature, ironically, is to do with the prevalence of immobility. When Rossi's (1955) seminal work was undertaken, mobility was seen as an urban problem, and the research was instrumental in establishing mobility as a normal part of changing household needs and demands (Rossi and Shlay, 1982). Nevertheless, it is now universally recognised that immobility characterises many people's housing history. Warnes' (1986) sample of couples included one pensioner, with two children living away from home, and had an average length of stay in their present dwelling of 24.2 years. Over a third of this sample had not moved out of the home they first entered after their marriage. A further third had moved only once. Patterns of mobility were class related; 62–66 per cent of all classes had moved not more than once, with skilled manual workers being the immobile exception: a full 47 per cent had never left their first marital home and a further 28 per cent had moved only once.

It is clear that mobility should not be the whole focus or definition of a housing pathway: a household that stays in one place over a long period continues to make decisions regarding maintenance, improvement and repair which are important elements of outcomes in the housing market. They are, implicitly or explicitly, taking a decision not to move, while the needs, demands and composition of the household may change. At the same time, the milieu in which the house is located may alter: transport, amenities and status will gradually alter both absolutely and relatively, changing the position of the dwelling in its neighbourhood context and in the wider urban structure. Thus, it is not enough to use cross-sectional analysis focused on the point of entry to a tenure or mobility within it because family circumstances as well as the condition and context of the house may change considerably for the majority who stay in one house for long periods of time.

Another lesson which should be drawn from the mobility literature relates to the importance of two levels of constraint. Economic analysis has focused on individual economic and other characteristics which limit the scope of 'free choice' in the housing market. An alternative perspective on housing mobility developed by urban managerialists has stressed the lack of choice available to many in the housing market and the control of opportunities exercised by 'gatekeepers' such as housing managers or building societies (Pahl, 1975). This approach highlights a broader, more structural, level of constraint and has resulted in robust criticism of work founded on the (neo-classical, economic) notion that households exercise free choice in the housing market. Rather, emphasis is placed on the very limited options that may face households and factors beyond their direct control which may prevent them from attaining a preferred solution.

Housing Careers and Housing Histories

One promising attempt to avoid the static approach of much housing analysis has been to use the concept of a housing career or a housing history to explore the progress of households in the housing system and factors which influence this progress.

Forrest and Kemeny (1984) started from a criticism of the concept of housing classes (Rex and Moore, 1967) which they argued lacked any sense of process and of the importance of access to different types of housing. This was partly remedied by Payne and Payne (1977) who attempted to track the pathways of young households in Aberdeen using a series of cross-sectional surveys of households at the birth of children. In this way they explored progress within and between tenures and looked at the influence of the changing housing system on the different pathways followed by households in different housing classes or status groups. However, they tracked path-ways over a relatively short timescale and over a limited range of the life-cycle and, as in the literature reviewed earlier, they concentrated on mobility. Their analysis also focused on housing constraints at the expense of wider economic and social factors.

Forrest and Kemeny (1984) attempted to remedy these deficiencies by bringing together the concepts of 'career' and 'coping strategies' which they felt were complementary. 'Careers concern long-term trajectories through social structures whereas coping strategies concern specific and usually short-term adaptations to contingencies without necessary reference to a career' (Forrest and Kemeny, 1984 p.1). The balance between the positive planning and purposiveness associated with a career and the reactive, defensive emphasis of a coping strategy was said to vary.

> In certain circumstances, some kinds of careers may be little more than a series of coping strategies, during which the individual moves from one crisis to another. At the other extreme, where powerful constraints are absent or less evident, conditions may be such that the individual may have to carry out long-term plans in relatively unproblematic circumstances. (Forrest and Kemeny, 1984 p.1)

Using this framework Forrest and Kemeny hoped to explore the interaction between structural constraints and individual perceptions, attitudes and behaviour. However, the framework was never fully developed and it remains unclear how the fusion of career and coping strategy and constraint and adaptation would have worked conceptually and whether it would have been possible to operationalise the approach sufficiently to undertake empirical work.

In later work with Murie (Forrest and Murie, 1985; 1991) the concept of career was dropped and that of housing history substituted. Their main focus was on the relationship between housing and labour markets and they attempted to highlight the complexity of these links through individual housing histories compiled through a mixture of a short questionnaire survey to ascertain key details and a longer semi-structured interview. Histories were traced back to birth to give a wider scope than previous studies such as Payne and Payne (1977). Through contrasting affluent and working class home owners the research showed clearly the important influence of employment histories in shaping housing histories. However, the concept of housing history was not developed and seems to have been used as a research method rather than a conceptual framework. It is unclear, for example, what emphasis is placed on constraint as against choice or to what extent the perceptions and attitudes of actors were important in shaping housing histories.

The idea of compiling an account of households' experience of housing over their life course is an important one which can help to counteract the cross-sectional emphasis evident in most housing research. Nevertheless, the approach used so far has been very rudimentary and under-conceptualised. Also, it has been exclusively backward-looking as the term history would imply, with no attempt being made to project forward to predict housing outcomes – a feature which is important in looking at housing outcomes in old age. It has also been largely event-based, concentrating, as much of the housing literature does, on moving house and changing tenure at the expense of a focus on the changing experiences of people staying in the same house. So, although the concept of housing history is an adequate starting point it needs considerable development before it can be used as a framework for studying housing and the life course. In seeking to move forward in this way we need to look outside the housing field to the social gerontology literature for guidance.

Social Gerontology and the Life Course

Social gerontology is not concerned solely with older people but rather the ageing process, although its emergence as a distinctive field of study in most countries is usually associated with government concern about an ageing population (Coleman and Bond, 1990). One might expect those concerned with human ageing to perceive a focus on the life course and life histories as pivotal to all their endeavours. However, much social gerontology research is confined by the realities of research funding. There are far more studies on the dependency characteristics of the minority of older people in some form of institutional care than there are studies concerned to forge an integrated life course perspective on ageing. Having said this, some notable exceptions do exist and three important strands will now be considered.

The first strand is that associated with the Cambridge Group for population and social structure, especially Peter Laslett (1984; 1987; 1989). Laslett (1989) argues that the emergence in developed economies of old age as a phenomenon which is experienced by the majority of individuals requires the creation of A Fresh Map of Life, which recognises the emergence of what he calls 'the Third Age'. Laslett defines the first age as that of dependency, socialisation and education and the second age as that of 'maturity, independence, familial and social responsibility' (p.144). Traditionally, the final age has been that of old age which is associated with 'dependence and decrepitude' (p.152). The argument of Laslett is that British society and most other developed economies have reached a population structure which allows the emergence of a third age of 'personal achievement'. In the third age, most individuals have reduced work and family responsibilities so they are free to pursue hobbies, enthusiasms and interests. The experience of the Third Age is most likely to be positive for those individuals who have 'used the period of his life in the Second Age to work out a plan which will bring final satisfaction in the Third when he or she is free, free to realise personal purposes completely' (p.152). The length of the Third Age and the staving off of the Fourth Age cannot be guaranteed because life expectancy varies so much from individual to individual. However, Laslett believes the onset of dependence can be put off by most people for a long time by appropriate behaviour during the Third Age.

Laslett's ideas are of central interest to our concerns because of his emphasis on developing life plans and strategies in the Second Age which are designed to help ensure fulfilment in the Third Age. It seems likely that housing is a major arena open to such strategies. For example, the unlocking of home equity can enable 'dreams' to be realised or hobbies to be continued despite declining income. At the same time, poor housing can undermine any pretence to self-fulfilment. However, we know little about whether people enter their sixties with homes that are a by-product of the Second Age requirements, a creative attempt to plan for the Third Age or a panic about possible dependency in the Fourth Age.

Perhaps the biggest criticism that can be levelled at Laslett is that he offers a purely middle class manifesto, with little awareness of the extent of poverty in later life and the way in which this diminishes choices and opportunities. This brings us to the second strand of social gerontology writing, namely the political economy perspective.

The major insight of the political economy writers relevant to this discussion was their recognition that class and gender differences do not disappear with old age. In particular, not all elderly people experience poverty in later life. Some had accumulated wealth through their life course or had access to sizeable occupational pensions. Nevertheless, reliance on state pensions meant the majority, especially women, remained poor (Walker, 1981; 1990; Ginn and Arber, 1991).

However, the emphasis in the political economy writings of the early 1980s was upon the structural pressures impinging upon older people. As Townsend puts it:

> Retirement, poverty, institutionalisation and restriction of domestic and community roles are the experiences which help to explain the structural dependency of the elderly' and it is society that 'creates the framework of institutions and rules within which the general problems of the elderly emerge or, indeed, are 'manufactured'. (1986 p.21)

Some authors have pointed out that this perspective carries the risk of elderly people being treated as passive victims rather than actors trying to make the best of their given circumstances (Dant et al., 1988). This issue is increasingly confronted within the political economy perspective. For example, Fennell, Phillipson and Evers (1988) juxtapose the need to ensure the continued visibility of poor and disabled elderly people against the necessity of recognising that 'where people have resources, they actively create and re-create their own lives' (1988 p.26). However, even this quote is problematic. It is certainly true that people with more resources (and these include health and friendships as well as money) tend to have more choices and options. However, this does not mean that poor, disabled or lonely elderly people have no choices, or that they lack the capacity to create and re-create their lives. They just do it under more trying and limiting circumstances (Means, 1988).

The importance of this point can be illustrated by looking at housing options in later life. Well-off elderly people who own high equity homes have multiple choices available to them. These include staying put, buying a winter home in the Canary Islands, trading down or taking out a home equity release scheme. A low income elderly person in a badly repaired, privately rented flat may not have the options in the previous example but options can still be numerous. These options might include moving in with a grown-up daughter, applying for council house accommodation, staying put but requesting repairs or seeking alternative private accommodation. The very act of putting together a case for council housing involves telling a story and attempting to grasp some influence over future housing outcomes (Means, 1990).

A third use of a life course perspective in social gerontology has involved the concern to understand processes of adaptation in later life. This has often involved carrying out in-depth interviews with small samples (Cornwell and Gearing, 1989; Thompson et al., 1990). For example, Di Gregorio (1987) looked at the strategies of 66 older people for managing their lives. Individual managing strategies were seen as flowing from external circumstances, such as labour market and household histories, but also certain more intangible factors such as the amount of self-determination which an individual had been able to exercise during his or her life. Di Gregorio's sample did not define themselves as good or bad managers but rather as individuals who had managed throughout their lives. However, the nature of these strategies varied enormously, in particular, the choice of some individuals was constrained throughout their lives as a result of labour market and household constraints. For example, it is well known that divorce for women can be associated with a loss of income and a restriction on housing choice (Watson, 1988).

Many of the studies draw upon a biographical research approach. Gearing and Dant (1990) and Fennell et al. (1988) provide useful summaries of the biographical research approach to social gerontology and both emphasise the influence of the mid-seventies writing of Johnson (1976). Johnson drew on both symbolic interactionism and the life history approach in sociology (see Plummer, 1983) to argue for the centrality of the concept of career when attempting to understand the lived experience of older people. As Gearing and Dant (1990) explain:

> Johnson proposes that the many intersecting careers and individual experiences in a lifetime and which may be shed compulsorily or voluntarily in later life, may in any case have differing degrees of significance for the individual. This significance is more likely to be known to the person concerned than to any outside observer, but it

suggests an approach to unravelling and integrating something varied and complex – the biography of the older person. By identifying main strands in a life ('careers'), how they have shaped and been shaped by significant biographical events (family, upbringing, marriage, work, parenthood, retirement, widowhood, and so on), we will better understand the way the individual concerned experiences 'old age', and his/her present needs, satisfactions and problems. (1990 p.144)

As such, the biographical approach in social gerontology draws on similar theoretical assumptions and research techniques to those ethnographic contributions to housing studies which have been outlined by Franklin (1990).

Gearing and Dant (1990) argue that the biographical approach opens up 'the rich variability of the lives of individual older people' (1990 p.159), but they also recognise that the sheer volume and complexity of the data generated creates considerable problems for analysis and reduces the ability to make comparisons between cases or to build up generalisations which are reliable for given populations. An attempt to overcome the problem of generalisation is represented by the work of Taylor and Ford (1981). Their sample of 619 men and women over 60 who lived in Aberdeen was used to explore individual differences in ageing, in terms of different coping and adjustment behaviour. Taylor and Ford expressed excitement at 'the possibility of viewing later life as a constant struggle to maintain cherished life-styles against the threatening impact of both external events and internal changes' (p.339). They drew on the existing life-style literature to develop ten life-style orientations which they tested out through vignettes with their respondents. The ten types were taking life easy, gregarious, solitary, spouse centred, invalid, altruist, hobbyist, family centred, work centred and full life. The central interest of Taylor and Ford is whether common life course experiences, such as retirement and widowhood, will have different implications for elderly people who have varying life-styles. For example, becoming housebound may be easier to cope with for someone whose life-style has always been home centred than for someone whose main interests have always been outside the home. This suggests that decisions about whether or not to move home may have different meanings for individuals according to life-style orientation.

Housing Through the Life Course

We can now piece together the major elements of a framework to examine housing through the life course. The first necessary element of this framework is the adoption of a biographical perspective. Both in gerontological studies and in Forrest and Murie's (1985) work on housing histories, the construction of a personal biography, usually through in-depth qualitative interviews with small samples, has been vital in exploring the links between various elements of people's lives. A biographical approach is vital if we are to understand how households reached their present housing situation. It is clear that housing circumstances in old age are crucially influenced by a household's previous history. For example, most households make a move into owner-occupation or public renting at an early stage in their housing lives and few change tenure later (although the right to buy council housing has had a considerable impact on tenure change over the last decade). Also, a great many people remain in the same home throughout their post-retirement lives. For those who do move, the choices available to them will be crucially dependent on their previous housing history including factors such as whether they have been able to build up housing wealth.

One major drawback of the biographical approach is that only small samples can be used and so the results are not easily generalisable. Nevertheless, it is important to start at this level to develop an understanding of how different experiences are shaped. It may be possible later, on the basis of this knowledge to build up topologies of experience which can then be applied to larger data sets in order to assess the relative importance of different kinds of experience.

Di Gregorio's work (1982) on the strategies of older people for managing their lives and Laslett's (1989) emphasis on planning for a long and active Third Age, alert us to the possibility that many households may have housing strategies in, and in preparation for, old age and may actively manage their housing circumstances. For others, as Forrest and Kemeny (1984) make clear, their housing experience is essentially reactive through a series of coping strategies designed to aid adaptation to changing circumstances. Any household may move from actively pursuing a strategy to coping and back again at different points of their life course. For example, a 65-year-old couple in good health may be actively managing a housing career, but may be adopting a coping strategy by the time the survivor is 85 years old and in failing health.

We do not know whether households have housing strategies in old age and what factors influence whether they exist and what they entail. There is evidence for instance of very different degrees of planning and strategic thinking at an earlier stage of the life course amongst newly forming households (Clark, 1991). Such questions should be at the forefront of the research agenda.

The political economy approach to ageing shows the importance of the constraints which structure households' progress on their housing pathway. For example, there has been an important recognition that class, gender and ethnic differences do not disappear with old age (Arber and Ginn, 1991a). Rather, one's circumstances in old age are crucially influenced by one's previous history. Thus, some people experience poverty in old age whereas others have accumulated wealth through their life course or have access to sizeable occupational pensions. Forrest and Murie (1985) have shown how a household's labour market position can influence housing circumstances throughout the life course.

It is important to distinguish in the biographical approach between the three different types of time in which housing pathways are structured: (i) individual time (how old the individual is, state of health and so on); (ii) family time (the stage of the family life-cycle) and (iii) historical time (what are the prevailing economic, social and political conditions) (Hareven, 1982a; Yeandle, 1987). Considering housing factors alone, households forming in the 1930s would have had opportunities to enter owner-occupation not available in the 1920s. Couples having children would face very different access to council housing in the 1950s than in the 1990s. Completely new housing options have emerged at different points in historical time. For example, the recent growth in private retirement homes has created an option for some older people which has not existed to any significant extent for preceding cohorts. Many other factors will influence the housing circumstances of different cohorts, such as changes in labour market conditions, evolving family structures, and cultural factors which can influence social attitudes, expectations and life-styles. Housing pathways may be predominantly influenced by non-housing factors such as these.

A danger with the biographical approach is that the focus on individual households leads to an over-emphasis on the choices which people have and neglects the constraints within which choices are made. This is particularly because of the 'taken-for-granted' nature of many of the societal constraints which influence the way that people perceive the options open to them. In the mobility literature reviewed earlier the constraints considered to limit household choice were usually narrowly defined in terms of the immediate factors which influence the options available, such as levels of income, prevailing prices or the actions of financing institutions. However, it is important to recognise, as the political economy approach does, that the focus needs to be wider than this to incorporate factors operating at the societal level. There has been no work which looks at the impact of such constraints on housing outcomes and which attempts to explore the relationships between constraints and the perceptions, attitudes and actions of individual households or at the way that attitudes and perceptions of the options available to households are formed.

Researchers have taken different views of the relative emphasis to be given to choice and constraint. In some instances, such as Forrest and Murie's work (1985) on the importance of labour market position, constraints are held to be all consuming. In other work, such as some of that on life-styles, the impression is given that few constraints on behaviour exist (Taylor and Ford, 1981). However, life-styles may be a product of dominant ideologies rather than choice and, therefore, be one way in which structural factors impact on housing outcomes. In practice it is very difficult to identify the relative importance of choice and constraints. Both are clearly important and combine together to generate the housing outcomes of older people. The problems to be resolved are how they combine and how they can be disentangled to help understanding of the possibilities for change.

Research directions

In order to solve these problems the relationship between choice and structural factors needs to be theorised. In other words, the micro and macro levels of analysis need to be combined within a linking conceptual framework. One possible framework from the sociological literature is that of structuration based on the work of Giddens. Structuration is a very complex and abstract framework and there are a number of differences between the approaches of various authors. It is not possible to do full justice to the ideas here, readers are referred to Giddens (1976, 1979, 1981), Bhasker (1979), Bourdieu (1977) and Bryant and Jary (1991).

The essence of structuration is the belief that the social structure exists prior to the individual agency because individuals are born into and grow up within an existing social structure which, through socialisation, permeates their thinking as well as surrounding them with structural constraints and opportunities. Therefore, structure has a major influence on the actions of individuals. However, social structures are not independent of individual actions and only continue insofar as individuals reproduce them through their actions. In most cases the effect of individual actions is to continue pre-existing structures unchanged, but there is argued to be some scope for changes in social structures usually brought about by the unintended consequences of many people's actions. However, despite their key role in reproducing social structures, individuals, according to Giddens, may not be consciously aware of what they are doing and, therefore, cannot be relied upon to give a complete account of what they do. Thus, the researcher has a key role in interpreting the meanings and actions of individuals in the light of structural forces.

Structuration has generally been welcomed as an approach but has been criticised for its lack of specificity, for example, it is not clear from Giddens by what mechanisms reproduction occurs. There is a large gap in the approach between abstract structure and individual practice which is not filled by any mediating concepts.

There are few prescriptions about appropriate empirical research methods in the structurationist approach but, following Sarre (1986), it is possible to identify four levels of research tasks as follows:
1. The elucidation of frameworks of meaning using ethnographic or biographical methods to clarify individual's knowledge of the social structure and their reasons for action.
2. Investigation of the context and form of practical consciousness.
3. Identification of the bounds of knowledgeability to discover the unacknowledged or unconscious meanings held by individuals and the unintended consequences of actions.

4. The specification of structural orders i.e. the structural factors which impinge on actions.

In other words, the research needs to employ ethnographic or biographic methods to understand the meanings of individuals and the conscious aspects of their behaviour. However, the unconscious meanings and actions also need to be explored bearing in mind the constraints and opportunities which structure them and are reproduced by them. In short the researcher has to interpret data in the light of an analysis of structural forces.

The intention is not to argue that structuration theory represents the only possible research framework, but to show that frameworks exist which, despite their abstract and problematic status, can provide some general guidance for a biographical life course analysis of housing. The hope is that empirical research in this area will not only advance understanding of housing in old age, but also play some part in helping to clarify major theoretical issues.

The biographical approach which is being put forward here would take as its primary focus the explanations given by older people about their housing circumstances. It would ascertain the options which older people perceived to be open to them and would seek explanations from them as to why certain options were chosen and others rejected. The reasons for rejection of options can be especially important in drawing attention both to immediate constraints and also to levels of understanding and knowledge of social pressures which structure behaviour. As an example an older couple may be interviewed who are living in an 'ordinary' owner-occupied house they have shared for 20 years and which is now in a state of disrepair. Why have they not taken advantage of other options?

The adoption of a biographical approach can help to provide a dynamic life course perspective. However, it is not by any means an unproblematic method. It rests on asking people to recall facts which may have happened a long time ago. Memories are far from perfect (Thompson *et al.*, 1990) and attitudes can be re-interpreted in the light of ongoing experience. The ideal approach would be a longitudinal study in which individuals were tracked through the life course and their experiences recorded at regular intervals. Such longitudinal studies exist, but the difficulties of organisation and funding mean that they tend to be wide-ranging in the scope of the topics covered and based on questionnaire surveys rather than biographical interviews. In addition, all the existing studies in Britain are at a relatively early stage in the life course of the individuals surveyed, so are not very useful in exploring the issues outlined here. Therefore, there is a need for longitudinal research focused on housing issues and based on biographical interviews.

This kind of research is difficult to organise, expensive to fund and requires considerable commitment over a long period of time from researchers. A more practicable research method is the cohort study in which the research focus is on groups of people in different cohorts usually on the basis of chronological age although other variables can be used. Thus, a sample of people could be interviewed aged 50–55, others aged 60–65 and others aged 70–75. The findings from the different cohorts can then be compared to give a longitudinal dimension to the research.

The key to the success of this approach is to be able to differentiate between 'cohort' properties, that is, previously acquired features of successive age cohorts which will be relatively stable properties of the cohort and, therefore, amenable to prediction, and 'period' effects, that is, historically specific factors. The operation of both these types of factors makes comparison between cohorts difficult because differences cannot simply be put down to age. Simple prediction is also misleading, for example, the assumption is often made that because some older owner occupiers today have problems in keeping their houses in good repair, and because there will be a higher proportion of owner occupiers among future cohorts of older people, these problems will become more common. However, future older owner occupiers will have entered this tenure at a different time from previous cohorts and will have had different housing and other life experiences which may mean that their experience of owner occupation in old age will be very different. In addition, changes in the nature of society and in public policies may mean that older owner occupiers in one period may face very different circumstances than those in other time periods. If factors such as these are adequately taken into account, a cohort research design can provide a longitudinal dimension, both in terms of understanding the past and predicting the future.

The emphasis in this paper on cohort and longitudinal research does not mean that cross-sectional research is not worthwhile. On the contrary, some insights can be gained through this means, although its value is increased considerably if it is combined with a biographical or longitudinal perspective. It can provide the contextual information within which individual biographies can be situated, thus providing the possibility of generalising from what is usually a relatively small number of life histories.

Finally, the approach outlined here need not be tackled in one single study. Indeed, such a task would be very difficult to achieve. Rather, the agenda and framework outlined can profitably be tackled at a variety of levels including, for example, biographical fieldwork on the one hand and the historical analysis of structural constraints on the other. Insights from research at these different levels should be integrated and this chapter has attempted to take the first steps in outlining a framework for this task.

Conclusion

The contention in this chapter is that there is a need to add a longitudinal or dynamic element to existing research on housing and old age which has been overly static and cross-sectional in design. There have been some attempts to remedy this situation through simplistic life-cycle models and more recently through the use of the idea of a housing history or housing career.

We have attempted to build on this latter approach by taking ideas and approaches from social gerontology. In particular, the life course perspective and the biographical research approach offer insights which when applied to housing can present a way forward. We have attempted to outline a way of integrating these perspectives into housing studies and to suggest that the housing biography should form the basis of future research. Nevertheless, it is necessary to counterbalance the biographical emphasis on individual attitudes and perceptions with an analysis of the many constraints and structural forces which shape and limit behaviour, and we have suggested that structuration theory is one possible way of doing this.

With the increasing visibility of housing problems in old age and the growing policy interest in this area, there has been more research on housing and old age, but it has been very restricted in scope. At first it was treated as a separate and distinct field with concentration on the evaluation of specific forms of provision such as sheltered housing. There are signs that it is now becoming more integrated into mainstream housing research, but this has not been associated with the conceptual development which is necessary if our understanding of housing outcomes in old age is to be increased.

One of the consequences of current modes of research has been to reinforce ageist assumptions about the problematic nature of old age. The focus on housing circumstances in old age has directed attention towards the characteristics of older people and away from the factors in early life which have such a profound influence on the experience of old age. Thus, policy intervention has been focused on ameliorating bad housing situations in old age through special forms of provision, such as sheltered housing and care and repair schemes, rather than on dealing with the factors in earlier life which have made some older people vulnerable (Clapham and Smith, 1990). For example, there is little if any policy discussion about the impact of the current housing subsidy system on the ability of future older people to obtain good housing. Issues such as the impact of changing tenure structures and the changing role of council housing on housing outcomes in old age could be addressed with an understanding of the dynamics of housing pathways through the life course. Adoption of the approach advocated here would shift the focus of attention away from specific forms of provision in old age and the problematic nature of old age and towards the workings of the housing system which structure the choices which households make and strongly influence housing outcomes in old age.

The adoption of a biographical research method should help to bring the views of older people themselves more to the fore in policy debates. Also, it should help to improve understanding of the choices open to households at various stages of the life course and the factors which shape the decisions made. For example, despite numerous studies of entrants to sheltered housing it is still unclear why some older people enter sheltered housing and others with similar characteristics reach very different destinations. Biographical research should help unravel issues which repeated cross-sectional surveys have failed to clarify.

Finally, a greater understanding of the factors which shape housing pathways is necessary if plans are to be made and policies drawn up to meet the needs of future cohorts of older people. At present, simplistic assumptions are made on the basis of simple demographic projections. For example, it is often assumed that, because many current owner-occupiers have problems in the upkeep of their houses, the greater number of owner-occupiers in future cohorts will mean that there will be more problems. However, this is not necessarily so as future cohorts will have entered owner-occupation at different times and had different housing experiences than previous cohorts. In addition, their attitudes towards factors such as releasing house equity may well be different as it will have been shaped by their own experiences, as well as changing ideologies and government policies.

CHAPTER 10

Class, Caring and the Life Course

Sara Arber and Jay Ginn

It is remarkable that within the extensive literature on informal care for elderly people (see Parker, 1990) there is virtually no mention of class divisions in informal caring. This chapter provides an initial exploration of class divisions in relation to caring for elderly people and how such caring varies over the life course, using secondary analysis of General Household Survey data.

Class Divisions in Health, Disability and the Need for Care

In this section we argue that the class of an elderly person is associated with their likelihood of becoming dependent and losing autonomy. Class differences arise, first, because class influences the likelihood of chronic ill-health and impairment, and second, because within any given level of impairment, class influences the likelihood of that person losing independence. Class is directly associated with the material, financial and cultural resources necessary to enable an elderly person to remain autonomous within their own home; those who lack resources, including access to caring resources, are most likely to experience entry into residential care, which is usually characterised as representing a marked reduction in the elderly person's autonomy and independence.

There is extensive evidence that the lower social classes have higher levels of morbidity and mortality, and that poor material circumstances and adverse working conditions lead to higher levels of disability and poor health status (Townsend *et al.*, 1988; Wilkinson, 1986; Fox *et al.*, 1983; Fox and Goldblatt, 1982; Power *et al.*, 1991). However, the implications of the differential distribution of ill-health for the class distribution of informal caring are rarely discussed.

Class differences in mortality have been found to persist among the 65–74 and over 75 age groups (Goldblatt, 1990; and Fox and Goldblatt, 1982), but analyses have been restricted to men in these two age groups. Grundy (1989) shows an association between housing tenure and mortality with elderly tenants of both sexes having higher mortality rates than owner occupiers. We examine later in this chapter the association between position in the labour market during working life and level of functional disability in later life, focusing on how this might give rise to class differences in caring.

Financial and material resources are related to disability and to dependence in a number of ways. With increasing age income declines (Ginn and Arber, 1991; 1992), while at the same time there is a greater likelihood of chronic illness and impairment. Thus, at the stage in their life course when individuals are most likely to suffer from a functional impairment they have the least financial resources to cope with living with it. The costs of coping with disability are considerable, for example, aids and adaptations may be required, and fuel and transport costs increase (Thompson *et al.*, 1988a, 1988b, 1990; Martin and White, 1988).

Health care costs which must be borne by the disabled individual are likely to increase in the future, with health care becoming more market-driven as in the US. In the US, the costs of health and nursing care frequently impoverish elderly people (Arendell and Estes, 1991). The restriction of Medicaid to financing nursing home care to those below specified poverty levels means that, to obtain state-funded nursing home care, elderly people must either already be poor or must deplete their financial resources to become eligible. The US situation is complicated by the lack of health insurance for domiciliary care. This means that frail elderly people have a stark choice of paying for their own domiciliary care, relying on informal carers or entering residential care (providing they have sufficient financial resources or are eligible for Medicaid).

Whether an elderly impaired person needs informal care is not simply a function of their degree of impairment, but is mediated by their material, financial and cultural resources, which are themselves intimately bound up with class. We have coined the term 'leverage' to denote how possession of these resources reduces a disabled person's need for reliance on informal care. For example, financial resources can be used to adapt or purchase more appropriate housing or aids and adaptations to promote independent living, as well as pay privately for substitute care. Cultural resources increase the elderly person's knowledge about available services and their ability to negotiate with providers and social welfare agents for desired services, which may obviate the need to rely on informal carers. The availability and adequacy of state support services are important intermediary factors between an individual's impairment and their need for informal care.

Where an elderly person requires daily care, their class may influence whether they are cared for in their own home, the home of their care-giver, or in a residential setting. Caldock's (1992) longitudinal study of elderly people in North Wales found that working class frail elderly people were more likely to enter residential institutions, and at a lower level of disability, than middle class elderly people. Caldock suggests this is both because elderly middle class people living alone were better able to support their independence by paying for needed help, and middle class carers were more likely to have the resources to enable them to carry on caring. Similarly,

Grundy (1989) shows that the likelihood of an elderly person entering an institution differs by their tenure and social class. Tenants of both sexes and men in manual occupations in 1971 were more likely to be in an institution in 1981 than owner occupiers or middle class men. Grundy states 'The predominance of those from working-class backgrounds in institutions... is undoubtedly related to their lower command of resources – including perhaps relatives ability to provide accommodation'. (1989 p.145). These issues are discussed in Higgs and Victor's chapter. In the US, Olson (1985) and Knight and Walker (1985) note that those without adequate income (predominantly women) are often unnecessarily placed in nursing homes. Thus, there may be differences in the ability of elderly people of different classes to stay in their own homes.

The Provision of Informal Care

There is extensive literature on the costs to the carer of providing care for elderly people, in terms of employment opportunities foregone and adverse effects on their mental and physical health (Nissel and Bonnerjea, 1982; Braithwaite, 1990; Wenger, 1990). This literature focuses particularly on how women are disadvantaged by policies of community care (Land, 1991), but we know little about other ways in which caring responsibilities are socially structured. How is caring distributed across the life course and among classes, and how does life course position and class influence the manner in which caring responsibilities are fulfilled?

Class may not affect the likelihood of an individual having to provide care for elderly parents, since we all have parents who will probably have one or more periods of disability during which they need care. However, class differences in health, disability and mortality in later life lead us to expect that the *timing* of care provision is class related; middle class elderly people, because of their better health and greater longevity, may require care when they are in their eighties and their children are close to retirement age, whereas working class parents may experience disability in their sixties and thus require care from their children who are in their forties or younger. (This timing difference may be partially offset by the shorter generation length of the working class). Differences in the timing of care provision within the life course may have profound implications for the development or re-estab-lishment of women's careers.

We suggest that the working class are doubly disadvantaged both by being more likely to be called on to provide care to elderly parents at an earlier age, when it conflicts with the demands of employment, and by having less material resources with which to ease their caring burden. Potential carers with adequate financial resources are able either to pay someone else to provide the required domiciliary support or to finance private residential provision, thus avoiding or reducing the constraint on their own time and energy. If the elderly person lacks financial resources and state services are not provided, the cost of aids and adaptations, laundry, special diets, transport, etc. may fall primarily on the carer. Thus, the financial resources of the carer may be crucial in influencing whether the elderly person is enabled to live independently, within the constraints of their own physical impairment.

Car ownership is another aspect of material resources which facilitates the provision of care to individuals living in other households. A car may allow informal care to be provided over fairly long distances and obviate the need either for the elderly person to move into the carers' own household or to enter residential care. We have argued elsewhere that care 'at a distance', which maintains the elderly person in their own home, is prefer-able for the elderly person compared with co-resident care in the home of the care-giver (Arber and Ginn, 1992). But, where 'care at a distance' is not appropriate to the elderly person's needs, carers with greater financial resources may be more easily able to accommodate an elderly relative in their own home because of having sufficient space, or being able to build or buy a property with a 'granny flat'. The latter arrangement may promote the independence and autonomy of an impaired elderly parent, whereas moving into shared common living spaces in a small dwelling would increase their dependence.

Evidence from the US indicates that elderly people with low incomes are more likely to live with adult children or other relatives (Wolf and Soldo, 1988; Wolf, 1990). Using longitudinal data from the British census, Grundy (1989) shows that between 1971 and 1981 moving to live with an adult child was greater in the owner occupied sector, including elderly tenants moving into the households of relatives who were owner occupiers. Grundy and Harrop (1992) show that co-residence of elderly parents with adult children is more likely in larger dwellings (with seven or more rooms). However, such co-residence often provides support for adult children and grandchildren rather than care for the elderly parent. Thus, classes may 'manage' the caring 'needs' of their relatives in different ways. Middle class carers have effec-tively more options as to whether to provide informal care themselves, pay for substitute care, purchase aids, or modify their own or the elderly person's housing to reduce the need for informal care. These strategies entail greater hardship or may be impossible for working class carers.

Middle class carers also have more 'leverage' in negotiating with social welfare professionals to obtain state supportive services or residential care. Current community care policies, as outlined in the 1990 NHS and Com-munity Care Act (Department of Health, 1989), give considerable discretion to care managers, who in future will put together packages of care in consultation with the elderly person and their care-giver. Class inequalities may be exacerbated if the middle class have greater skills in negotiating an advantageous care package.

This chapter provides a preliminary analysis of class, caring and the life course. First, we examine class differences in disability, marital status and living arrangements of elderly people, and second, we examine the pre-valence of adults providing informal care to elderly people according to their stage in the life course, class and access to material resources in the form of car ownership.

Data and Methods

The data used in this chapter are from the General Household Survey (GHS), which is an annual nationally representative interview survey of all adults aged 16 and over living in about 10,000 private households (OPCS, 1989). The GHS obtains a response rate of 82–84 per cent each year. For the first part of the analysis, we have combined together the GHS for three years, 1985–87, yielding a sample of over 11,000 people aged 65 and over. For the second part, we use the OPCS Informal Carers survey, which was conducted as part of the 1985 GHS and provided a sample of approximately 2,400 carers aged 16 and over (Green, 1988). The survey excludes informal care provided to people living in residential settings.

Carers were identified in the GHS using two screening questions (Arber and Ginn, 1990). The first screening question was – 'Some people have *extra family responsibilities* because they look after someone who is sick, handi-capped or elderly... Is there anyone living with you who is sick, handi-capped or elderly whom you *look after or give special help* to?' The second screening question identified people with caring responsibilities outside the household – 'And how about people not living with you, do you provide *some regular service or help* for any sick, handicapped or elderly relative, friend or neighbour not living with you?' (authors' emphasis). The *'regular service or help'* may be no more than regular gardening or purchasing some item of shopping for a relative. Both of these would be included as 'caring' in the OPCS survey, yet may have little to do with the dependency of the recipient. Thus, the range of activities through which a respondent is classified as a 'carer' for someone in another household (extra-resident care) is more inclusive than for co-resident care, where 'normal' services are excluded (Arber and Ginn, 1990).

Carers were asked a detailed set of questions about their caring tasks and the characteristics of the dependent(s) they assisted. In this chapter we focus on adults who said they cared for a person aged 65 and over. Ten per cent of women and seven per cent of men provide extra-resident care, according to the OPCS definition, and two per cent each of women and men report providing co-resident care to elderly people.

Class and Disability of Elderly People

Economic position during adult life has a lasting impact on health and disability which persists up to the oldest age groups (Arber and Ginn, 1991a; 1993). We consider the effect of class position on a measure of functional

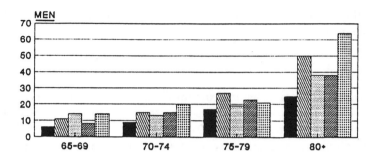

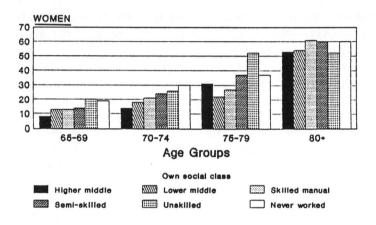

Source: General Household Survey, 1985 (authors' analysis)

Figure 10.1 Percentage with disability by social class for elderly men and women

impairment based on a series of six activities of daily living; getting up and down stairs, getting around the house, getting in and out of bed, cutting toenails, bathing or washing all over, and going out and walking down the road. These items were found to form a Guttman scale (Arber and Ginn, 1991a). A measure of three or more on this scale represents 'moderate' or greater disability, such that an elderly person has difficulty going up and down stairs or going out and walking down the road. These individuals will generally need some help, for example with shopping. Questions on functional ability were only asked in the 1985 GHS, so the analysis of disability is restricted to 3600 elderly people interviewed that year.

The impact of their previous economic role on elderly people's disability is measured using their main occupation during working life. This was coded into five classes, plus a category for elderly women who have 'never worked' (for details see end of chapter). An individualistic approach was used (Arber, 1990). This may be questioned for elderly women, as many have not worked since they married, and 16 per cent have never worked. It is all the more surprising that, despite these drawbacks, strong class trends emerge. Figure 10.1 shows that for men and women aged 65–74 there is a clear class gradient relating to position in the labour market during the life course. Elderly people previously in unskilled occupations are twice as likely to have a moderate or greater level of disability as those previously in higher middle class occupations. Class differences above 75 are still evident but the gradient is less clear.

The persisting influence of role in the productive labour force shows that an elderly person's earlier biography has a lasting impact on their level of functional impairment and thus on how long they are likely to be able to remain independent and autonomous in later life. This association of disability and class will have an impact on the need for care and on the living arrangements of elderly people.

Class, Marital Status and Living Arrangements of Elderly People

The marital status and living arrangements of elderly people affect who provides care, if it is needed: whether it is provided in the elderly person's own home by another household member; whether the elderly person is able to continue to live alone with help provided by informal carers or the state; whether they move to live in the home of an informal care-giver; or whether they enter residential care. The location in which care is given and who provides that care has profound implications for the elderly person's self-concept and for their feelings of independence and autonomy (Arber and Ginn, 1992).

Independence is likely to be greatest where the elderly person remains within their own home cared for by a close relative, particularly a spouse. For the widowed and never married, living alone is a preferred option, particularly for those who have sufficient financial resources to enable them to live autonomously (see Wilson, this volume), and/or have the support of informal carers on whom they can rely. Howarth (this volume) shows that independence is promoted where support is based on reciprocity and interpreted as part of a neighbourhood support system, rather than being conceptualised as 'care' which implies dependence and a lack of reciprocity. State support services in Britain are particularly targeted at elderly people who live alone (Arber et al., 1988; Arber and Ginn, 1991a), and are important in promoting continued independent living. However, there may be negative connotations in having to 'depend' on the state (see Wilson, this volume). Elderly people generally prefer to move into residential care than move to live in the home of a younger relative as a dependent, particularly if the relative is a married child (Thompson and West, 1984; Connidis, 1983; Finch, 1989). In this setting, they are most likely to become dependent and

Table 10.1 Class differences in marital status among elderly men and women by age group (column percentages)

Men	Higher middle	Lower middle	Skilled manual	Semi-skilled	Un-skilled	All
65–74						
Single	5	6	5	11	10	7
Married	84	81	77	71	69	78
Widowed+	11	14	18	18	21	16
	100%	100%	100%	100%	100%	100%
N=	(883)	(309)	(1113)	(578)	(174)	(3057)
75+						
Single	4	8	6	6	8	6
Married	70	57	63	61	58	64
Widowed	26	35	32	33	34	31
	100%	100%	100%	100%	100%	100%
N=	(464)	(176)	(542)	(298)	(120)	(1600)

Women	Higher middle	Lower middle	Skill manual	Semi-skilled	Un-skilled	Never worked	All
65–74							
Single	16	10	8	7	4	5	9
Married	48	51	50	50	49	54	50
Widowed+	36	38	42	43	47	41	41
	100%	100%	100%	100%	100%	100%	100%
N=	(565)	(1139)	(368)	(1145)	(427)	(199)	(3843)
75+							
Single	23	13	12	10	5	5	11
Married	19	25	22	20	19	25	22
Widowed+	58	62	66	70	76	71	67
	100%	100%	100%	100%	100%	100%	100%
N=	(399)	(620)	(352)	(916)	(361)	(370)	(3024)

NB. Percentages may not add up to 100% because of rounding in this and subsequent tables.

Social class is measured by own last main occupation for both men and women.

+   'Widowed' includes a small number of elderly people who are divorced or separated.

Source: General Household Survey, 1985–87 (authors' analysis)

to have little autonomy, unless the living arrangements are separated, as in a granny flat.

Should married people become frail and in need of care, marriage usually ensures care by their spouse, a situation which is likely to maximise their level of independence within the constraints of their physical impairment, especially for men (Arber and Ginn, 1992). Class is associated with an elderly person's marital status (Table 10.1), although the pattern of association differs by gender. For men aged 65–74, there is a linear class gradient: 84 per cent of higher middle class men are married compared with 69 per cent of unskilled men. The class trend is similar among men over 75, although lower middle class men have a greater likelihood of being widowed. Widowed, unlike single, men will often have children who provide support should they become impaired.

Entry into residential care is strongly associated with marital status (Arber and Ginn, 1991a). For example, in their late 70s, single men have a 17 times greater chance of being in residential care than married men, and widowed men have a six times greater chance. The differentials are more marked among the young elderly and persist even among men over age 85, where the differentials are six times higher for single men and four times higher for widowed men than for married men.

Differences in marital status among elderly people reflect three different life course processes, each of which is associated with class. We have already considered class differences in health and mortality: the wives of higher middle class men are likely to be healthier than the wives of unskilled men, resulting in class differences in widowhood. Second, there are class differences in marriage rates. These can be seen among young elderly men, where twice as many semi- and unskilled men have never married compared with men in other classes. The third trend relates to re-marriage following widowhood, which is much higher for elderly men than elderly women (Arber and Ginn, 1991a). We suspect that widower's likelihood of remarriage is associated with their health and their financial resources, which are both associated with their occupational class.

Elderly womens' marital status is associated with their class in a different way from men. The proportions of elderly women who are married differ little by class, but class differences are in opposite directions for the widowed and single. Women in higher middle class occupations during their working life are least likely to have been married (Table 10.1). The class gradient is linear in both age groups, four to five times *more* higher middle class than unskilled women have remained single. Widowhood varies inversely with class. Three-quarters of over 75-year-old unskilled women are widowed compared with 58 per cent of higher middle class women.

Widowhood and single status differ in their likely impact on an elderly woman's independence and autonomy, because of two factors which pull in opposite directions. Single women have greater financial resources than widowed women (Ginn and Arber, 1991) and are thus more likely to have the resources to remain independent in their own homes for longer. On the other hand, widowed women are more likely to have children who can be called upon to provide informal care should they need it. Differences in the likelihood of living in residential care by marital status are less for women than for men but are in the same direction. The chance of being in residential

Table 10.2 Living arrangements+ of elderly men and women by class and age group (column percentages)

Men	Higher middle	Lower middle	Skilled manual	Semi-skilled	Un-skilled	All
65–74						
Lives Alone	13	16	16	22	19	16
Md couple	84	80	77	71	69	78
Other elderly	2	2	3	4	5	3
Young adults	1	2	3	3	7	3
	100%	100%	100%	100%	100%	100%
N=	(882)	(309)	(1110)	(578)	(174)	(3053)
75+						
Lives Alone	20	32	27	28	33	26
Md couple	70	27	63	60	54	63
Other elderly	4	5	3	5	3	4
Young adults	6	5	8	7	9	7
	100%	100%	100%	100%	100%	100%
N=	(464)	(176)	(540)	(298)	(120)	(1598)

Women	Higher middle	Lower middle	Skill manual	Semi-skilled	Un-skilled	Never worked	All
65–74							
Lives Alone	40	40	38	40	38	28	39
Md couple	48	51	50	50	49	54	50
Other elderly	8	6	7	4	5	5	5
Young adults	4	3	5	7	9	12	6
	100%	100%	100%	100%	100%	100%	100%
N=	(564)	(1138)	(368)	(1143)	(424)	(198)	(3835)
75+							
Lives Alone	64	61	60	63	63	50	61
Md couple	19	25	22	20	19	25	22
Other elderly	11	7	7	6	5	7	7
Young adults	6	7	11	11	13	18	10
	100%	100%	100%	100%	100%	100%	100%
N=	(399)	(618)	(350)	(911)	(365)	(369)	(3012)

Social class is measured by own last main occupation for both men and women.

+ The four categories of 'living arrangements' are:

Lives alone

Lives as part of a married couple (may be including adult children in the household)

Other elderly – Unmarried elderly person living with other elderly people (may also include younger adults)

Young adults – Unmarried elderly person who lives only with younger adults (mainly adult children).

Source: *General Household Survey, 1985–87* (authors' analysis)

care is 7.5 times greater for single than married women in their late seventies, and 3.5 times greater for widowed women. The comparable figures for women over age 85 are 3.3 times higher for single women and twice as high for widowed as for married women.

The living arrangements of elderly people have a critical influence on whether informal care is provided by another household member, someone living in another household or whether formal care is provided by the state. These different locations of care have implications for the elderly person's likely level of autonomy and dependence. Research suggests that the two living arrangements most likely to precede entry into residential care are living alone and living with younger relatives, particularly a married daughter (Seale, 1990; Sinclair, 1988).

Table 10.2 shows class differences in the living arrangements of elderly men and women in private households. The majority of elderly men live as part of a married couple (some couples also live with others, mainly adult children), as do half of women aged 65–74. But the majority of women over 75 live alone (61%), and only a fifth live as part of a married couple.

A higher proportion of higher middle class men live with their spouse. Among men aged 65–74, 13 per cent of the higher middle class live alone, compared with a fifth of unskilled men (Table 10.2). Unskilled men are more likely to live with younger adults (mainly adult children), seven per cent compared with only one per cent of higher middle class men aged 65–74. We suggest that this living arrangement is the least desirable from the point of view of the elderly person; it is most likely to result in a dependent relationship and in the elderly person being considered a burden by the care-giver (Arber and Ginn, 1992; Nissel and Bonnerjea, 1982). Thus, higher class for elderly men is associated with living arrangements which are likely to maximise their autonomy and independence.

For elderly women, there is very little class difference in the proportions who are married or living alone, although women who have never worked are less likely to live alone. The main class difference is that twice as many unskilled as higher middle class women live in the same household as younger adults. We suggest that this relates to two factors; first, the health and financial resources of elderly women which vary according to their class, enabling middle class elderly women to remain living independently (either alone or with other elderly people), rather than with younger kin and second, the differential ability of their relatives to provide informal care 'at a distance'. The somewhat higher proportion of elderly middle class than working class women who live with other older people, largely reflects the higher proportion of never married women living with their siblings. This living situation is likely to involve greater reciprocity and mutual care than where an elderly person is living with adult children.

The cross-sectional data provided by the GHS on elderly people living in private households suggests that middle class elderly people may retain their independence for longer than the working class for several reasons:

**Table 10.3 Informal care for an elderly person (65+) and
time spent in caring, (a) within the same household and
(b) in a different household, by age and gender of carer**

Percentage providing any care, care for 10+ hours per week, and care for 20+ hours per week.

	(a) % Caring for elderly person within the household Co-resident Care			(b) % caring for elderly person in another household Extra-resident Care			N=
	Any	10hr+	20hr+	Any	10hr+	20hr+	
Under 45							
Men	1.0	0.5	0.3	4.8	1.0	0.3	4582
Women	0.7	0.6	0.4	7.5	2.1	0.7	5015
45–64							
Men	2.4	1.6	1.0	10.5	2.5	0.8	2483
Women	3.5	2.9	2.3	16.0	5.6	1.7	2769
65+							
Men	4.8	4.3	3.7	6.9	1.7	0.4	1419
Women	3.6	3.2	2.8	7.0	2.5	0.7	2060
All ages							
Men	2.0	1.4	1.1	6.8	1.6	0.5	8484
Women	2.1	1.8	1.5	9.8	3.2	1.0	9844

NB. The small number of people providing care both to an elderly person living in their own household and to an elderly person living elsewhere have been categorised as both co-resident and extra-resident carers.

Source: General Household Survey, 1985 (authors' analysis)

they have better health, living arrangements which give preferential access to informal carers, and greater financial, material and cultural resources. However, to provide more conclusive answers longitudinal data is needed, for example, to trace changes in living arrangements and entry into residential care for elderly people as they become impaired, and to analyse how these transitions vary with the resources of the elderly person and of their potential informal carers.

Caring and the Life Course

Informal care provided within the household (co-resident care) differs on a number of dimensions from care provided to an elderly person living in a separate household (extra-resident care), and therefore discussion of caring should distinguish these two locations. Under 10 per cent of adults caring for an elderly person in another household spend more than 20 hours per week on informal care, compared with over two-thirds of adults caring for someone in their own household. We examine how the likelihood of providing informal care to an elderly person (age 65+) varies over the life course, and how the kin relationship between carer and care-recipient differs between these two locations of care and at different stages of the life course.

Table 10.4 Provision of informal care to elderly people who is being cared-for by age and gender of carer and location of care (column percentages)

	Age of Carer			
	Under 45	45–64	65+	All
Co-resident Care				
Men Care for:				
Spouse	-	8	78	34
Parent/in-law	70	85	13	53
Other relative	30	7	9	13
	100%	100%	100%	100%
N=	(44)	(60)	(68)	(172)
Women care for:				
Spouse	-	30	75	41
Parent/in-law	73	58	7	42
Other relative	27	11	19	17
	100%	100%	100%	100%
N=	(37)	(96)	(75)	(208)
Extra-resident Care				
Men Care for:				
Parent/in-law	61	72	22	59
Other relative	24	11	27	19
Friend/Neighbour	15	18	51	22
	100%	100%	100%	100%
N=	(217)	(260)	(98)	(575)
Women Care for:				
Parent/in-law	57	60	10	51
Other relative	22	13	26	19
Friend/Neighbour	21	26	64	30
	100%	100%	100%	100%
N=	(377)	(440)	(145)	(962)

Source: *General Household Survey, 1985* (authors' analysis)

The likelihood of providing co-resident care for an elderly person increases with age, whereas for extra-resident care it peaks in the 45–64 age group (Table 10.3). The highest probability of being a co-resident carer is among older men, nearly five per cent provide such care, mainly for their wives. There is a greater gender difference in extra-resident than co-resident care, with women predominating among extra-resident carers below retirement age.

As well as measuring caring based on whether an individual provides any care at all, Table 10.3 includes two additional measures of the likelihood of being a carer: whether more than 10 hours of informal care are provided each week, and whether more than 20 hours are provided. It is clear that the majority of extra-resident care consists of caring for less than 10 hours per week, and is therefore less likely to have a major impact on the life of the carer than is co- resident care. Taking a more stringent definition of being a carer, based on a time commitment of over 20 hours per week, increases the gender imbalance; for example, in each stage of the life course, women are twice as likely to be extra-resident carers as men.

Care to an elderly person living elsewhere is least likely in the youngest life course stage (under age 45), it peaks in late middle age (45–64), and then falls. The gender differential is smaller among elderly than younger carers. This suggests that men's role in paid employment during the earlier part of their working life leads to lower levels of extra-resident care than following retirement.

Co-resident care for elderly people increases over the life course with the highest level of provision by carers who are themselves elderly. This increase is particularly sharp for men: 12 times more elderly men than men under 45 provide at least 20 hours of care, and seven times more elderly women than younger women provide this level of care. In the earlier phase of the life course there is little gender difference in the provision of co-resident care, but among 45–64-year-olds over twice as many women as men provide care for over 20 hours per week. In contrast, a higher proportion of elderly men than women provide co-resident care.

The kin relationship between the elderly care-recipient and the care-giver varies at different stages of the life course. Among women and men who care for an elderly person, Table 10.4 shows the proportion who care for a parent (or parent-in-law), their spouse, other relatives, and friends or neighbours at different stages of the life course. Earlier in the life course, and for men in mid-life, co-resident care is dominated by care for parents and parents-in-law. Among mid-life women nearly a third of carers support an elderly husband. Three-quarters of elderly co-resident carers are caring for their spouse.

The majority of extra-resident carers below retirement age are caring for their parents (or parents-in-law). Even among elderly carers, a fifth of women and two-fifths of men provide extra-resident care to a parent. Thus parent care is still evident in the latter stage of the life course. Women at all

Table 10.5 Percentage of men and women caring for an elderly person (65+) by social class and age of carer – (a) caring within the same household (b) caring in a different household

	Social class of carer*					
	Higher middle 1	Lower middle 2	Skilled manual 3	Semi- skilled 4	Un- skilled 5	Ratio 5/1
(a) Co-resident Care						
16–44						
Men	0.2	1.7	0.9	1.7	3.3	16.5
Women	0.6	0.8	0.6	0.9	1.5	2.5
45–64						
Men	2.1	3.1	1.4	3.6	5.9	2.8
Women	3.2	5.7	2.4	3.3	3.5	1.1
65+						
Men	4.9	2.0	5.2	3.9	10.4	2.1
Women	6.0	3.3	6.0	1.5	1.7	0.3
All ages						
Men	1.6	2.1	1.7	2.7	5.4	3.4
Women	2.2	2.5	2.1	1.7	2.2	1.0
(b) Extra-resident						
16–44						
Men	5.6	3.8	5.9	4.6	4.7	0.84
Women	7.6	6.0	10.1	6.7	7.6	1.00
45–64						
Men	11.2	15.0	11.0	6.5	8.5	0.76
Women	18.4	15.9	16.9	12.0	9.8	0.53
65+						
Men	8.6	5.8	6.8	5.0	6.5	0.76
Women	11.6	8.8	7.3	4.2	5.6	0.48
All ages						
Men	7.9	6.8	7.2	5.2	6.1	0.77
Women	11.5	8.9	11.9	7.4	7.5	0.65

*   Social class is measured by own current (or last) occupation for men and unmarried women, and for married women by their husband's class.

Source: *General Household Survey, 1985* (authors' analysis)

stages of the life course provide more care to neighbours and friends while men's care is more confined to their family. With increasing age more care is provided to neighbours and friends. Among elderly people providing extra-resident care, half of men and nearly two-thirds of women care for neighbours and friends. Here we would expect a higher level of provision among middle class elderly people who have greater resources at their disposal with which to facilitate such care.

Because the likelihood of being a carer varies across the life course stages, the analysis of class and caring in the next section focuses on each of the six

Table 10.6 Percentage of men and women providing informal care (a) within the same household, (b) in a different household, by carer's car ownership and age

	(a) % caring within the same household Co-resident Care			(b) % caring in a different household Extra-resident Care		
	No car	1	2+	No car	1	2+
Under 45						
Men	1.3	0.6	1.4	4.1	5.1	4.7
Women	1.1	0.4	1.0	5.9	8.1	8.0
45–64						
Men	4.0	1.8	2.1	7.7	11.0	12.0
Women	4.2	2.9	3.6	10.8	17.0	20.5
65+						
Men	4.5	5.0	5.6	4.2	9.2	10.1
Women	3.4	4.2	3.3	5.8	9.3	14.8
All	2.84	1.65	1.87	6.2	9.2	9.8
N=	5770	8598	3960	5770	8598	3960

Source: *General Household Survey, 1985 (authors' analysis)*

age-sex groups in Table 10.3.

Class and Caring

Class is conventionally assumed to be unrelated to the likelihood of providing informal care. Indeed the OPCS Informal Carers report states 'There was very little variation between the percentages of carers among non-manual and manual socio-economic groups...' (Green, 1988 p.11 and Table 2.7). We show below that this was because the OPCS analysis combined together all caring rather than separately analysing co-resident and extra-resident care, which are associated with class in opposite ways. To measure the carers' class, for men and unmarried women we used their own (current or last main) occupation, and for married women their husband's occupation. Table 10.5 shows how class influences the likelihood of providing informal care to an elderly person, for men and women in three stages of the life course.

At the earlier stages of the life course, the unskilled are more likely to be co-resident carers than other classes. Unskilled women are two and a half times more likely and unskilled men are sixteen times more likely to be co-resident carers than higher middle class women and men. This greater propensity to be a co-resident carer among the semi-skilled and unskilled remains for men throughout the life course. However, for middle aged women, 45–64, a class gradient is not apparent, and for women over 65 the class gradient is reversed. For all men, the class trend is approximately linear, falling from 5.4 per cent of unskilled men to 1.6 per cent of higher middle class men. This class pattern is partly associated with marital status, since never married and previously married men have a greater likelihood of being a co-resident carer largely because of remaining in the parental home (Grundy and Harrop, 1992).

The class pattern with extra-resident care is quite different. Among younger women and men, there is no clear association between class and providing care to someone in another household. In the middle age group, 45–64, middle class and skilled manual women are most likely to provide extra-resident care. There is a strong class gradient among elderly carers, with middle class women most likely to be extra-resident carers: 12 per cent of higher middle class women compared with 4–6 per cent of semi- and unskilled women. This pattern of greater provision by the middle class is also found among mid-life and elderly men.

In summary, in the middle and later stages of the life course the middle class are more likely to provide extra-resident care (both to their elderly parents and to friends and neighbours). Counterbalancing this there is a greater tendency for caring within the household among the unskilled, with the greatest class differences in the earlier stages of the life course.

An important aspect of class and caring is the resources associated with being middle class, which can be used to facilitate or alter the task of caring. A key resource which can be used to advantage by those in higher social classes is possession of one or more cars. The association between car ownership and the likelihood of providing extra-resident care to elderly people is very strong, especially for women (Table 10.6). Twice as many women aged 45–64 with two cars in their household are extra-resident carers compared with those without a car, and this differential is even greater for elderly women. Over twice as many elderly men who are car owners provide extra-resident care compared with those without cars. However, there is no association between car ownership and extra-resident care among men in the earlier stage of the life course.

Men and women without access to a car are more likely to be caring for an elderly person within their household compared with those with a car. This may be because co-residence is forced on adult children lacking a car. However, it may also reflect the fact that a higher proportion of those without a car are also unskilled workers, and that class is the critical factor in being a co-resident carer rather than lacking a car to facilitate provision of extra-resident care.

Discussion and Conclusions

The marital status and living arrangements of elderly people influence whether care, if required, is provided by a household member, someone living in another household or the state. These varying locations of care have implications for the elderly person's likely level of autonomy and independence. Elderly men and women who were previously in unskilled occupations are more likely to be sharing a home with younger adults, which we consider is a less preferred living arrangement. The two living arrangements most likely to precede entry into residential care are living alone and living with younger relatives, particularly a married daughter. Among elderly men, those who worked in higher middle class jobs during earlier stages of the life course are more likely to be married than other men, and thus cared for by their wife if they should need it.

The likelihood of providing informal care varies at different stages of the life course; this sequencing differs for men and women and for co-resident and extra-resident care. The involvement of men in paid work during earlier life stages leads to lower levels of care provision compared with women of comparable age. In later life elderly men are more often co-resident carers than elderly women, but less often provide care to older people living elsewhere. Throughout the life course women are more likely than men to provide care for friends and neighbours.

If informal caring responsibilities are taken on by a woman in mid-life, her opportunity to re-build her career and pension entitlements will be severely constrained. Such women have been termed 'Women in the middle' (Brody, 1981), their child care responsibilities barely over before elder care makes demands on their time and energy. Although the state pension scheme allows credits for caring years (Home Responsibility Protection), there is no compensation for lost opportunities to acquire occupational pension rights (Ginn and Arber, 1993). Informal caring may therefore threaten financial well-being in later life.

The contribution of elderly people to informal care is largely unacknowledged (Arber and Ginn, 1990). Co-resident care by elderly care-givers is mainly for their spouse. Although caring may be a constraint on their lives, it is less likely to conflict with other role demands in terms of paid employment and the needs of family members, and is thus less likely to be experienced as a burden. Elderly people who provide extra-resident care do so primarily for friends and neighbours and other elderly relatives. Such care may represent activities which are valued by the carers rather than being perceived as a constraint on their lives.

Although informal carers as a whole are drawn equally from all classes, if co-resident and extra-resident care are examined separately opposing class trends emerge. Among younger men (under 45), class has a marked effect on the likelihood of being a co-resident carer: working class men are far more likely than middle class men to provide care to an elderly person in the same household. For older men and for women of all ages, the effect of class on co-resident caring is less clear; this is mainly because a higher proportion are caring for their spouse, which we would not expect to be related to class.

In mid- and later life, more middle class people provide care for an elderly person in a separate household. The resources possessed by the middle class enable them to care 'at a distance'. Working class people, with fewer options easily available, are more likely to provide informal care within the household. It seems likely that class differences in the resources of carers combine with class differences in elderly people's own resources to influence the likelihood of residential admission.

Women are likely to be disproportionately affected by current government policies which shift a greater responsibility for the care of elderly people onto relatives. Women in the middle stage of the life course bear a heavy burden of informal care, both caring for parents and husbands within the household, and for elderly parents and parents-in- law living elsewhere. This is the time when many women seek to rebuild their careers following childbearing, and this aim may be adversely affected by informal caring. Elderly people themselves provide significant amounts of care to other elderly people. If shifts in policy reduce state domiciliary and support services, this may have detrimental consequences for the physical health and well-being of older carers, who are often themselves frail.

Current changes in care policies are likely to have particularly adverse effects on the working class, who not only have higher illness rates, but also the least resources to cope with the demands of caring. Unskilled men are particularly likely to be co-resident carers, and reduction in state support could make their already weak employment situation even more precarious. Not only do the middle class have more resources to cope with the demands of caring, but they are likely to have greater 'leverage' with care managers, which may in future exacerbate their irrelative advantage.

Acknowledgment

For access to the General Household Survey data for 1985–87 we are grateful to the ESRC Data Archive, University of Essex, and to the Office of Population Censuses and Surveys for permission to use the GHS data. The paper is based on research funded by the Economic and Social Research Council (Grant No. R000231458).

Note

For Figure 10.1 and Tables 10.1 and 10.2, the elderly person's main occupation during working life was classified into the Registrar General's socio-economic groups (OPCS, 1980) by the GHS, and we grouped these into social classes in the following way. For Table 10.5, married women were classified by their husband's occupation and all other women by their own current (or last) occupation. The coding was as follows:

Higher middle class: (1–4,5.1,13)	Higher professionals Employers and Managers Lower professionals
Lower middle class: (5.2,6)	Intermediate and Junior Non-Manual
Skilled manual: (8,9,12,14)	Self employed own account workers Foremen Skilled manual workers
Semi-skilled: (7,10,15)	Personal service workers Semi-skilled manual workers Agricultural workers
Unskilled: (11)	Unskilled manual workers
Never worked:	Women who have never been in paid work

CHAPTER 11

Policies and Perceptions of Identity
Service Needs of Elderly People from Black and Minority Ethnic Backgrounds
Janet Askham, Lesley Henshaw, and Maryrose Tarpey

All people acknowledge their individuality as well as their membership of various groups. For some purposes they have an identity which they see as totally unique, for others, as one they share; sometimes with everyone else (as a human being), sometimes with millions of other people (such as that of 'woman' or 'Asian'), sometimes only with a few (such as member of a local organisation). In addition, they of course have constellations of identities. Since so many different identities can be combined in any one individual they may see this combination as a source of their unique individuality. Different identities are given primacy in different circumstances or contexts, either in the way people decide they want to behave or in the way they are treated by others. Conflicts or dissatisfactions arise when the identities a person wants to emphasise (the way he or she behaves or indicates that she wants to be treated) differ from the identities accorded to her by others.

People stress different types of identity to indicate both what they have in common with and how they differ from others. In any social context people stress some types of identity rather than others. This may be done for many reasons: in order to achieve particular kinds of end; because they believe it is expected of them in that particular context; because it is one with which they feel comfortable or which they see as their most important identity; or because it is an identity which they see as constrained by, or imposed upon them by, the way they are treated.

Service providing organisations will accept as a service user anyone who can demonstrate needs which their organisation is designed to meet, as long as they have the appropriate characteristics (for example, being a British citizen) and use the correct means for obtaining the service (such as applying through the appropriate channels). Some organisations claim that all clients are treated equally within those parameters whereas others give priority to some clients over others. It is part of the ideology of large bureaucracies such as the National Health Service or local authority Social Services Departments not to treat all users equally but to ensure that they are all treated according to 'individual need'; individual treatment plans, individual assessment, and individual packages of care are important tenets of these services (Dalley,

1991; Brown, 1989). For example, in the Report which formed the basis of recent community care legislation (NHS and Community Care Acts 1990), Sir Roy Griffiths stated that Social Services Departments should:

> Identify and assess individuals' needs, taking full account of personal preferences (and those of informal carers), and design packages of care best suited to enabling the consumer to live as normal a life as possible. (Griffiths, 1988 p.1)

Perhaps one would not therefore expect group identities (as opposed to 'individuals') to play a part in the vocabularies either of the users or of the service providers.

However, large bureaucracies must categorise people, otherwise their work would be impossible. They do this, first, when they see certain groups of individuals as having, or as likely to have, certain kinds of care or treatment need; they must therefore 'target' that group for special attention, for example screening of women or of elderly people, or the provision of culturally sensitive services. For instance the White Paper on community care stated, 'Government recognizes that people from different cultural backgrounds may have particular care needs and problems' (DoH, 1989 p.10).

Second, service agencies categorise people when they see certain groups as having to be cared for within a communal setting (such as a ward, day centre or residential home), which must necessarily impose a more or less uniform environment which may not entirely suit the needs of any one individual. Third, in areas and times of scarce resources service agencies must prioritise clients if they cannot treat them all (or not all at once). It could be argued that such prioritisation is carried out according to individual rather than group characteristics. This, however, would be very hard to achieve; for in order to develop rules or guidelines for prioritisation and to act with the necessary speed, organisations must categorise. Fourth, some treatments must for reasons of cost be provided in a more or less uniform way, for example, an information booklet cannot be written afresh for each person using it.

These examples show that organisations cannot treat people as unique individuals, and that they depart from this in two ways – either by treating people in a uniform way or by classifying them into groups or categories on the basis of one or more characteristics, and arranging these characteristics in order of service priority.

The object of this chapter is to examine the ways in which identities are used by service providers and by elderly people from black and minority ethnic populations. It explores the extent to which black or ethnic identities are used to account for the way in which people are or should be treated within the health and social services.

Although research interest in ethnicity and ageing is growing, it is still very limited. Much of it has focused on the extent of service needs (see for example, Bhalla and Blakemore, 1981; Ebrahim *et al.*, 1987; Farrah, 1986; Fenton, 1988; McFarland *et al.*, 1989; Norman, 1985) and the uptake of services (Badger *et al.*, 1989; Blakemore, 1982, 1983; Holland and Lewando-Hundt, 1987; Johnson, 1987; Mays, 1983). There has also been a long debate about whether there should be any differences in services, or the way in which they are provided, to people from black or minority ethnic populations compared with the white indigenous population (for example, Atkin *et al.*, 1989; Connelly, 1989; Daniel, 1988; Moledina, 1987; Murray, 1985; Patel, 1990). The issues discussed have included, for example, whether they should attend the same day centres, have the same hospital catering service, or whether they should receive at least some specific or separate services, such as separate day centres for people from one ethnic group or specific prayer facilities in hospital.

With the ageing of the black and minority ethnic population in the United Kingdom, and at a time of considerable change in the way social and health services are provided, this is an extremely important subject for study. For instance, within these populations the proportion aged sixty and over was estimated at approximately five per cent during the latter part of the 1980s, but a much larger proportion (approximately 13%) was in the age group 45–59 years (Shaw, 1988; Haskey, 1990). With the implementation in 1993 of the new community care arrangements in which local authorities move towards a purchaser rather than provider role in social services, and a bigger part is to be played by the voluntary and private sectors, black and minority ethnic communities may be expected to provide more of their own care services than before. Whether this is what they want or need is therefore being even more hotly debated.

The Study

The data used in this chapter are taken from an investigation into health and social services provision for elderly people from black and minority ethnic populations in England and Wales. The aim of the study, which was funded by the Department of Health, and carried out between 1990 and 1992, was to examine the extent to which elderly people from black and minority ethnic groups received separate, specific or mainstream services, and the views of both staff and users. The investigation has involved firstly, a review of current social and health service provision, through postal surveys of local authority Social Services Departments, District Health Authorities, Family Health Service Authorities and general practitioners. These surveys have been carried out in areas with significant elderly black and minority ethnic populations; namely all those which in the 1981 Census had 400 or more people over the age of fifty whose head of household had been born in the New Commonwealth or Pakistan. Second, the investigation has included a series of interview studies with small samples of both service providers and users. This chapter uses data from two of these studies.

The first was an interview study of 172 people from Asian and Afro-Caribbean groups; its aim was to identify their service provision perceptions, experiences and preferences. These interviews were carried out in six counties or boroughs in England amongst a quota sample of people living in the community aged 50 years and over. The areas were selected from among those which had responded to the postal survey of providers, and chosen to provide both a geographical spread and a spread of authorities with specific policies on the employment and provision of services to black and minority ethnic communities. Age quotas were set to obtain approximately equal numbers of those approaching retirement age, young elderly, and older elderly people. The questionnaires were translated into three Asian languages and administered, where necessary, by interviewers who spoke the required language.

The second interview study examined the views and experiences of 90 members of staff working for Social Services Departments and District Health Authorities. Six further areas were selected; again these provided a geographical spread, and spanned a variety of approaches to service delivery. Staff were selected to include senior and middle rank practitioners as well as administrative and managerial officers together with any staff recruited specifically to work with people from black and minority ethnic populations. All respondents had responsibilities which included elderly people from these groups.

The Importance of Ethnicity and Age in Accounting for Preferred Health and Social Service Treatment

Although little research has been devoted to older people's perceptions of identity, some researchers have argued that other identities are more important than age to elderly people in general. For example, Kaufman (1986) in a small scale interview study of elderly Americans found that people continued to see themselves, and act in accordance with, themes or identities developed much earlier in adulthood. Gubrium (1986) used the metaphor of the 'mask' of age to conceptualise how age related to people's sense of identity. These findings would suggest that ethnicity, if it had been an important source of identity to people in earlier life, would be more salient to them than age in later life. Interest in objective measurement of the relative importance of age and ethnicity in influencing health, service receipt, life satisfaction and social networks is growing but such studies have not yet been carried out in the United Kingdom. However, as Blakemore concludes in a review of the evidence, there is little to suggest that age acts as a leveller in later life, and much to indicate that 'as people age they remain ethnically different from each other, or perhaps become more different from each other' (1989 p.172). However, in thinking about health care and social service provision both age and ethnicity may be seen as relevant.

Table 11.1 Ethnicity and preferred form of health and social service provision

Qu: Do you think people from Asian/Afro-Caribbean backgrounds should be treated in a special way when receiving health and social services?

	Afro-Caribbean %	Asian %
In a special way	-	40
Not special but:		
fairly/equally	12	3
kindly/with respect	1	7
effectively	8	1
Not special/same way	47	18
No preference	23	27
Not answered	8	3
Total %	**99**	**99**
N=	**(83)**	**(89)**

NB. All respondents reported some contact with health or social services, for example general practitioners. All were therefore asked this question.

Table 11.2 Ethnicity and Preferred Form of Provision by Hospital Staff

Qu: Do you think hospital staff should treat you in a special way because you are an Asian/Afro-Caribbean person in your 50s/60s/70s/etc.?

	Afro-Caribbean %	Asian %
In special way:		
unspecified	-	1
because needs differ	1	45
because elderly	7	4
Not special but:		
fairly/equally	12	3
effectively	4	-
Not special/same way	65	15
No preference/don't know	4	26
Not answered	7	6
Total %	**100**	**100**
N=	**(83)**	**(89)**

This section examines the importance of ethnicity compared with age (or indeed other identities) in what older Asian and Afro-Caribbean people say about how they would like to be treated by the health and social services. The Asian and Afro-Caribbean older people interviewed were asked whether they thought they should be treated in the same way as elderly people generally or whether they thought they should be treated in any special way because they were elderly/in their fifties or were Asian/Afro-Caribbean. Table 11.1 shows that, although nearly one-third said they could not answer or had no preference, 40 per cent of the Asian sample, compared with none of the Afro-Caribbeans, said they would prefer to be treated in a special way. (Detailed terminological issues, such as how terms like 'specific' or 'special' were translated are not addressed here). When asked specifically about care and treatment in hospital (Table 11.2) the pattern of answers was much the same, though with a slightly higher proportion of the Afro-Caribbeans stating firmly that they did not want to be treated in a special way, and a slightly higher proportion of the Asians saying that they did.

Such figures of course mask the inherent complexity of views about the relevance of ethnicity to service provision. People's more detailed comments about the relevance of age and ethnicity were therefore examined in greater depth. What did people mean when they said they did or did not want to be treated in a special way? Why did some appear to have difficulty in expressing a preference? What circumstances were they thinking of when they did express a preference? Was age a more or less important identity to them than ethnicity, or indeed were there other identities which they called on to justify treatment in one form rather than another?

Among those who said they did not want to be treated in a special way, a frequent view, particularly amongst the Afro-Caribbean sample, was that all people should be treated equally. In referring to equality they called upon common characteristics such as common humanity, being a member of 'the British family' or a British citizen, one of God's children, or a tax-payer. For example:

> Everybody is equal in the sight of God and should be treated accordingly. I don't think it happens, but it should. (56-year-old, Afro-Caribbean man)

> I don't think there should be any distinctions… I don't give a jot for people who can't adapt…they've been here long enough to have adapted to sausages and chips…everyone should have attention, and you should look after the black ones the same as the white ones. (67-year-old Afro-Caribbean woman)

> I don't mind how I'm treated as long as I'm treated like a human being, and not by the colour of my skin. (55-year-old Afro-Caribbean woman)

Of course these are only very general statements about fairness; they do not give any guide to action or awareness of differential circumstances.

This universal identity was used by Afro-Caribbean interviewees but only very rarely by Asians. Less frequently, but this time by Asians as well as Afro-Caribbeans, interviewees stated that everyone should be treated as an individual. For example:

Nowadays you are just a number – we should be treated as individuals. (64-year-old Asian woman)

What I'm saying is I wouldn't like to see separation *(separate treatment)* because it depends on individuals how they get on with each other. (67-year-old Afro-Caribbean woman)

The difficulty or impossibility of individual treatment was, however, recognised. As one man said:

Hospital staff can't possibly switch to cater for each type of person, or colour, or religion, etc. They just haven't the time. (62-year-old Afro-Caribbean man)

Age itself was grounds for special treatment to a small minority (though to slightly more Afro-Caribbeans than Asians). For example:

Whether you are black or white, as a pensioner you should all be treated the same way as you more-or-less suffer the same fate...Black elderly, Jamaican elderly, Asian elderly, White elderly, we are all pensioners. (83-year-old Afro-Caribbean woman)

Yes *(I should be treated in a special way)* not because of my colour but because of my age. (64-year-old Afro-Caribbean woman)

(I need special attention because) I am old – I don't go out that often – and I don't understand any of the system. (83-year-old Asian man)

Only one other kind of identity was called upon to justify some kind of special treatment; this was health or disability status. For example an elderly Asian man discussed the fact that he was blind:

I am blind and therefore I need support. (75-year-old Asian man)

Another said:

(I should be treated in a special way) because I'm disabled. (82-year-old Asian woman)

Overall, the main single ground for special treatment was ethnicity, though sometimes in conjunction with other special grounds, such as age or health status. As already stated ethnicity was mentioned by Asians but not by Afro-Caribbeans, none of whom when asked specifically said they thought they should be treated specially by reason of their ethnic background. However they did occasionally mention it at other points in the interview, showing that it was a factor not without significance for them. For example:

I'm not sure about special centres for Afro-Caribbean elderly. I think it's best to have a centre where everyone can go, and where they arrange activities to suit Afro-Caribbean people, like Calypso music...people say we are noisy but we just act differently. (59-year-old Afro-Caribbean woman)

All should be treated equally, and I should not be treated less favourably because of my skin. *(At another point in the interview she said)* GPs should know about people's cultural background before giving certain treatments – some of the doctors are not very helpful, because our needs are very different. (55-year-old Afro-Caribbean woman)

Among the Asians, however, there was much less uncertainty and inconsistency. For instance they used common or universal characteristics to justify specific rather than similar treatment:

Everybody must respect other human beings for their religion and customs. (82-year-old Asian woman)

We pay our tax like anybody else, so they must be kind to us...they should be patient and explain things...they should provide interpreters and employ Asian nurses. (58-year-old Asian woman)

Yes *(we should be treated in a special way)* because I don't speak English, and I don't eat the food that the majority eat...also taking into account my culture and so on. (57-year-old Asian woman)

Yes *(I should be treated in a special way)* because I cannot speak English and my culture and religion is different. (68-year-old Asian woman)

As some of the above quotations show, people were thinking about a variety of different facilities or needs when they discussed differential treatment or care. They mentioned the kind of facilities usually discussed by community groups or professional service providers in connection with the needs of people from black and minority ethnic groups. Both Asian and Afro-Caribbean respondents mentioned day centres specifically for different ethnic groups, and meals services for those with different culturally determined dietary needs from those of the majority white population. Some Asians also mentioned doctors and nurses of the same gender because of particular cultural or religious prohibitions. Another specific facility mentioned was interpretation and translation for those who speak languages other than English; this was seen not as a need for special treatment but for a facility which would help to ensure similar or equal treatment.

Sometimes what was seen as needed was not a specific service but a specific set of attitudes or understandings by those providing mainstream services:

We need more understanding about our culture – we are human too – our needs are the same as anybody when you go into a different place where you can't speak or understand. They must be patient and teach us what to do. (52-year-old Asian woman)

The GPs don't really understand the problems of the black people. (60-year-old Afro-Caribbean woman)

District Nurses need to be taught how to nurse black people because their needs are different from the White community. (55-year-old Afro-Caribbean woman)

Sometimes the change of attitude seen as needed was one which would not so much ensure sensitivity to different cultures as prevent discrimination and thus ensure equality of treatment or care. Also specific facilities were mentioned; for instance a room for death and bereavement practices, prayer mats, somewhere where specific entertainment needs or preferences can be catered for (such as Calypso music).

People's more detailed comments also suggest reasons why, when asked specifically how they preferred to be treated, a significant minority said they had no preference or did not know how to answer. Clear preferences may have been difficult to voice, because people have available to them two common but inconsistent views – that all people should be treated alike, or that each person should be treated as an individual. Second, the issue of 'individual need' brings with it the question of what sorts of identity or characteristics are relevant to care or treatment; if health status provides a relevant need then perhaps so does age, religion, culture, or language. Uncertainty about the relevance of different identities may also make it hard to voice a clear opinion about how people should be treated.

The questions used the terms 'treat' and 'be treated'; these may also have led to some difficulties. Where they were seen to mean an outcome of an assessment or consultation the interviewees stated that in certain circumstances ethnicity should have relevance, for example with respect to day centres and meals services. Where 'being treated' meant the means to the end or the nature of the interaction involved in the consultation, or the environment within which the treatment took place it was also viewed as relevant but in somewhat different ways, for example, where people found it hard to communicate with those they were consulting or from whom they were receiving treatment. 'Ethnic group' was also a complex concept, with some people acknowledging that even within groups there were many differences in preferences, beliefs, skills, and so on. As one woman said: 'We are not a homogeneous group, just as English people are not'. Finally there could be worries about the implications of 'special' or 'separate' treatment; the same woman said:

I would be totally against having separate clinics; because once you have separatism established, to me that's the road to apartheid; and when you have an economic squeeze, as is bound to happen at some time, those things are seen as on the periphery and not in the mainstream, and those are the groups who would feel it most...and what happens is like in South Africa, the poorest provision is on the periphery. (60-year-old Afro-Caribbean woman)

Such views are similar to those raised by other minority groups, such as disabled people (see, for example, Oliver, 1990).

Biography and Ethnic Identity

Do older people use biography to account for how they feel they have been or should be treated? As other research among older people from minority ethnic groups has shown (Hazan, 1980; Francis, 1984) personal biography influences people's perceptions and behaviour, though not in a simple way. The 'limbo people' of Hazan's study of a day centre for elderly Jewish people in London put an embargo on discussion of most aspects of people's individual past but emphasised common religious beliefs and interests. Francis' elderly Jewish parents had different relationships with their adult children, according to whether they lived in Leeds (UK), or Cornell (USA), even though the latter's behaviour was similar in the two areas; the difference appeared to be related to the extent to which in the past the parents had adopted the values and expectations of their host society. For present purposes 'using biography' is taken to mean accounting for preferred treatment not purely by reference to membership of a current, broad group such as 'elderly people' or 'people of minority ethnic background', but by employing conceptions of the past, the course of one's own life, or of the future, to contextualize current preferences.

There was no evidence in this study of a denial of the past as among Hazan's sample. Biography was used in three major ways: through references to past behaviour and the passage of time; the continued use of values and cultural practices learned and adopted at earlier stages in life; and conceptions of social changes over time and their impact upon oneself.

Some elderly people claimed the right or desire to be treated like everyone else as a consequence, not necessarily of seeing the United Kingdom as their home, but viewing it as a place where they have lived for a long time and therefore contributed to through their work, tax and national insurance payments. For example:

People like me who've lived and worked here for so long do not want separate provision. (64-year-old Afro-Caribbean woman)

This pattern was particularly common among the Afro-Caribbeans, all of whom had been living in Britain for more than ten years, and none of whom wanted to be treated in a special way.

A second use of biography was demonstrated by the Asian interviewees. For example, in stark contrast to the Afro-Caribbeans mentioned above, were those Asians who had come to the United Kingdom more recently, said they had come to stay permanently, and that they would prefer to be treated in a special way. For example, a sixty-four-year-old Indian woman, who had been in the United Kingdom for five years said that she and her husband had no intention of returning to India (they had made that decision before they left). When asked directly she said she did not want to be treated in a special way but she went on to say that she thought there should be special facilities for people of her ethnic group:

> Some of the services need to have Asian people working for them. The rest of the staff need to be educated about Asian cultures and needs. More interpreters should be available – and then some research work should be undertaken to see if these things have helped.

She also emphasised, as did 83 per cent of the Asian sample, compared with 39 per cent of the Afro-Caribbean, that having the culturally preferred diet when in hospital would be 'very, very' important to her:

> This matters very much as the diet for Asian people is completely different even if they are non-vegetarians. I would rather not eat than be forced to eat something I do not like. (64-year-old Asian woman)

There was little difference between the views of those Asians who had been in the United Kingdom for less than ten years and those who had been here longer. Five of the eleven Asian respondents who had been in the United Kingdom for less than ten years said they would prefer to be treated in a special way, and only one said he wanted to be treated in the same way as other kinds of service user.

Ethnicity also seemed more important than people's intentions or hopes about remaining in the United Kingdom or returning to their country of origin. Table 11.3 shows that the difference between Afro-Caribbeans and Asians remained whether or not they said they intended to stay in this country. In accounting for their preferences, therefore, Asians who wanted specific facilities referred mainly to cultural differences between themselves and the indigenous population, to values and practices carried through from earlier to later life (as in Francis, 1984).

Third, biography can be used in the sense of placing one's own life experiences within the context of wider social changes (or lack of change). People may contextualise their current lives by comparing them with the past or future, and by taking a more or less distant perspective. This gives them enormous scope and can allow reference to some past or future 'dark' or 'golden age'. In this study long-term changes were used by those who saw them as relevant to relationships between black and white people or majority and minority ethnic groups. More recent changes tended to be used by those who wanted to relate them either to age or to ethnic identities. Most (though not all) of those who used the longer time perspective presented positive or optimistic accounts; those with the shorter perspective were more pessimistic. Among the former, for instance, were the following:

Table 11.3 Ethnicity and preferred health and social services response by intended permanent residence

Qu: Do you think people from Asian/Afro-Caribbean backgrounds should be treated in a special way when receiving health and social services?

	Afro-Caribbean		Asian	
	Intend to stay in UK	Will not stay/DK	Intend to stay in UK	Will not stay/DK
	%	%	%	%
In a special way	-	-	39	45
Not special but:				
fairly/equally	12	12	4	-
kindly/with respect	2	-	7	5
effectively	7	10	2	-
Not special/same way	46	48	15	23
No preference	22	24	31	14
Not answered	10	7	2	14
Total %	99	101	100	101
N=	(41)	(42)	(67)	(22)

I was born in Barbados, and we were under British rule until we got independence. So we always learned to cope with white people...we grew up with them. It's all to do with how the person feels about white people... When I lived there they were a bit aloof, but nowadays they mingle together and live as one people...so there's no difference as far as a lot of Barbados people are concerned so I don't see a need for separate provision... Years ago it seemed there was one set on one side and another on the other side, but now the world seems to be changing, and I think it is absurd for a black person to tell me that they want a ˙black nurse or doctor...I find it ridiculous...my grandchildren were born here and they know nowhere else. (67-year-old Afro-Caribbean woman)

and another Afro-Caribbean woman:

Some people like to go to an Afro-Caribbean day centre because of the cooking but things have improved a lot...my daughter buys Caribbean spice...in hospital it used to be potato morning, noon and night...but now you can get all the things you want. In hospitals things have changed and you can have special foods. They're trying and things have improved. (70-year-old Afro-Caribbean woman)

An Afro-Caribbean woman in her sixties talked about the long-term future rather than the past:

Some of the arrangements, like providing interpreters or separate clinics for Asians who do not speak English are expedient, but expediency is not a long-term thing...in twenty years time when you have the third generation of black and Asian people born here and if you speak to them on the phone you won't know whether they are black or white there's no problem. Therefore I would be totally against them having separate clinics...(64-year-old Afro-Caribbean woman)

People with such views used them to justify treating everyone in the same way. The more bleak view of those who took a shorter-term perspective could be used to justify special or compensatory treatment (though this was mainly implicit). To such people life had become, or was likely to become, worse for elderly people in general or for themselves in particular. For instance some people were concerned about the recent economic recession, the curtailment of public expenditure and the way it might affect them:

At present all I hear is cost-cutting in all services. (67-year-old Afro-Caribbean woman)

The Housing Department are having a problem and they've been closing down Homes – I think the future looks very bleak for the elderly. (56-year-old Afro-Caribbean woman) There will be more elderly living alone in ten years time – the young generation don't want the burden and the restrictions. (71-year-old Asian man)

Several people were also very concerned about their personal future. They were concerned partly about problems connected with their ethnicity, such as 'What will life be like for me as an Asian who cannot speak English?'. Their concern was also expressed in terms of their identity as an old person or as an ill or frail person. For example:

My wife still cooks so it is O.K. But I am old, and I'm worried when she gets ill what will happen. (71-year-old Asian man)

Interviewees therefore used both past and future, their own as well as that of their group (their ethnic group or age group) within which to place their views and experiences of health and social services. If they took a long-term view Afro-Caribbeans were generally positive, and used universal or individual identities; for instance in the long-term they saw a decline – or a likely decline – in discrimination. For them a long period of residence in the United Kingdom encouraged universalistic identity. For Asians with a strong, separate cultural identity this was not true. For all respondents the short-term perspective (whether of past or future) was generally linked to more pessimistic views and to the focus upon either age or ethnic identity; for instance recent changes in provision were said to have affected elderly people; recent move to the United Kingdom was seen to explain the need for specific treatment; and coming changes were seen as worrying for people in later life or for those from a black or minority ethnic group.

Service Providers' Views About Special Treatment

The ninety health and social services department staff interviewed were asked specifically about the way in which services were provided in their area to elderly people from various black and minority ethnic groups, as well as the way in which they thought services should be provided. Although the six areas chosen spanned a variety of approaches to service delivery, in all areas the provision of separate or specific services and facilities was extremely limited. The views of the staff did not necessarily accord with the way services were actually provided, although this was more likely among staff in decision-making positions.

All staff were asked whether they thought elderly people from black and minority ethnic groups should receive mainstream services only, some specific facilities but within a mainstream service, or at least some completely separate services. The interviewees showed a great deal of awareness of special needs (Askham *et al.*, forthcoming). For example, they identified a number of problems in providing for elderly people from black and minority ethnic groups solely through mainstream services.

Communication with people who spoke languages other than English featured as the main concern; this was followed by concern about lack of cultural sensitivity, the particular difficulties of providing residential care, racism, inaccessibility of services, and the poor facilities for elderly people in general. It is therefore not surprising that, when asked whether they generally favoured mainstream, specific or separate service provision only a tiny minority of those interviewed (one in ten) said they supported providing solely mainstream services. All but one of these were health authority staff; the one exception was a member of social services staff (in one of the areas with a lower proportion of minority ethnic elders), who said that there were insufficient numbers to warrant any special provision. This view was echoed within the health authorities, as was the opinion that services should be mainstream but should take account of individual need.

The majority of staff favoured specific provision within a mainstream service, making comments such as:

> They've got to have the mainstream service but with interpreters. (Speech Therapist)

> Mainstream but with special needs catered for. (Social Services Department/District Health Authority Liaison Officer)

> Special – for instance special clinics with an interpreter. (Psychologist)

> Some special services such as meals-on-wheels; but we mustn't raise their expectations too much – white clients don't get a lot either. (Social Worker)

This last quotation clearly indicates an awareness of the difficulties and dangers of treating service clients at anything other than the universal level:

special provision has to be justified, understood and seen not to discriminate unfairly either in favour or against the interests of any group.

Ethnicity may be seen as relevant or irrelevant in any aspect of service provision: service planning, assessment of applicants, treatment, long-term care, and so on. Where appropriate each of these was covered in the interviews. For instance, most respondents were asked about assessment for services of elderly people from black and minority ethnic groups. Statements were complex and cannot easily be fitted into categories. The most common answer, however, was that there was no difference in the type of assessment carried out, but that since people were all assessed as individuals then any special needs resulting from ethnic background should be picked up. Answers of this kind were given by approximately one third of all respondents. About one in five said there was no difference, and that all *elderly* people were assessed in much the same way. Only about one in seven said that assessment was carried out so as to take ethnic background or cultural needs into account.

Two-thirds of the health authority staff, as compared with one-third of the social services department staff, said that there was no specific difference in the assessment of indigenous white and black or minority ethnic groups. This difference between the two agencies appeared to be mainly accounted for by the tendency for health authority staff to talk in terms of individual or unique identities (as would be expected within the medical model) whilst social services staff seemed more conscious of the legitimacy of the ethnicity identity. For example:

> We have to think about elderly people from ethnic minority groups at fifty-five years and over – they grow older quicker because of the isolation, poor health, poverty. We've set up a client planning group on ethnic minority elders to set a series of objectives for our services. (Deputy Director, Social Services Department)

> We have a universal assessment form for everyone. But we are white and they are black; we are not totally aware of their needs. (Home Care Organiser)

> From a practical point of view assessment is the same as for anyone else. (Health Visitor)

> All patients are assessed in terms of their assets and deficits. There's very little difference in that all elderly people are subject to communication problems and cultural variations. (Consultant Psychogeriatrican)

Differences among staff within as well as between agencies are also noticeable. Within the programme of research a postal survey of 280 general practitioners has been carried out in areas with significant black and minority ethnic populations (Pharaoh, forthcoming). The objectives of this study were to examine the extent of general practitioners' involvement with elderly people from black and minority ethnic groups, the kind of services they offered, and any problems or difficulties they perceived in their care. Among its findings it showed that Asian doctors were more likely than white doctors to see ethnicity as affecting the need for services. For example, when the general practitioners were asked to comment on the low uptake of community health and social care services by elderly people from black and minority ethnic groups, while the overall response patterns were similar for white and Asian general practitioners, the Asians were much less likely to say that it was due to the existence of family support, and more likely to mention lack of client awareness and knowledge of services, and problems due to language barriers.

Like the Asian service users and potential users, therefore, health and social services staff tended to want specific services or facilities for minority ethnic groups. As stated earlier, service provision implies generalisation about the kind of people for whom that service is provided, so it is not surprising that staff generalized. However, using the example of assessment for services it was clear that Social Services Department staff were more likely to identify people with black or minority ethnic identity as having specific needs than were Health Authority staff; the latter were more inclined to use individual or universal identities. In this their views were similar to those of the Afro-Caribbean user sample but less like those of a substantial proportion of the Asian older people.

Conclusion

Older people from different ethnic backgrounds do feel differently about the importance of ethnicity in aspects of social life. More of the people interviewed in this study used ethnicity than age in explaining or justifying why they thought they should be treated in one way rather than another when receiving health and social services. But ethnic background was not used in this way by all; Afro-Caribbeans used it less than Asians, with the former more likely to call on common or universal characteristics or on age itself. People's unique or individual identities were also cited by both Asians and Afro-Caribbeans. Long residence in the United Kingdom helped to confer a sense of common identity, but particularly for Asian people cultural background appeared of greater significance. The use of different identities was very complex; for example, when people phrased their comments within the context of shorter timespans they often emphasised age identities, but when in addition they had lived in this country for only a relatively short period (ie. some of the Asian interviewees) this encouraged them to empha- sise their ethnic identity.

The majority of service providers interviewed identified black or mi- nority ethnic groups as requiring some specific services or facilities. Health Authority staff, however, were more inclined than those in Social Services

Departments to refer to individual or universal identities rather than to generalise about such groups.

This research illustrates some of the tensions, ambiguities and difficulties in the provision of health and social services, particularly within the current context of policy changes in the United Kingdom. Community care policies emphasise on the one hand individual identities, but on the other the need to consider the specific requirements of black and minority ethnic groups. The re-structuring of services is likely to reinforce the latter perspective by encouraging provision by community groups and voluntary organizations.

This ambiguity is compounded by the variation in, and complexity of, views among both health and social services staff and older people from black and minority ethnic groups. Where people's views differ, and especially where there are differences between service users and providers, dissatisfaction or conflict may occur unless people are sensitive to those differences.

Service agencies cannot treat people as individuals; they must classify and categorise. However, these research findings suggest that such categorisations need to be developed with great care, and their relevance explained and justified. As research in other fields also shows, 'special' may be seen either as discriminatory or as taking special care to ensure that all get the same treatment. 'Individual' may be seen either as taking special needs into account or as not providing facilities which one group of individuals requires. 'Treating everyone the same' may be perceived as fair and just or as ignoring the specific requirements of an individual. The increasing sensitivity to ethnicity in policy documents, may be masking an insensitivity to other categorisations which are also important to the way people see themselves and their circumstances.

CHAPTER 12

Institutional Care and the Life Course

Paul Higgs and Christina Victor

Introduction

> 'Without a genuine commitment to community care, there remain a
> number of bleak alternatives for elderly people. There may be no care
> at all or perhaps inadequate services from either families with other
> responsibilities or from hard pressed social services departments. For
> others it may entail institutionalization (Rossiter and Wicks, 1982; 82).

In Britain the image of the institution and of institutional living for older
people is one that figures highly in the collective consciousness. Institutional
care is perceived as a highly negative setting, involving regimentation, loss
of autonomy and are perceived as being set apart from 'the community'.
Means and Smith (1985) provide a description of the conditions in which a
frail 84-year-old woman lived which encapsulates many of the popular
images about institutional care for older people '...down the side of each
ward were ten beds facing one another. Between each bed and its neighbour
was a small locker and a straight backed wooden uncushioned chair... No
library books or wireless... No easy chairs... No pictures on the
walls...'(1985 p.80). More recently these negative stereotypes have been
reinforced by scandals concerning the abuse of older people in both public
and private sector homes.

What factors have determined the development of institutional or communal care for older people and what distinguishes those older people who
live in the institutional sector from those who remain in the community?
How important are factors such as age, gender, marital status and socio-
economic status in distinguishing those older people who are in institutions
from those who remain in what is termed the community? How do life
course experiences impact on this distinction? In this chapter we will
examine the broad pattern of provision of institutional care for older people
and consider the nature and characteristics of those older people who live
in this sector. We will also consider the policy issues surrounding the area
of institutional care, discussing the extent to which fiscal imperatives have
been the over-riding influence upon recent reforms of the social care system
(DoH, 1989). The chapter concludes by considering future policy develop-

ments which are likely to arise from the introduction of the community care reforms in April 1993.

Institutional Care Provision in Britain

There are three main forms of institutional care provision for older people in Britain; (i) residential care (which can be provided by either the local authority or the private and voluntary sector), (ii) long-term continuing care wards for the mentally and physically frail provided by the NHS and (iii) Nursing Homes, which are mainly provided by the private sector. First we briefly consider how the different forms of provision have developed. Comprehensive histories of the development of institutional care provision are provided by Means and Smith (1985) and Parker (1988).

The origins of institutional care

Institutional care for older people in the United Kingdom has its roots in the evolution of the English Poor Law (Means and Smith, 1985). However it is the reform of the Poor Law in 1834 and the development of the 'workhouse' which has had such a lasting and negative effect upon the image of the institutional care sector. Parker (1988) draws attention to the role which institutional provision played as an element of social control and the failure to distinguish between the different types of institutional care; prisons and workhouses were categorised in the same group by policy makers and society alike.

The social discipline instilled by the threat of the workhouse was in accordance with the values of the ruling elites of the period (see Parker, 1988). The threat of the workhouse and a pauper's grave was a significant worry to the labouring classes of the nineteenth century and underlay the foundation of the friendly societies who were to play a key role in the early twentieth century oganisation of health care.

Institutional care and the creation of the welfare state

Up to at least the onset of the 1939-45 war, old age was seen as a disease in itself, one that was incurable. Illness and old age were seen as inseparably entwined. Because of exclusion from the voluntary hospitals, often the only place for infirm and chronically ill old people was the poor law infirmary; an adjunct of the workhouse with much the same connotations (Wilkin and Hughes, 1986).

A distinction developed between 'hospital care' for the acutely ill, which has greatly improved its 'public image' over the last century, and the infirmaries caring for those with chronic health problems. The distinction has had an important bearing on the image of long-term care for older people. Care which is perceived as necessary on medical grounds is perceived much more positively than other forms of care.

The division of institutional provision between NHS long-stay or continuing care wards and local authority residential homes arose from the services developed with the creation of the welfare state in the post-war period. Under Part III of the 1948 National Assistance Act, Local Authorities were given the duty to provide 'residential accommodation for persons who by reason of age, infirmity or any other circumstances are in need of care and attention which is not otherwise available to them' (Tinker, 1984 p.319). The National Health Service was given the responsibility for the care of the sick older person. Within the NHS a further division was drawn between older people with acute problems and those with chronic or long-term problems.

This fundamental division of responsibility was based on the perceived different needs of the chronically sick and of the physically frail (Sinclair, 1988). Local authorities were given responsibility for those who were seen to need social care. The rationale for the form of care chosen, namely the Old People's Homes, was based on the idea of them acting as sunshine hotels for older people (Thomson, 1983). Care was to be based on older people's frailty and not their need for medical or nursing attention.

Essential to this distinction was the notion that old age brought about conditions which in themselves could be cured and that often all that was needed was rehabilitation. If older people were given the benefit of medical intervention they could be restored to an acceptable level of functioning, thus, avoiding an institutional placement. Similarly those whose main needs were the result of frailty could be provided for in environments that would avoid the medicalisation of their situations as the poor law infirmaries had not done. Simplistic in its conception, in practice the distinction has become difficult to maintain; at what point a frailty became a medical condition is still a dispute that affects all health service / social service interfaces.

The development of community care and the rise of the nursing home

Although the legislation which created the post-1945 welfare state gave considerable emphasis to the institutional care sector, the importance of community care was recognised from the outset (Means and Smith, 1985). It was not, however, until the early 1970s that the current antipathy to institutional provision on the part of policy makers really gained prominence. Concerns about the ageing of the population and the perceived expense of institutional forms of care were two of the most important factors underlying the popularity of the general policy objective of community care. Although the term 'community care' has remained constant in the post-war period its meaning has undergone subtle changes from 'care in the community' to 'care by the community'. In its current manifestation community care envisages that the bulk of care required by those with long-term care needs will be provided by family, friends and neighbours with state services being used as a last resort (DoH, 1989).

Despite the rhetoric and policy statements extolling the virtues of community care the residential sector expanded through out the 1960s, so that by 1970 there were 244,800 places for elderly people in the institutional care sector of which 172,500 (70%) were in the residential sector (see Table 12.1). In addition there were approximately 52,000 'geriatric' beds. As Table 12.1 shows the vast majority of the long-stay provision was provided by the public sector; in 1970, 63 per cent of places in residential care were provided by the local authority sector.

Table 12.1 Institutional places for elderly people in the UK by sector, 1970–1990

	Residential home			Nursing home	Long-stay geriatric hospital	Total
	LA	Private	Voluntary			
1970	108700	23700	40100	20300	52000	244800
1980	134500	37400	42600	26900	46000	287500
1990	13050	155600	40000	123100	49100	498300
% change	+20%	+656%	-1%	+606%	-6%	+203%

Source: Henwood 1992, table 7

12.2 Institutional care – places per 1000 population UK 1970–1990

	Places per 1000		
	65+	75+	85+
1970	34	96	529
1980	36	94	520
1990	56	127	568
% change	+64%	+32%	+7%

Source: Henwood 1992, tables 7 and 8

Since 1970 there have been significant changes in the number and type of long-stay care places for older people. Since 1970 the total number of places has doubled reaching nearly half a million in 1990 (see Table 12.1). Within this broad pattern of increase there have been important changes within the different sectors. Over the last two decades there has been a decrease of 6 per cent in the number of long-stay geriatric beds whilst the number of nursing home beds in the private sector has increased six-fold (from 20,300 to 123,100). Overall the number of residential places has increased by 89 per cent from 172,500 to 326,100. Within the residential sector there has been a small decrease in the number of places provided by the voluntary sector and a modest increase in the local authority sector.

Some increase in long-term care provision would have been expected in order to keep pace with the demographic changes over these two decades. We will, therefore, examine the number of places per 1000 people in the older age groups. Table 12.2 shows that there has been an increase in the number of places in the long-stay care sector over and above that which would be expected from demographic change. However the size of this increase depends upon the population base which is used in the calculation. If we calculate the number of places per 1000 aged 65 and over there has been an increase of 64 per cent compared with 7 per cent if the calculation is based on the number of people aged 85 and over.

Both Firth (1987) and Bosanquet et al. (1990) consider that the increase in the volume of long-stay provision has exceeded that which would have been expected from demographic change alone. For example between 1988 and 1989 applying the 1981 age-specific rates of long-stay care provision would suggest an increase of 11,500 places in England whereas the actual increase was 30,000 places (Laing and Buisson, 1990).

What has brought about this increase in the number of places in long-stay care in the private sector? The very rapid growth in number of private residential and nursing home places during the 1970s resulted from a change in the Supplementary Benefit (SB) (renamed Income Support from April 1988) regulations which enabled older people with low incomes to enter private care at no cost to themselves. In 1980, regulation nine introduced discretion to local SB offices which enabled them to pay board and lodging allowances to older people in private homes at rates which were 'reasonable' for that area. This resulted in an increase in such claimants from 12,000 to 25,800 between 1980 and 1983 and increased annual expenditure from 18 million pounds to 102 million (Challis and Bartlett, 1988).

This element of local discretion meant that there were significant variations within the country in how the system was applied. For applicants, entry to care and payment of fees was not based upon an assessment of their 'need' for care but upon a means-test of their financial status. Two issues developed from this public funding of private care. First, both nursing and residential homes became attractive business propositions because of the 'guaranteed' income from the state. Second, the geographic variation in the interpretation of the SB regulations was an important factor in the geographical variations in the growth of private care. It was not until early 1985 that this element of local discretion was removed and central government imposed maximum payments permissable which were to apply across the country. Despite restrictions and changes in regulations imposed by the government the expenditure upon private care has continued to increase to over £1,000 million in 1990. Table 12.3 shows that the total cost of caring for older people in institutions in 1990 was £5.5 billion.

Table 12.3 Total numbers of elderly people in institutions and cost, Great Britain, 1990

Type of institution	Places	£million
Private nursing homes*	112,600	1,330
Private residential homes*	155,600	1,275
Voluntary nursing homes	10,500	122
Voluntary residential homes	40,000	305
NHS long stay geriatric	49,100	897
NHS elderly mentally ill	31,000	567
Local authority Part III	130,500	1,108

* Home registered with the Local Authority, that is with four or more beds.

Source: Laing and Buisson, (1991)

The unexpected and, initially, out-of control growth in public expenditure on private institutional care is the total antithesis of the stated policy objective of community care. It demonstrates how policies from the same administration can be in complete conflict. Although government policy sought to encourage the growth of private institutional provision they did not envisage the rapid increase of public expenditure on this type of care. The growth in public expenditure on the private long-term care sector which, it was argued existed as a 'perverse' incentive favouring institutionalisation rather than community care (Audit Commission, 1986) was the stimulus for the enquiry into community care which resulted in the reforms which will come into force in April 1993.

Institutional care provision after 1993

The community care element of the NHS and Community Care legislation will come into force in April 1993 (DoH, 1989). From this date local authorities will become responsible for the public funding of residential and nursing home care via the transfer to them of social security money used to fund older people in private sector care. 'Free access' to private nursing and residential homes will be abolished with the handover of these income support monies to the local authorities. Currently the amount of money local authorities will receive to implement community care is unclear. However such funds will not be protected from use in other areas, that is ring-fenced.

Existing residents will not be effected by this transfer but all new residents will become the financial responsibility of the local authority.

Like the introduction of the internal market in the NHS, reforms to the community care legislation will result in the separation of providers of care from those purchasing care. However whereas contracts in the NHS are largely block contracts local authorities will be contracting 'packages of care' for individual clients. The key to accessing services will be the assessment of client's care needs. As from 1st April 1993 dependent elderly people will be assessed by the local authorities (DoH, 1989). Having profiled the care needs of the individual, appropriate forms of intervention based on the availability of resources in relation to the needs of the client will be purchased. For all services local authorities are to be encouraged to make as full use of the private sector and informal care as is possible. This will legitimise reliance on the informal sector and promote the use of the private-for-profit sector.

This legislation maintains the important distinction between older people with health needs and those with social care needs. Whilst those with long-term health needs remain the responsibility of the NHS there is an increased use of private sector nursing homes as the NHS seeks to divest itself of the 'long-stay' geriatric wards. Henwood (1992) criticises the NHS for abandoning longstay provision (Association of Community Health Councils, 1991) and for not developing nursing homes despite their proven value (Bond et al., 1989; Bowling and Formby, 1992). Another manifestation of the desire by the NHS to divest itself of continuing care wards is the use of dedicated professionals known as 'home finders' to obtain placements for dependent elderly people in private nursing homes.

The Prevalence of Institutional Living

There is a common misconception that the majority of older people live in institutional care. Victor (1992) reports that 29 per cent of medical and nursing staff in an inner London health district thought that nearly one third of those aged 65 and over lived in institutional care. The 1981 census ennumerated approximately five per cent of those aged 65 and over were resident in institutional care. The amount of data concerning the characteristics of older people in institutional care are severely limited. First, there are few British studies which have attempted to compare all forms of institutional care using a standardised research instrument. There is an implicit tendency to treat the institutionalised population as a homogeneous social group. Second, the majority of research concerned with the institutionalised population in Britain has been cross-sectional in nature. We may speculate that the institutionalised population is composed of three distinct elements; those who die shortly after admission, those who return to the community after a short stay and those who are long-stay. In any cross-sectional study this latter group will be over-represented. Furthermore, s ome older people may experience various types of institutional care but again such older people are difficult to identify.

Demographic characteristics

Detailed analysis of data from the 1981 census, highlights important variations among older people in the prevalence of institutional living. The likelihood of living in an institution increases with age from about 0.5 per cent of those aged 65–69 to 16 per cent of those aged 85 and over (Arber and Ginn, 1991a). Among the 'oldest old' those aged 90 and over, Bury and Holmes (1991) report that 50 per cent are resident in communal establishments. However this illustrates that even amongst those of very advanced age half are still resident in the community. Data from the OPCS disability survey show that 67 per cent of disabled people resident in institutions are aged over 75 (Martin *et al.*, 1988).

Residence in institutional care is not a simple function of age, as demographic factors other than age also appear to be important. The OPCS disability survey demonstrated that 69 per cent of disabled people living in institutions were women (Martin *et al.*, 1988). Up to the age of 74 there is little difference in the percentage of men and women living in the various types of communal establishments. However, from age 75 onwards the percentage of women living in such settings exceeds that of men. The 1981 census showed that for those aged 85 and over, 12 per cent of men and 20 per cent of women were resident in communal establishments (Arber and Ginn, 1991a).

For both sexes the highest percentages of people resident in institutional settings are never married, while the still married are least likely to be resident in such environments (Arber and Ginn, 1991a). Cross-sectional studies have consistently identified the over-representation of the never married, widowed and married (but without surviving children) in the institutional sector (Townsend, 1962). The OPCS disability survey reported that 66 per cent of disabled people aged 75–84 living in institutions were widowed and a further 22 per cent were single (Martin *et al.*, 1988).

As yet there are few longitudinal studies which enable us to examine the influence of age, or indeed any other variable, upon the probability of moving into institutional care. One of the few sources available are the analyses of the OPCS Longitudinal Study undertaken by Grundy (1992). However these data are limited because they only examine census information and cannot include important parameters such as health status or the availability of informal care. Grundy (1992) examined the movement into institutions between 1971 and 1981. She shows that two per cent of men aged 65–69 in 1971 were resident in institutions by 1981; for men aged 75 and over in 1971 9.8 per cent were in institutions by 1981. For women the respective percentages were 3.2 per cent and 23.6 per cent.

In the United States, elderly people from minority backgrounds are under-represented in communal establishments (Kane and Kane, 1991). However there are few data available for Britain to enable us to examine the ethnic characteristics of the institutional population.

Housing and socio-economic status

Two distinct aspects of housing may be important in precipitating entry into institutional care; quality and tenure. Data indicating the percentage of people in institutional care from different types of housing and housing of different quality are not available. Grundy (1991) reports that housing quality, as measured by access to standard housing amenities, seemed to have little value as a predictor of entry into institutional care. However tenure seemed to be of more importance. For men and women aged 65 and over in 1971, 2.8 per cent and 6.1 per cent of owner occupiers had entered institutional care by 1981, compared with 8.1 per cent and 5.1 per cent of private renters respectively. These differences may simply reflect the differential age profile of the different segments of the housing market; for example home owners may be younger than those in the rented sector. To take out the possible effect of age, Grundy (1991) calculates for women aged 65 and over in 1971 an age-standardised institutionalisation ratio. This was 91 for owner occupiers, 109 for local authority tenants and 112 for those renting property in the private sector. This suggests that the higher pre-

Table 12.4 Severity of disability and communal living by age, Great Britain, 1984–85

Disability severity category	Total disabled (000's)			% resident in communal establishment		
	60–69	70–79	80+	60–69	70–79	80+
10	22	47	97	32	51	60
9	64	86	139	11	21	33
8	81	104	117	6	12	26
7	87	124	147	3	7	13
6	187	158	125	1	6	11
5	148	182	147	1	3	8
4	158	187	112	2	4	11
3	175	218	117	1	3	7
2	227	268	111	1	2	5
1	311	313	141	1	1	2
Total	1334	1687	1254	3	9	17

Source: Martin et al. (1988) Table 3.3

Table 12.5 Percentage of residents in disability categories 7–10
by type of establishment and age

	Types of Establishment				
	NHS	LA	Voluntary	Private	All
65–74	64	50	60	55	58
75–84	90	58	41	62	65
85+	97	74	60	70	76

Source: Martin et al. (1989) Table 9.9

valence of institutionalisation amongst older people in rented accommodation is not simply a function of age.

Townsend (1962) reported that amongst males, those from manual backgrounds were over-represented in the institutional sector but for women the pattern was unclear. Grundy (1992) using data from the OPCS Longitudinal Study has shown an association between class and institutionalisation for men aged 65–74. She reported that 2.5 per cent of those in social classes one and two entered care by 1981 compared with 4.1 per cent of those in classes four and five. She did not pursue the analysis for women or men aged 75 and over in 1971 because of the limitation of the data source.

Physical impairment

We have already shown that the prevalence of institutional living increases with age, and this may be taken as a proxy for health status. Data from the OPCS survey of disabled adults conducted in 1984–85 is a useful data source for describing the profile of disabled elders living in community compared with institutional settings (Martin et al., 1988). The survey estimated that there were 4,275,000 disabled people aged 60 and over in Great Britain of which 351,000 (8%) were resident in communal establishments. The percentages of disabled elders living in institutions increased from 3 per cent of those aged 60–69 to 17 per cent of those aged 85 and over (see Table 12.4). This illustrates that at all ages the majority of disabled elders are resident in the community rather than communal settings.

The OPCS disability survey devised a ten point disability scale ranging from one (least disabled) to ten (most disabled). At each level of disability there is a higher prevalence of communal living amongst those aged 80 and over than those aged 60–69 (Table 12.4). For those aged 65 and over, 3 per cent of those in institutional settings were in disability category one compared with 25 per cent in category ten whilst in the community 19 per cent were in category one and 2 per cent in category ten.

Given the policy context within which the various sectors developed, we would expect a gradient in frailty from the residential sector to the continuing care wards provided by the NHS, with nursing homes occupying an intermediate position. The OPCS disability survey distinguished between the different elements of the institutional sector and allows preliminary examination of this hypothesis. Confining our attention to those in disability category seven and over, the NHS has very few elderly residents who are not in this very severe disability category (see Table 12.5). This is not surprising given that within the continuing care hospital sector, control by doctors over beds means that high levels of physical dependency are virtually universal. We may speculate that those who remain in hospital long-stay care have come to the end of the rehabilitation and care career and are in need of extensive nursing care. Table 12.5 shows that at all ages, levels of disability are lower in the non-NHS establishments. Darton and Wright (1992) found that levels of dependency were higher amongst nursing home residents than those in the residential care sector. They report that 14 per cent of private and 17 per cent voluntary nursing home patients could walk at least 200 yards outdoors compared with 36 per cent and 45 per cent in the respective residential home sector.

Another illustration of the degree of disability characteristic of the institutional sector is incontinence. Incontinence is one of the most difficult problems which informal carers have to deal with and one which they often find impossible. Campbell *et al.* (1990) report rates of severe incontinence of 11 per cent in private/LA residential care and 72 per cent in long-stay wards. Darton and Wright (1992) report the prevalence of incontinence at 20 per cent in the private and voluntary residential sector and 38 per cent among the private nursing home sector, while Victor (1992) reports the prevalence of double incontinence at 56 per cent on psycho-geriatric wards.

Mental impairment

Mental frailty, especially that related to dementia has consistently been identified as a factor precipitating entry into institutional care. Waldren (1991) in her review identifies mental frailty as a key reason in many studies which have looked at the types of older people who enter care. However there are insufficient data to determine accurately the prevalence of institutional living amongst the different manifestations of mental health problems. The OPCS disability survey estimates that there are 1,475,000 people with intellectual functioning problems of whom 20 per cent were ennumerated as resident in institutions. Of the 537,000 people aged 75 and over with intellectual problems 35 per cent were in communal establishments (Martin *et al.*, 1988).

Rates of confusion and cognitive impairment are high in the institutional sector, especially NHS continuing care and nursing homes (Victor, 1992). For those aged 85 and over in the NHS, 80 per cent had problems with intellectual functioning compared with approximately 50 per cent across the other types of institutional care.

Access to caring resources

It is difficult to establish with certainty why some older people enter communal care whilst others with comparable degrees of disability remain in the community. These difficulties are compounded by the limited longitudinal data available and by the strong probability that different factors may facilitate entry into the different forms of care.

A surrogate indicator for the availability of informal care is household composition. Grundy (1992) reports that for women aged 65 and over in 1971, 9.9 per cent of those living alone entered care compared with 4.6 per cent of those living in married couples and 2.2 per cent of those living as a couple with one (or more) of their children. For men the respective percentages were 8.1 per cent, 2.7 per cent and 1.1 per cent. Although these data are not controlled for age, they do suggest that the presence of a spouse and/or children are very important in reducing the likelihood of institutionalisation. The government's policy of community care envisages harnessing the caring resources of the 'community', by which they mean neighbours and friends as well as relatives. This is at odds with the reality whereby few friends and neighbours are significant providers of care to older people (Arber and Ginn, 1990).

In her review of residential care Waldren (1991) points out that many applicants for residential care have an informal care network which has collapsed under the strain of looking after a person with high levels of disability and/or mental impairment.

Challis and Bartlett's (1988) survey of private nursing home residents shows that 31 per cent of their sample entered nursing homes because they lived alone and a further 29 per cent because relatives or friends were unable to cope. They also point out that such admissions were often arranged in a hurry, at a time of crisis and with little involvement on the part of the older

**Table 12.6 Length of stay of residents in homes
for elderly people – England 31 March 1988
(column percentages)**

Length of stay	% LA Homes	% Voluntary	% Private
<1 month	10	11	12
1–6 mths	14	10	19
6–12 mths	11	11	17
1–3 years	33	29	35
3–5 years	14	14	12
5+ years	18	25	6

Source: Department of Health (1988) Table 3–9.

person. Indeed they suggest that the older person actively did not wish to be involved in the process and expected this to be undertaken by professional workers. Victor (1992) describes a similar set of factors in the admission of older people to continuing care wards. In addition transfer from acute wards and from residential and nursing homes were important reasons for finally entering an NHS long-stay ward.

Previous place of residence

Another factor of importance in the debate about the future of institutional care is the older person's previous place of residence. Darton and Wright (1992) report that 40–50 per cent of those in private/local authority homes had come from hospital or other communal establishments as did 60 per cent in the survey of private nursing homes reported by Challis and Bartlett (1988). This indicates that for many individuals entry into a nursing or residential home and presumably a hospital long-stay ward is the culmination of a lengthy process as the consumers of care. Entry into care for many therefore appears to be transfer between different caring sectors rather than the result of a new episode. Although it is not evident from the cross-sectional data, it seems likely that older people frequently move between different sectors of long-stay care.

Length of stay

There are no representative data about mobility between the different long-stay sectors or the length of time older people remain in the long-stay sector. Table 12.6 shows that over half of people in residential care had been resident for 12 months or more. However as was indicated earlier, any cross-sectional study of length of stay will over-represent the proportion who are 'long long-stay' residents. The lower percentage of residents of five years or more duration in the private sector illustrates the fairly recent development of this sector.

Do Life Course Factors Influence Admission to Care?

A tentative conclusion to this summary of who is in institutional care is that there are life course factors which appear to be related to entry into care. The data presented earlier indicate that marital status, household composition and social class are associated with institutionalisation. The elevated rates of institutional living amongst the widowed and those living alone illustrate the importance of family care in supporting dependent older people in the community. Socio-economic status as measured by social class and tenure was also important. This could reflect the greater resources of more 'affluent' older people which may enable them to purchase private domiciliary care and so delay or prevent entry into an institution. In addition, socio-economic differences in health status at all ages of the life course mean than older people from manual occupations experience higher rates of morbidity that those from non-manual occupations.

However the lack of detailed data about the 'care careers' whereby older people enter institutional care means that it is difficult to map precisely how life course factors may influence entry into different types of care. The local authority residential sector has an over-representation of people from manual occupational groups. Within the private sector, only a minority, probably under 25 per cent, pay all their own fees. With fees for single rooms in private residential and nursing homes at an average weekly charge of £190 and £265 (Laing and Buisson, 1991) it is only the most affluent who could freely make the choice to enter care (annual fees of £9,880 for residential care and £13,780 for nursing homes). Clearly this option is available only to those with substantial assets.

Choice and the entry into care

The crisis driven nature surrounding entry into all forms of communal care calls into some doubt the policy objective of increasing the choice of older people in the decision-making process. Indeed we should, perhaps, be rather more realistic about the nature of the choices older people may have to make if long-term care is considered. As Wilkin and Hughes (1986) note, older people may be choosing between a difficult and unpleasant struggle to stay at home and the perceived disadvantages of communal living. The notion of choice is further restricted by the lack of equity in provision across the country, the presence of waiting lists and the failure to provide 'subsidies' for home care services.

Conclusion: Is There a Role for Institutional Care?

While much has been made of the existence of unnecessary institutionalisation for many older people (Booth, 1985), the earlier section has demonstrated the high levels of physical and sometimes intellectual impairment of the older population in all sectors of institutional care. As a consequence when examining care options for this group, the need for institutional provision should not be rejected out of hand because of an ideological objection to such forms of care. However in proposing that there is a positive role for the institutional sector in the care of frail older people we must emphasise the need to develop the quality of the care provided by this sector through such devices as monitoring and staff training.

The general thrust of government policy is that support to dependent people should be provided in the community. Assuming there were unlimited funds, this might possibly work; but the provision of 'around-the-clock' supervision is prohibitively expensive. Furthermore would this be the best environment for the extremely physically dependent? Would it not simply re-create the very features of institutionalisation it is designed to overcome? For example being woken up and put to bed at specific times designated by professionals, having a series of different people coming in at different times attending to different tasks. Would this really be preserving autonomy and independence? Similarly, would allowing an individual to stay in their own home result in a more enriched experience if they were extremely isolated than if they were on a ward in a hospital or in a nursing home? Gavilan (1992) argues that there is little difference between the experience of community and institutional care for very frail housebound elderly people.

Higgins (1989) argues that there is a false dichotomy being drawn between the institution and the community. Often individuals receive institutional type care in their own homes in the community in that it is routinised and impersonal, or they may live in institutions that are part of the community and which have a flexible regime.

Similar points are made by Foster (1991) who suggests that residential care needs a positive re-assessment. Hockey (1989) has pointed out the importance of the negotiation process in residential care which allows individuals to situate their present situation in the context of their understandings of their previous lives. An example provided by Haire (1990) demonstrates how even the concept of privacy has different meanings in different settings. Two individuals in identical ward environments experiencing the same care activities can have totally different views of what is occurring. One might feel that her privacy has been invaded while another that these activities are happening 'backstage' and do not constitute any loss of privacy.

As was shown earlier in this chapter, the main characteristic of older people in the long-stay sector is their high prevalence of physical and social disability. Social and economic differences in the life experience of older people may influence their risk of experiencing serious long term disability. These factors in combination with health and social policy influence older people's ability to construct forms of care to cater for their needs and limit their dependency. How individuals needs are met, however, is a matter of the social and caring context they find themselves in. Individuals may not be able to alter their physical condition, but how they are cared for is an issue which could be altered and should be a 'real' option for all.

CHAPTER 13

Social Security and the Life Course
Developing Sensitive Policy Alternatives

Maria Evandrou and Jane Falkingham

Individuals in society do not enter old age equal. Life course events prior to retirement influence the social and economic position of people well beyond the age of withdrawal from the labour market. Factors such as the accumulation of pension rights, access to and participation in pension schemes and the availability of housing wealth as a potential source of income in old age, all act to differentiate people at later stages of the life course. These are in turn influenced by gender, previous occupational group and experience of caring responsibilities. Yet to what extent does British welfare policy recognise the diversity of life course experience?

This chapter first discusses current Social Security policies in Britain with reference to pensions and social care, in particular the changing balance in the mixed economy of welfare. It then evaluates the effectiveness of these policies by examining the financial position among older persons today. To what extent have current policies, particularly pensions, served to accentuate or perpetuate existing inequalities among elderly people, in particular inequalities based upon gender, social class and previous labour market position? Which groups are systematically disadvantaged by the current structures? In the light of the heterogeneity of income position amongst the elderly population and the persistence of the experience of poverty, how realistic are government policies in the area of health and social care? Finally, proposals for reform which adequately take into account the heterogeneity of older persons' life experiences are examined.

Major Policy Developments

Income in later life

A key objective of policies concerning income support of the elderly population throughout the twentieth century has been to reduce poverty and dependence on means tested social assistance through the provision of a basic state pension in old age. Indeed a central goal of the Beveridge reforms after the Second World War was to provide an adequate living standard in old age.

The main question that has exercised policy makers is how best to achieve that goal without discouraging self-help, via private provision and savings, and at the same time controlling public expenditure. The historical development of pensions policy has been catalogued in detail by several commentators (Brown, 1990). The debate has centred around the relative merits of three policy options: contributory pension schemes; universal non-contributory pension granted as a right of citizenship; and means-tested non-contributory pension.

Policy has shifted over time between these options. First introduced in Britain in 1909, old age pensions were paid on a *means-tested* basis to people aged 70 or over. From 1928 *contributory* pensions were paid under the national insurance scheme to insured workers over 65 who had paid the requisite number of contributions. There was no means test for these insurance pensions and no retirement condition, payment was made irrespective of income or employment. The 1946 National Insurance Act introduced the requirement that workers must be retired from full-time employment in order to qualify for a pension. A retirement rule or earnings limit continued to be applied to all recipients of state pensions until 1989.

Perhaps the most far-reaching innovation in *state* financial provision for older persons was the introduction of *earnings-related* pensions. The 1959 National Insurance Act, implemented in 1961, introduced a graduated element to the hitherto flat rate pension. The principle of relating both contributions and pensions to earnings was fully developed in the State Earnings Related Pension (SERPS) which was adopted as part of the 1975 Social Security Act, came into force in 1978 and was further modified in 1986.

The rationale behind the introduction of state earnings related pensions was to extend to those persons not in occupational pension schemes the perceived benefits of such schemes. Implicit in this was a reduced role for the NI retirement pension. The tacit assumption is that as SERPS comes to maturity and as more people have income from private sources, the importance of the NI pension in income support in later life will diminish. The result of this is that past labour force participation and earnings will have a greater effect on present levels of economic resources (Ginn and Arber, 1991).

In parallel with many other areas of welfare policy there has been a shift in the balance between public and private provision. The 1980s witnessed increased financial incentives for occupational and private pensions; such as the introduction of two subsidies for personal pension contributions in 1988. Around half the labour force has now 'contracted-out' of SERPS. These changes have tended to favour those groups that have 'excess' income and who are able to save for retirement.

At the same time other changes in *state* policy have acted to reduce the value of the NI Retirement (Basic) Pension. Table 13.1 shows that the initial replacement rate of this pension, just under 20 per cent of average male manual earnings, barely changed in the first 25 years, rose marginally during the 1970s but has declined sharply during the 1980s. Since 1980 the pension

Table 13.1 Retirement pension as a percentage of average male earnings, UK 1948–2030

	as % male manual earnings	as % male earnings
1948	19.1	-
1955	18.4	-
1961	19.1	-
1965	21.4	-
1971	19.5	17.5
1975	21.5	19.6
1981	22.9	19.8
1985	22.5	19.2
1990	-	16
2000	-	14
2010	-	12
2020	-	10
2030	-	9

Note: Projections from 1990 assume that pension is uprated in line with prices and that real earnings grow at 1.5% per annum

Source: DHSS (1986), pp.262–3, Government Actuary (1990), p.18.

has been uprated in line with prices rather than average earnings. With the purchasing power of the pension fixed at its 1980 level, if real incomes rise at 1.5 per cent per annum the NI pension will wither to a mere 10 per cent by 2020.

Community Care

A series of government documents on community care over the last decade have redefined the role of local authorities, leading to the 1990 NHS and Community Care Act (DHSS, 1988; DoH, 1989). This Act essentially confines the role of the state to one of manager and coordinator of care provision rather than 'provider', thus leaving the informal, voluntary and private sectors to take on greater responsibility for providing care and support. This legislation continues to emphasise domiciliary rather than residential care services, characteristic of government policy over the last 20 years (Evandrou et al., 1990), but a more fundamental change is the stress on contracting-out and the extension of consumer choice (Leat, 1990).

Local authorities will allocate their funds to become 'enablers', relying upon a 'mixed economy' of care largely based on the private and voluntary sectors. The role of local authorities will be establishing and assessing the needs of their differing client base, advising clients of the range of options available to them in terms of available care, managing and purchasing 'packages of care', and controlling budgets. The lack of guidelines as to how to define needs and what level of provision would be considered adequate has been criticised (Harding, 1992; Schorr, 1992).

The aim to develop a range of social care service providers is based on the assumption that introducing markets within social care will improve efficiency in service provision as well as consumer responsiveness. The extent to which the consumer will have a *real* choice will be dependent upon markets within social welfare performing competitively given a variety of providers, the provision of an adequate *range* and *quality* of services across the country, and the negotiating skills of the social care manager (Bosanquet, 1987; Knapp, 1989; Hoyes and Means, 1991).

The debate over the adequacy of 'quasi-markets' within the delivery of welfare services has embraced education, housing, and health (Cahn and Barr, 1986; Le Grand, 1990; Le Grand and Robinson, 1984). A major criticism of markets is their tendency to create inequalities. As Hoyes and Means point out, 'discrimination is likely to affect disproportionately the poorest and minority ethnic groups' (1991 p.5). In rural areas, ensuring a sufficient variety of suppliers would be difficult, thus providing a competitive service is unrealistic. Given the prescribed objective of profit maximisation, some services may not be provided at a price which could be afforded.

A key focus of the new community care legislation is on ability to pay. The extent to which users of care services or carers are able or willing to contribute to the costs of care support is a crucial question in the light of government legislation. It has recently become a major issue for discussion (Leat, 1990; Craig, 1992; Glendinning and Craig, 1992) and one which we will address later.

Employment Histories and the Link with Income in Later Life

The decline in value of the state pension has meant that a large minority of pensioners have continued to live in poverty. The continuing prominence of the contribution principle and the expansion of earnings related pensions, both via SERPS and occupational pensions, have served to reproduce in retirement the income differentials that have existed in employment. This has resulted in increasing diversity in the income position within the retired population and growing polarisation.

Diversity in income levels

People do not enter old age equal. Furthermore, progression through the later stages of the life course does not have an equalising impact upon access to material resources. We first examine men and women within ten years of the state retirement age. Table 13.2 shows that the median usual gross income of men is nearly three times that for women. However, there is as much

Table 13.2 Median usual gross weekly income of women aged 50–59 and men aged 55–64 by various socio-economic indicators, Great Britain, 1989

	Women		Men	
	Usual Gross Income (£s)	N=	Usual Gross Income (£s)	N=
All	62	1107	179	1020
Social Class[1]				
I	208	9	332	66
II	143	91	267	219
IIINM	78	478	222	127
IIIM	51	103	148	382
IV&V	46	408	101	222
Housing Tenure				
Owns Outright	59	374	195	401
Owns mortgage	78	429	242	318
Local Authority	45	238	80	231
Other renters	54	66	140	70
Employment				
Working	108	629	234	616
Not working	62	478	84	404
Pension Entitlement				
In occupational pension scheme	157	232	257	364
NOT in occupational pension scheme	71	355	186	154
Not applicable[2]	25	518	96	502

[1] Social class is defined using the Registrar General's Classification as follows: I – Professional; II – Employers and managers; IIINM – Intermediate and Junior non-manual; IIIM – Skilled manual (inc foremen and supervisors) and own account non-professional; IV – Semi-skilled manual and personal service; V – Unskilled manual. Class related to own current (or last occupation).

[2] Not in employment, self-employed or did not know if a member.

Source: Authors' own analysis 1989 General Household Survey

diversity within each gender as there is between men and women. There is a clear gradient of income by occupational class with individuals in professional occupations receiving three (for men) to four (for women) times as much income as their counterparts in semi-skilled and unskilled manual jobs. Levels of income also vary widely between the tenures; owner- occupier men with a mortgage receive a median net weekly income of £242 in 1989 compared with male local authority tenants who could have expected on average £80. Membership of an occupational pension scheme has a marked effect on median income. Women who are members of such a scheme receive

Table 13.3 Pensioner household[1] income by source, Great Britain, 1987 (£ per week)

| | Quintile group | | | | |
	Bottom	2nd	3rd	4th	Top
All Social security benefits	42.80	55.10	62.60	71.10	64.50
Occupational pensions	1.66	4.30	10.40	21.70	78.40
Savings and investment	2.70	3.80	6.10	13.10	78.60
Employment	0.20	0.50	1.40	3.90	33.30
Total Gross Income	47.50	62.30	80.50	109.80	254.80
Social Security as a percentage of total gross income	90	87	78	65	25

[1]   Pensioner households are defined by the CSO as one where the head of the household is over the state pensionable age.

Source: *Hansard*, written answers col. 307–10, 25 July 1990.

a median net income of £157 and men £257 compared to £71 and £186 respectively for those employed individuals who are not members.

Membership of an occupational pension scheme also has a significant effect on income at older ages. Table 13.3 shows the mean level of household income by source for pensioner households. The most striking difference between income quintile groups is the contribution social security benefits and occupational pensions make to total gross income. For the bottom 60 per cent of the pensioner income distribution social security payments comprise well over three-quarters of their income, whereas for the top 20 per cent state benefits contribute only one quarter. This is despite the fact that the absolute amount of social security benefits received by the more affluent group is higher than that received by the lowest 60 per cent.

In contrast, receipt of income from occupational pensions increases across the income distribution. The weekly amount received rises sharply for those in the top quintile, comprising around a third of their total gross income. Incomes from savings and investments follow the same pattern, as does income from employment. The proportion of households in receipt of income from occupational pensions varies across quintile groups, with only 23 per cent of the bottom quintile receiving an income from this source, compared to 53 per cent of households located in the middle quintile and 81 per cent of those in the top. However, *amongst* households in receipt of income from an occupational pension there remain marked differences in the level of income received. In 1987, those households in the top quintile group received on average 13.6 times more (£96.80 in 1989 prices) than those in the bottom (£7.10) and over twice as much as the average across all groups (£44.80) (Hansard, 1990). Thus previous labour market experience, and the

Table 13.4 Employment histories of women and men aged 55–69, Great Britain, 1988

	Women	Men	All
Never worked	2	0	1
Continuously employed	10	56	31
Not continuously employed	88	44	66
Always full time	32	93	60
Always part time	3	1	2
Employed part-time and full-time	63	6	36
N=	1840	1660	3500

Source: Bone *et al.* (1992), Tables 2.3 and 2.7, p.6

ability to accrue occupational pension contributions as well as the accumulation of savings and investment assets, appear to be the key determinants of a higher income stream in later life.

The main reason for the income heterogeneity amongst elderly persons lies in the fact that income in later life is related to previous labour market experience via the *contributory principle* and the *earnings-related* elements of public and occupational pension schemes. The contributory principle is predicated on the assumption of participation in paid employment. However as Lister (1992) points out the contributory principle is based on standard notions of employment. These notions are of a male standard which significantly differs from existing patterns, especially for women. This has been echoed by other commentators (Groves, 1988; Ginn and Arber, forthcoming) and is illustrated by the information on the work histories of persons aged 55 to 69 in 1988 from the OPCS Retirement Survey (Bone *et al.*, 1992) presented in Table 13.4.

Only a tiny minority of individuals have never been in paid employment since finishing continuous full-time education; less than 0.5 per cent of men and only 2 per cent of women aged 55–69 in 1988 reported that they had never worked (Table 13.4). However, there are significant gender differences within employment patterns. Over half (56%) of all men had uninterrupted work histories compared to only 10 per cent of women. Conversely, very few men had ever worked part-time (7%) whereas nearly two-thirds (66%) of women had at some stage during their working life had a part-time job.

Not surprising, respondents who had been employed continuously during their working lives have higher total incomes than others. This reflects, in part, differences in opportunities to build up state and occupational pension contributions. Retired men who had previously worked continuously had a median net weekly income of £92 in 1988 compared to £68 for men whose work was not continuous and who were not working before retirement (Bone *et al.*, 1992).

Strikingly, even for the minority of retired women who had worked continuously their median net weekly income of £56 was below that of men who had been out of the labour market prior to retiring. Women whose employment was not continuous but who were in work prior to retirement received £44, whilst those whose work was not continuous and who were not working before retirement received a mere £36.

To explain these differences in income we will briefly examine how past labour market experience influences entitlement to, and level of receipt of, the three main forms of pension income in later life: NI retirement pension; state earnings related pension and occupational pensions.

NI retirement pension

Eligibility for receipt of a Category A NI Retirement pension is based upon an individual's own contribution record. To satisfy the contribution requirement the contributor must have paid or been credited with contributions equal to a given amount in each of a requisite number of years. The number of years necessary to satisfy this condition depends on the length of the 'working life'. This is taken to be the period inclusive of the tax year in which the individual reached age 16 but exclusive of the year they reach pensionable age. In effect this means that most women have a working life defined as 44 years and for men 49 years, and so require a contribution record of 39 and 44 years respectively (length of working life minus five).

The fact that present state pensions are dependent on a contribution record means that a significant number of elderly people do not receive the full pension, either because they are 'dependent' on their spouse's contribution or because of incomplete contribution records. In September 1990 over four million married women or widows were claiming on their husband's insurance rather than in their own right (DSS, 1992). It is unlikely that this pattern will persist into the next century. Prior to April 1977 married women were allowed to opt for paying a 'reduced rate contribution'. These contributions did not qualify them for any NI benefits in their own right but instead they qualify for a pension at 60 per cent of the rate of the basic pension when their husband retires. Since 1977 this is no longer an option for new contributors. As Davies and Ward note 'reduced-rate contributors are a dwindling and steadily ageing group' (1992 p.13).

However, many people who earn below the lower earnings limit for NI will continue to fail to qualify for a full rate pension. Of the 6.1 million men in receipt of a basic state pension in 1990, 89 per cent (5.4 million) received a pension of 100 per cent of the basic rate. In contrast, less than three-quarters (72%) of the 2.2 million women who were in receipt of a pension on the basis of their own insurance received the full amount. Nearly half a million women received less than 75 per cent of the full basic pension rate and 308,000 received a pension of less than 50 per cent (compared to 48,000 and 15,000 men respectively) (DSS, 1992).

Although there are a number of ways in which credits towards NI contributions can be obtained, they are far from providing a universal protection to persons with gaps in their employment histories – either because certain groups of people continue not to qualify under any of the categories prescribed or because those entitled fail to claim them.

Currently, women in receipt of State Maternity Allowance or Statutory Maternity Pay are entitled to NI credits under the home responsibility protection scheme. However, this is not automatic but has to be claimed. Additionally, if a low paid woman takes a period of unpaid maternity leave beyond the statutory period and does not make sufficient contributions in the remainder of the year, this will result in the year as a whole not counting as a qualifying year towards the pension. Thus the effect of the credits are lost altogether. There are similar problems with Home Responsibility Protection (HRP). HRP only applies to complete years. Thus if a low paid woman ceases to work part-way through a tax year she is likely to find herself neither having a 'qualifying year' nor receiving HRP (Davies and Ward, 1992).

Protection in the form of NI credits is provided for those persons whose employment record is interrupted due to spells of unemployment. However, in order to qualify the claimant must be registered as unemployed. Many women do not sign on because an inadequate contribution record in the past does not qualify them for Unemployment Benefit and they are not eligible for means-tested Income Support because of their spouse's income. Reform of the current mechanisms for protecting contribution records could do much to alleviate the present vagaries of the contribution principle. This issue is discussed at greater length below.

Even where people do qualify for a full basic pension, there remains the issue of its adequacy. As shown in Table 13.1, the replacement value of the state pension has not followed a simple upward trend since the Second World War, and the indexation of the basic state pension to prices rather than earnings since 1979 means that the replacement rate is now falling and is projected to fall further in the future. The level of the basic pension for a single elderly person now stands at just 15 per cent of average male earnings. A pensioner whose only source of income is the basic pension is now automatically eligible for Income Support.

We have shown that persons with interrupted work histories are disadvantaged with regard to entitlement to the basic state pension but this disadvantage is magnified in the case of the other two forms of pension income discussed below: the State Earnings Related Pension Scheme (SERPS) and occupational pensions.[1]

---

1 Although around four million people have now taken out personal pensions this form of income is only likely to have an impact on those retiring from 2020 onwards.

Table 13.5 Occupational pension histories of women and men aged 55–69 by (i) own usual occupation and (ii) disability

	Women			Men		
	Non-manual	Manual	All	Non-manual	Manual	All
No schemes joined	47	72	59	16	22	20
One or more schemes joined:	53	28	41	84	78	80
No retained rights	15	8	12	9	13	11
Total with retained pension rights	38	20	29	75	65	68
N=	(948)	(695)	(1840)	(638)	(951)	(1660)

	Not disabled	Disabled	Not disabled	Disabled
No schemes joined	57	64	19	24
One or more schemes joined:	43	36	81	76
No retained rights	12	11	10	13
Total with retained pension rights	31	25	71	63
N=	(1216)	(624)	(1068)	(592)

Source: Bone *et al.* (1992), Tables 6.5 and 6.7.

Earnings related pensions

By definition any earnings related pension will perpetuate into old age the relatively poor position of those with low earnings during their working life. Moreover, the changes to SERPS as a result of the 1986 Social Security Act have served to accentuate this effect. When originally introduced in 1978, the SERPS pension was to be based upon the best 20 years' earnings. However this condition was abolished in 1986 and now calculation depends on all years. The result is that years of no earnings or low earnings, such as part-time years or partial years, will reduce the average amount of 'lifetime' earnings. There is no contribution protection for persons who suffer episodes of unemployment nor periods of receipt of Statutory Maternity Pay. HRP does however count to reduce the number of years in the denominator for calculation.

For the present generation of elderly people SERPS entitlements are very small. The main source of pension income in later life in addition to the basic state pension comes from occupational pensions. In 1990 60 per cent of male and 38 per cent of female employees were members of occupational pension schemes (OPCS, 1992). The majority of these are 'final earnings' schemes where the level of pension is based upon earnings at, or within a few years of, retirement and years of pensionable service (contributions). The remainder of this section will concentrate on differential patterns of access to occupational pensions given different lifecourse experiences.

Evidence from the OPCS Retirement Survey (Bone *et al.*, 1992) provides an indication of the way *occupational* pension entitlements are accumulated over people's working lives. It highlights an important, but often overseen, point that membership of an occupational pension scheme at some point during working life does not necessarily mean that those rights are retained into retirement. Table 13.5 shows while 80 per cent of men aged 55–69 had belonged to an occupational pension scheme only about half as many women (41%) had done so. Over a quarter of women and an eighth of men had forfeited their entitlement to a pension from one or more schemes to which they had once belonged, and just over 10 per cent no longer had any occupational pension entitlement although they had formerly belonged to a scheme. There is a clear relationship between retaining rights to an occupational pension and socio-economic status. Amongst those aged 55–69 both men and women who had usually been employed in a non-manual occupation were more likely than others to have ever belonged to an occupational pension scheme and to have retained rights. This relationship holds for persons still currently in the labour force.

Evidence from the General Household Survey (GHS) (OPCS, 1992) regarding current membership shows that 81 per cent of men in intermediate non-manual occupations belonged to their employer's scheme compared with 45 per cent of men in unskilled manual occupations. The pattern of association between membership and socio-economic group was similar for employed women, although the proportion was lower in each group being 74 per cent and 32 per cent respectively. Unsurprisingly, persons working part-time (90% of whom are women) were much less likely to be covered by an employers scheme than full-time employees. Only 16 per cent of women working part-time were members compared with 55 per cent of women working full-time. Thus, arguments that the current pattern observed amongst today's elderly population is the result of cohort effects are not sustainable. Inequalities by socio-economic group and gender in access to income from non-state pensions are likely to persist into the next century.

Persons who have interrupted work histories through disability, chronic illness, periods of unemployment or home responsibility are also likely to experience lower levels of economic security in later life. Martin *et al.* (1988) found that only 31 per cent of disabled adults below pensionable age were in paid employment compared with 69 per cent of the population as a whole.

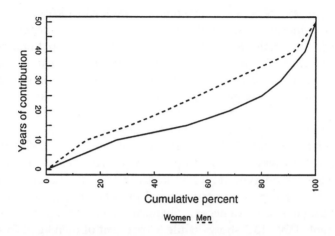

Source: Bone *et al.* (1992), Table 6.23

Figure 13.1 Number of years of pension contributions by sex:
persons aged 55–69 with retained rights to occupational pension schemes

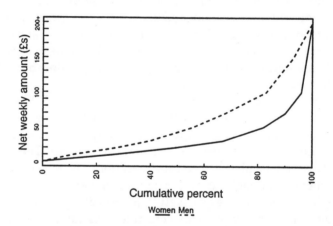

Source: Bone *et al.* (1992), Table 6.54

Figure 13.2 Net weekly amount of occupational pension by sex:
persons aged 55–69 drawing occupational pension

For those in a job, level of disability was found to be related to the level of
earnings, with those more severely disabled having lower hourly rates of
pay than both full-time employees generally and the less severely disabled.
The OPCS Retirement Survey found that individuals aged 55–69 who currently experienced some level of disability had lower incomes (of which state
benefits constituted the main component) than individuals without such

impairment (Bone *et al.*; 1992). Individuals currently with disabilities were less likely to have ever joined an occupational pension scheme or to have retained entitlements to one (Table 13.5).

The difference in membership of such a scheme is more marked where the person is affected by their disability prior to retirement. Of men currently aged 55–69 who had experienced some disability prior to age fifty, 66 per cent had ever joined a pension scheme, and only 53 per cent had retained some or all rights compared to 80 per cent and 68 per cent respectively of all disabled men. Women who had suffered some pre-retirement disability before reaching 50 were similarly disadvantaged, with 31 per cent ever having been a member of an occupational scheme, but only 19 per cent now retaining any rights (Bone, 1992, Table 8.35, p.205). Thus, the likelihood of ever having joined an occupational pension scheme, and of having retained rights to a pension from that membership, is related both to current disability and the length of time affected by the disability. The earlier the onset of disability, the greater the likelihood of income insecurity at a later stage in the life course through lack of access to an occupational pension.

Another group of individuals disadvantaged by interrupted employment patterns and inadequate protection of pension contributions are informal carers. The extent to which their caring experience at one stage of the life course impacts on their income security in later stages, is discussed in the following section.

Membership of an occupational pension scheme does not in itself guarantee enhanced income in later life. As mentioned above many people forfeit rights by moving jobs or breaks in contributions. The *level* of any pension drawn depends on duration of contribution record and earnings whilst in employment, resulting in variations both within and between genders. Figure 13.1 shows the years of contributions for those women and men who have occupational pension entitlements. Over a quarter of women have a contribution record of less than ten years and over half (52%) have less than 15 years. Only 20 per cent of women have accumulated 25 or more years of contributions, compared to 44 per cent of men.

Women are not only less likely to have retained entitlements to an occupational pension scheme of their own but they are also much less likely to have as long a contribution record as men. This in turn is reflected in the net weekly amount of occupational pension received, as shown in Figure 13.2. The median amount received by men (£40.62) was exactly twice that received by women (£20.31).

It is clear that differentials in later life with regard to income are strongly correlated with experiences undergone during working life. Payments of premiums for private and occupational pensions are clearly related to the income and employment history of the individual. Unemployment, part-time work and early retirement may well preclude the building up of non-state pension contributions for certain groups. Present pensioning arrangements do not cope well with diverse life course experiences of different individuals, especially women.

Social Care, Policies and Life Course Implications

The above discussion on pensions policy and the income position of the elderly population has several implications for current health and social care policy: both in terms of the changing balance in the *provision* of care between the formal and informal sector; and between state and personal *financing* of care. The provision of informal care has implications across the life course which extend beyond the time period of actual car-giving. This section discusses both the *current* costs of caring and the indirect *long-term* care costs in terms of the ability to build up contribution records and acquire secure forms of non-state income after retirement. The implications for developing consistent and coherent social security and community care policies in the future are also discussed.

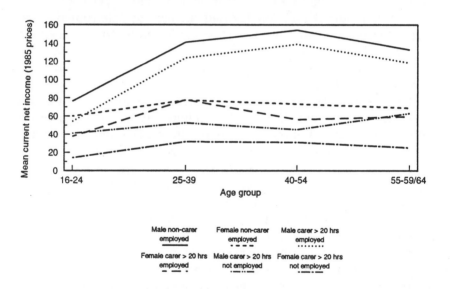

Source: GHS 1985 own analysis

Figure 13.3 Mean current net income of carers versus non-carers by employment status

The long-term costs of care

The role of the state in the provision of care and support for disabled and frail elderly people has historically been restricted compared to that of family support. The implication of recent government legislation is to further increase reliance upon informal care and support. *Caring for People* (DoH, 1989) stresses the importance of informal care and proposes that local authorities should 'arrange the delivery of packages of care to individuals building first on the available contribution of informal carers and neighbourhood support' (DHSS, 1988; para 1.3.3).

The 1990 Community Care legislation has been critically received (Allen *et al.*, 1992; Harding, 1992; Schorr, 1992). Policy planning explicitly relies upon the valuable contribution made by informal carers (DHSS, 1988), yet this is not paralleled by a recognition of the financial implications this may have to the care-giver or their family, currently or in the long term future. There are short-term and long-term economic effects on the income and employment of individuals providing such care. For example, current employment status, levels of earnings, savings, and additional expenditure incurred from caring may all affect income resources in later life. Disrupted employment histories of carers, many of whom are women, may affect their economic status in *their own* old age in terms of income and pensions forgone, and lower earnings related benefits in later life.

Analysis using the 1985 GHS revealed that 3.7m adults in Britain care for someone *on their own*, 1.4m spend at least 20 hours per week providing such care, and 700,000 carers care for 50 hours or more per week (Baldwin and Parker, 1991; Evandrou, 1992). Over a third (35%) of people caring for someone within their own household report incomes which are in or on the margins of poverty (140% of SB level), compared to 25 per cent of individuals without caring responsibilities. The greater likelihood of these carers experiencing poverty remains even after taking into account their employment status (Evandrou, 1992).

Studies investigating the employment and economic impact of caring, using the 1985 GHS, have documented the following. First, full-time participation rates of carers of working age are depressed compared to those of non-carers, and the employment effect was found to be greater for male carers (Parker and Lawton, 1990). However, the employment effects of caring are also dependent upon the time and intensity of care provided. Full-time employment rates amongst married women of (working age) were 28 per cent for non-carers, 23 per cent for carers looking after someone outside their household, and 13 per cent for those caring within their home (Evandrou and Winter, 1992). Second, female carers were more likely to be working part- time than women who were not carers. Third, the average weekly earnings, as well as the mean hourly wage of employed carers, were found to be lower than that of employed persons who were not carers (Baldwin and Parker, 1991; Evandrou and Winter, 1992).

Parents of disabled children reported lower employment participation rates, fewer hours worked and lower average earnings than families without such responsibilities (Baldwin, 1985). Furthermore, the likelihood of experiencing below average (net) earnings was found to be greater amongst parents of disabled children from non-manual rather than manual work backgrounds (Smyth and Robus, 1989).

The position of carers in relation to social security policy was not considered in the 1990 White paper *The Way Ahead* (DSS, 1990). In fact, Baldwin and Parker (1991) point out that the Social Services Committee report (House of Commons, 1990) is the only place where the issues of cash and care in providing support to carers are fully discussed. Thus it is important to consider the employment, earnings, income of carers and the related costs incurred, within the objectives and structure of current government policies.

To what extent does receipt of social security compensate carers' financial position and place them on a par with individuals who do not have caring responsibilities? Figure 13.3 shows that the mean (net personal) income of carers in employment is lower than that of employed non-carers'. This difference was found to be generally consistent for different types of carers in various age groups.

Introduced in 1975 as an earnings replacement benefit, Invalid Care Allowance (ICA) acknowledged the likely impact on employment of providing significant levels of hours of care per week and as McLaughlin (1991) points out, recognised the 'considerable savings to health and personal social services'. The aim was to provide long-term financial security by crediting national insurance contributions. However, the proportion of carers in receipt of ICA has remained very small even following reform and extension to married women in 1986; 110,000 carers receive it nationally, representing a mere two per cent of all carers (HM Treasury, 1989). This is not surprising given the strict eligibility regulations; the carer must provide a minimum of 35 hours of care per week to someone who is entitled to Attendance Allowance (i.e. with severe disabilities), must be aged 16–59/64 years when first claiming, not in full-time employment (or if in part-time employment, not earning more than £40 per week) or full-time education. Set at £32.55 per week (1992 rate for a single adult), ICA is lower than the basic state pension (£54.15) and unemployment benefit (£43.10) (Mathewman, 1991; Caring Costs, 1992). Furthermore, households which are in receipt of ICA and which receive no other income except from state benefits, or where the carer's spouse is unemployed, may be faced with a situation in which overlapping benefit regulations lead to a deduction of the ICA amount in full from their benefit income. Given the objectives of the introduction of ICA as an earnings replacement benefit, for many carers it is unlikely to meet its aims. As Baldwin and Parker stress, '[ICA] is not payment for caring, simply a recognition that the carer is not free to take up paid work' (1991 p.187).

Given the depressing effect of caring on earnings, low take-up of ICA, and consequent low protection of NI credits, the consequences of caring will extend beyond the caring process into the carers' own old age through their reduced ability to build up contributions and lower earnings related benefits. We do not know what proportion of informal carers in Britain who have been caring for periods of time earlier in their life course, will be faced with reduced or no occupational pensions, or the impact on carers' health status from long-term caring. Further research is required to answer such questions. However, what is crucial is *recognition at policy level* of such longer term costs of caring to the individual.

Personalising the costs of care

Although there are a number of issues in the cash versus care debate (see Craig, 1992), our focus here is limited to assessing the extent to which care users should and can be responsible for financing their own care provision. Explicit in the White Paper *Caring for People* (DoH, 1989) was the expectation that increasingly local authorities will, and should, charge for services. In doing so, it is important that policy makers are aware that the financial resources available to older people and other care users are a function of life course events as illustrated above.

For the majority of older people, retirement is not a period of affluence. In 1990, 1.7 million people aged over 60 were in receipt of Income Support, two million qualified for means-tested Housing Benefit and 3.6 million were drawing Community Charge Benefit because of their low incomes (DSS, 1992). A number of recent studies have shown that it is unlikely that many older people are affluent enough to finance their own care (Falkingham and Victor, 1991; Gibbs, 1991; Henwood, 1990a; Oldman, 1991b).

Similarly it is unlikely that many disabled people will be in a position to purchase their own care requirements. As discussed above, people who experience some level of disability are generally faced with lower incomes than those who do not. Furthermore disabled people frequently incur additional expenditure due to their incapacity (Martin and White, 1988). This varies with severity of disability and relates to both 'normal' and 'special' items. The OPCS Disability Survey estimated an average of £5.70 per week (in 1985) additional cost incurred for all disabled persons, which ranged from £3.60 amongst the lowest severity group to £10.60 for those in the highest category (Martin and White, 1988).

Local authority charging practices are justified on a variety of grounds. It is argued that they increase efficient rationing of resources by limiting excessive demand, raise revenue and encourage values such as 'independence' and 'choice'. However, studies show that the resources raised by charging are usually very small. For example, the proportion of expenditure on home helps covered by charges was a mere six per cent in 1985–6 (Oldman, 1991b). In 1968, Titmuss (1968) argued that price was a barrier which prevented people, especially poor individuals, from using services. In 1980, Judge and Matthews (1980) found that the implementation of flat-rate charges resulted in some clients refusing services and a decade later Sinclair *et al.* conclude that 'the imposition of charges could distort demand, deterring the poor who need home help from applying for it and deflecting services to somewhat richer pensioners who need them less'. (1990 p.56)

These poorer pensioners will be those with the life course experiences identified above, namely women, those with manual occupations during their working life, the long-term unemployed and persons suffering from disabilities. Carers' financial positions may also be affected by charging, particularly when they care for someone within the household where the joint financial resources of that household are low or precarious (Glendinning, 1990; Parker, 1990).

Alternative sources of personal financing of care have been receiving increased attention within research and the policy arena. A life course approach provides insights into the likely availability to elderly people of income from two sources, in particular, the use of housing equity and long term care insurance (LTC). In Community Care: Agenda for Action, Griffiths (DHSS, 1988) advocated for older owner- occupiers the use of resources currently tied up in housing equity to fund their care needs. However, work by Bosanquet and Propper (1991), Gibbs (1991) and Oldman (1991b) all shed doubt on the efficacy of such a course of action. Owner-occupation is related to previous labour market status and social class (Evandrou and Victor, 1989) and equity release schemes would not be an option for poorer groups of elderly people.

Long-term care insurance has been seen by some as one potential solution to the financing of social care needs of the growing elderly population (Henwood, 1990b; Oldman, 1991b). The last two years have seen a burgeoning in the number of financial products aimed at providing long term care insurance (see Oldman, 1991b). However, the expansion of such schemes whilst providing a means for people to plan for their health care needs in later life, may serve to increase inequality within the elderly population.

Just as receipt of an occupational pension is dependent on previous labour market experience, so too will these new financial market products. Some of them assume that the client already has a personal pension plan, with the long-term care insurance being an addition to that pension. Others require the availability of a substantial capital sum out of which a policy can be bought. As we have seen both home ownership and non-state pensions are related to labour market experience. Thus access to these products will clearly be limited to those at the upper end of the income distribution.

Certain groups of people, particularly women, carers and persons with a disability, are less likely or able to have accumulated sufficient contribution records for a full state pension or high occupational pensions. As early as 1958 Titmuss identified two nations in old age, those with decent occupational pensions and those without. The introduction of charging and increased private provisioning of care services may result in a two-tier care system in old age and a new cleavage in later life (Baldwin and Parker, 1989). To avoid this, the link between access to social care and income in later life should be weakened not strengthened.

The Way Forward

The majority of older people in Britain continue to live on incomes well below average for the total population (DSS, 1988, 1992). The continuing poverty of many British pensioners is the clearest evidence available of the failure of the British public pension system to provide an adequate income in old age.

Failure to achieve the goal of poverty elimination is associated with the different life course experiences amongst individuals and the failure of policy to respond to these differences. As Hancock and Weir (1992) note 'the heterogeneity of pensioners' incomes is such that policy options may need to be more detailed, to be more tailored to the variety of situations' (1992 p.3) and 'proposals must acknowledge the diversity which is at the heart of both state provision and pensioners' incomes' (1992 p.10).

As earlier sections have shown, current policies towards income support in later life are far from life course neutral. They give undue weight to particular prior life course events and in doing so are sexist and exclusionary. The switch to a contribution based basic pension and the introduction of an earnings-related component (SERPS) have served to extend the influence of labour market experience on income beyond the age of retirement. As social insurance has moved towards earnings- related benefits the protection of unpaid or low paid workers has become increasingly inadequate. It is important therefore that proposals for policy reform include flexible approaches that are sensitive to this link between the past and the present. 'As long as retirement is earnings related, something is required in the policy package to help restore the earning power and pension-earning power of those whose pension rights have taken second place to caring responsibility' (Joshi and Davies, forthcoming).

There are three alternate, but not necessarily exclusive, approaches that can be adopted. At the extreme, one can pursue policies that sever the link between past work and present (minimum) income altogether. Alternately if this relationship *is* maintained, policies can be adopted that: a) act to ameliorate the impact of prior life course experience on income in old age; and b) directly impact upon the life course experiences of individuals themselves. The former set of policy options would include the augmentation of the basic NI pension and the concomitant reduction in the relative importance of earnings-related components, as well as measures to circumvent the exclusionary and sexist nature of the contribution principle, for example through the extension of home responsibility credits. The latter would involve reducing the inequalities in labour market participation, and consequent earnings and contributions records, between different groups. Active labour market policies such as provision of child and elder care are an example of this type of approach. The strands of policy identified need not be mutually exclusive. Owen and Joshi (1990) conclude that equitable treatment of women in pensions requires both an enhancement of labour market opportunities for carers and an enhancement of the recognition given to unpaid contributions.

Two main policy alternatives are outlined: (i) radical rethinking, which severs the link between labour market history and an adequate income in later life, and (ii) reforming the current system.

Radical rethinking

One alternative would be to abandon the concept of an age related pension altogether, in favour of a benefit that was payable to *all* members of society regardless of economic status. Such a strategy approximates a full *Basic (or Citizens') Income Scheme* (Rhys Williams, 1989). In such a system, whether a person's non-participation in the labour market was due to retirement, ill-health or unemployment would be irrelevant. The basis of entitlement would be citizenship rather than contribution record or chronological age. This solves the problem of inter-generational equity as all age groups are assured of the same treatment throughout different stages of the life course. By removing an age threshold of entitlement it also provides complete flexibility in choice of retirement age.

A citizen's income would involve the abolition of the present dual system of separately administered state cash benefits and income tax reliefs, and their replacement by a new integrated system of personal basic incomes, which would convert automatically from cash benefit to tax relief and *vice versa*. All earnings rules would be abolished and individuals would be able to build on their basic incomes through employment earnings, subject to tax. Under a Citizen's Income scheme each individual in society would have the unconditional right to an independent, non means tested, and tax-free income, sufficient to meet basic living costs, irrespective of age, gender, occupation or marital status. Such incomes schemes would thus achieve a greater equality between men and women, and married and single persons. They would also remove the stigma from unemployment and the compulsion from retirement.

Although a full Citizen's Income scheme may not be realistic in the short-term future, research is being conducted into the funding feasibility and political acceptability of such a scheme, in particular by the *Citizen's (formerly Basic) Income Research Group* (Basic Income Research Group, 1985; Parker, 1992). However, examples of partial Citizen's Income systems already exist. In Britain the payment of child benefit is unrelated to the labour market participation of the parents. Other countries have already adopted policies which resemble Citizen's Incomes for elderly people, for example, Denmark's residence based old age pension and Canada's Old Age Security (OAS) pension.

An alternative solution is proposed by Johnson and Falkingham (forthcoming) in their Unified Funded Pension Scheme (UFPS). This scheme is designed to replace the existing NI basic pension and the majority of state, occupational and personal earnings-related schemes with a single pension that combines minimum pension guarantees with earnings-related provision. By combining individual based contributions to a personal retirement fund with a system of annual tax-financed capital transfers to people on low income or not in the labour market the link between past employment and *minimum* pension entitlement is eliminated. The scheme provides a guaranteed income for all elderly people irrespective of their past labour market history or marital status.

Both of the above policy scenarios involve a radical re- thinking of the current system of income support in later life. Other policy alternatives operate within the current framework. They involve altering the balance between existing benefits, and/or modifying the benefit structure.

Reforming the current system

As discussed above, present measures to protect contributions for groups outside the labour market are not comprehensive. Extension of Home Responsibility Credits to other groups and to years of low earnings whilst caring for children or adult dependents would serve to mitigate the contribution principle. At present credits for home responsibilities are only awarded automatically to persons who are not in paid employment and claiming child benefit. Award is *not* automatic for persons whose caring responsibility precludes their participation in the labour market. Currently only those who care for over 35 hours a week for beneficiaries of Attendance Allowance and who themselves are recipients of Income Support are entitled to apply for HRP. Widening eligibility criteria to persons with caring responsibilities who are on low pay, and increasing take up by automatic accreditation (rather than via application) would reduce disadvantage to these groups.

Present policy places an increasing stress on earnings related pensions in later life. This disadvantages those with periods of low pay due to part-time work. Measures that reduce the relative importance of earnings related pensions by increasing the real value of the NI pension such as restoring the indexation of the basic pension to earnings, which was abandoned in 1980, would help to redress this disadvantage.

Another strategy to ameliorate the pension penalties inherent in the contribution principle of unpaid reproductive and caring work is to initiate a comprehensive system of child and elder care. Evidence from other European countries suggests that provision of child care reduces the time out of the labour force for women after the birth of a child and so acts to help preserve her earnings and hence her pension rights (Joshi and Davies, 1992).

Current British social security policy does not encourage the labour market participation of informal carers nor does it support them to maintain full-time employment, given the exclusion of carers who are 'gainfully employed' from ICA eligibility. Social security and Community Care policies need to be made fully consistent and to support of each other. Arguments for improvements and reforms have been made by many. For example, McLaughlin (1991) outlines a number of recommendations to improve the targetting and effectiveness of ICA; by raising the level at which ICA is set, allowing ICA recipients higher earnings levels from part-time employment, disregarding ICA (in part or whole) from assessing income support entitlement, and by extending those in receipt of Attendance Allowance. The case is also made for a strategic incomes policy for carers and people in need of care and assistance in order to maximise their independence and choice (Caring Costs, 1992).

In summary, future government policies should:

1. Provide an adequate income replacement at a level which recognises short-term but also longer-term economic impact of providing informal care. In addition, it should not preclude carers taking up or continuing paid employment.
2. Ensure that policies (regarding cash and services) at national and local level reflect the diversity of caring experiences and socio-economic position of carers and cared- for persons.
3. Encourage labour market policies and practices which do not disadvantage individuals with interrupted paid work histories; in particular, individuals with disabilities, women with child care responsibilities, individuals with caring responsibilities for sick or disabled adults or children, or frail elderly persons.
4. Extend home responsibility credits beyond groups caring for a child or adult dependent to individuals on low pay and assign such credits automatically, without the necessity of an application.

Conclusion

Titmuss' observations about 'two nations' in retirement (Titmuss, 1958) are more relevant to the 1990s than they were to the 1950s, and may be more relevant still in the early decades of the next century. Fifty years ago to be old and retired meant to be poor for nearly everyone. In the future, retirement living standards increasingly will reflect past labour market status and life-time earnings trajectories, and the income and wealth distribution of the elderly population will more closely resemble that of the working population. Such changes in the economic circumstances of older people may alter the extent of poverty in old age, but they will not eradicate it.

The evidence discussed in this chapter demonstrates the tremendous heterogeneity of older people in terms of the level and sources of their income and wealth, their state of functional ability, and their overall welfare. Part of the relative impoverishment of the very old may be a function of age, but much of it is a cohort effect, since the majority of people who retired in the late 1960s left work with at best only modest occupational pension entitlements, and may well have seen the value of other savings fall during the rapid inflation of the 1970s. The more comprehensive pensioning arrangements available for large parts of today's workforce makes it probable that more people will in the future enter retirement with high incomes and substantial assets. On the other hand, the existence of many marginal workers in temporary and short-term employment, high unemployment and greater reliance upon informal carers makes it likely that large numbers of people will reach the end of their working life having accumulated few pension entitlements and few other realisable assets, and that they will have to rely upon a basic state pension which has declined in real value.

It is clear that there is a case for British government policies to recognise and take into account the reality of individuals' life course experiences; that is, that a person's social and economic position and experience earlier in their life course, has major consequences for their resources and well-being in the latter part of their life course. How and when people are able to make up the lost ground is dependent upon the form in which welfare and employment policies are developed.

References

Acton, W. (1862) *Functions and Disorders of the Reproductive Organs.* London: John Churchill.

Ahmad, A. (1988) *Social Services for Black People.* London: National Institute of Social Work.

Allen, I., Hogg, D. and Peace, S. (1992) *Elderly People: Choice, Participation and Satisfaction.* London: Policy Studies Institute.

Altman, I. and Werner, C. (eds.) (1985) *Home Environments.* New York: Plenum Press.

Anderson, M. (1971) *Family Structure in Nineteenth Century Lancashire.* Cambridge: Cambridge University Press.

Anon (1986) 'In England Now.' *The Lancet,* January 18th, p.147.

Anthony, K. (1984) 'Moving experiences; memories of favourite homes', *Environmental Design Research Association (EDRA) 15 Proceedings,* pp.141–149.

Anthony, K. (1989) 'Breaking up is hard to do; The meaning of home to parents and children of divorce.' Paper prepared for International Housing Symposium, *The Meaning and Use of Home and Neighbourhood.* Alvakarleby, Sweden.

Arber, S. (1990) 'Opening the "Black" Box: Understanding inequalities in women's health.' In P. Abbott and G. Payne (eds.) *New Directions in the Sociology of Health.* Brighton: Falmer Press.

Arber, S., Gilbert, M. and Evandrou, M. (1988) 'Gender, household composition and receipt of domiciliary services by disabled people.' *Journal of Social Policy,* 17 (2), 153–175.

Arber, S. and Ginn, J. (1990) 'The meaning of informal care: Gender and the contribution of elderly people.' *Ageing and Society,* 10(4), 429–54.

Arber, S. and Ginn, J. (1991a) *Gender and Later Life: A Sociological Analysis of Resources and Constraints.* London: Sage.

Arber, S. and Ginn, J. (1991b) 'The invisibility of age: Gender and class in later life.' *Sociological Review,* 39(2), 260–291.

Arber, S. and Ginn, J. (1992) 'In sickness and in health: Care-giving, gender and independence of elderly people.' In C. Marsh, and S. Arber (eds.) *Families and Households: Divisions and Change.* London: Macmillan.

Arber, S. and Ginn, J. (1993) 'Gender and inequalities in health in later life.' *Social Science and Medicine,* 36(1), 33–47.

Arendell, T. and Estes, C. (1991) 'Older women in the post-Reagan era', pp.209–26. In M. Minkler, and C.L. Estes (eds.) *Critical Perspectives on Aging: The Political and Moral Economy of Growing Old.* New York: Baywood Publishing Company Inc.

Askham, J. *et al.* (forthcoming) 'The provision of health and social services for elderly people from black and minority ethnic groups.' Research Report, King's College, London, Age Concern Institute of Gerontology.

Association of Community Health Councils (ACHCEW) (1991) *NHS Continuing Care of Elderly People.* London: ACHEW.

Atkin, K., Cameron, E., Badger, F. and Evers, H. (1989) 'Asian elders' knowledge and future use of community social and health services.' *New Community,* 15 (3), 439–445.

Audit Commission (1986) *Making a Reality of Community Care.* London: HMSO.

Badger, F., Atkin, K. and Griffiths, R. (1989) 'Why don't general practitioners refer their disabled Asian patients to district nurses?.' *Health Trends,* 21, 31–32. .

Baldwin, S. (1985) *The Costs of Caring: Families with Disabled Children.* London: Routledge Kegan Paul.

Baldwin, S. and Parker, G. (1989) 'The Griffiths Report on Community Care', pp.143–65. In M. Brenton, and C. Ungerson (eds.) *Social Policy Review 1988–9.* Harlow: Longman.

Baldwin, S. and Parker, G. (1991) 'Support for informal carers – the role of social security.' In G. Dalley (ed.) *Disability and Social Policy*. London: Policy Studies Institute.

Barnstone, W. (1962) *Greek Lyric Poetry*. London: Bantam Books.

Basic Income Research Group (BIRG) (1985) *Basic Income*. London: BIRG.

Bassey, E.J., Patrick, J.M., Irving, J.M., Blecher, A. and Fentem, P.H. (1983) 'An unsupervised "aerobics" physical training programme in middle aged factory workers: Feasibility, validation and response.' *European Journal of Applied Physiology*, 52, 120–5.

Batty, M. (1989) 'Europe and the Mature Consumer'. An address to the National Council of Women. London: March.

Begum, N. (1992) *Something to be Proud of: The Lives of Asian Disabled People and Carers in Waltham Forest*. London: Waltham Forest Race Relations Unit.

Bellow, S. (1970) *Mr Sammler's Planet*. London: Viking.

Belsky, J. (1992) 'The research findings on gender issues in aging men and women.' In B.R. Wainrib (ed.) *Gender Issues Across the Life Cycle*. New York: Springer.

Bengston, V. L. (1986) 'Comparative perspectives on the microsociology of aging: Methodological problems and theoretical issues', pp.304–36. In V.W. Marshall (ed.) *Later Life: The Social Psychology of Aging*. London: Sage.

Benson, M. (1980) *Serbo-Croatian-English Dictionary* (2nd ed.) Belgrade: Prosveta.

Bertaux, D. (1991) 'From methodological monopoly to pluralism in the sociology of social mobility', pp.73–92. In S. Dex (ed.) *Life and Work History Analyses*. London: Routledge.

Bhalla, A. and Blakemore, K. (1981) *Elders of the Minority Ethnic Groups*. Birmingham: All Faiths for One Race (AFFOR).

Bhaskar, R. (1979) *The Possibility of Naturalism*. Brighton: Harvester.

Blakemore, K. (1982) 'Health and illness among the elderly of minority ethnic groups living in Birmingham: some new findings.' *Health Trends*, 14, 69–73.

Blakemore, K. (1983) 'Ethnicity, self-reported illness and use of medical services by the elderly.' *Postgraduate Medical Journal*, 59, 668–70.

Blakemore, K. (1989) 'Does age matter? The case of old age in minority ethnic groups.' In B. Bytheway, T. Keil, P. Allatt, and A. Bryman (eds.) *Becoming and Being Old*. London: Sage.

Bond, J. Gregson, B. and Atkinson, A. (1989) 'Measurement of outcomes with a multicentred randomised controlled trial in the evaluation of the experimental NHS nursing homes.' *Age and Ageing*, 18, 292–302.

Bone, M., Gregory, J., Gill, B. and Lader, D. (1992) *Retirement and Retirement Plans*. London: HMSO.

Booth, T. (1985) *Home Truths*. Aldershot: Gower.

Bosanquet, N. (1987) 'Buying care', pp.23–8. In D. Clode (ed.) *Towards the Sensitive Bureaucracy*. London: Gower.

Bosanquet, N., Laing, W. and Propper, C. (1990) *Elderly Consumers in Britain: Europe's Poor Relations? Charting the Grey Economy in the 1990s*. London: Laing and Buisson.

Bosanquet, N. and Propper, C. (1992) 'Charting the grey economy in the 1990s.' *Policy and Politics*, 19(4), 269–281.

Bourdieu, P. (1977) *Outline of a Theory of Practice*. Cambridge: Cambridge University Press.

Bowlby, J. (1981) *Attachment and Loss (Vol 3): Loss: Sadness and Depression*. Harmondsworth: Penguin.

Bowling, A. and Formby, J. (1992) 'Hospital and nursing home care for the elderly in an inner city health district.' *Nursing Times*, 88(13), 51–54.

Braithwaite, V. (1990) *Bound to Care*. Sydney: Allen and Unwin.

Brecher, E.M. (1984) *Love, Sex, and Aging: A Consumer Union Report*. Boston: Little, Brown and Co.

Brody, E. (1981) '"Women in the Middle" and family help to older people.' *The Gerontologist*, 21(5), 471–9.

Brok, A.J. (1992) 'Some thoughts on gender role issues for men in later life.' In B.R. Wainrib (ed.) *Gender Issues Across the Life Cycle*. Boston: Little, Brown and Co.

Brown, J. (1990) *Social Security for Retirement*. York: Joseph Rowntree Foundation.

Brown, R. (1989) *Individualised Care: The Role of the Ward Sister*. London: Scutari Press.

Bryant, C. and Jary, D. (eds.) (1991) *Giddens Theory of Structuration: A Critical Appreciation*. London: Routledge.

Bulmer, M. (1986) *Neighbours: the Work of Philip Abrams*. Cambridge: Cambridge University Press.

Bury, M. and Holme, A. (1991) *Life after Ninety*. London: Routledge.

Butler, A., Oldman, C. and Grieve, J. (1983) *Sheltered Housing for the Elderly*. London: George Allen and Unwin.

Butler, R.N. and Lewis, M.I. (1988) *Love and Sex After 60*. New York: Harper and Row.

Byers, J.P. (1983) 'Sexuality and the elderly.' *Geriatric Nursing. (New York)* 4, 293–297.

Cadwallader, M. (1986) 'Migration and intra-urban mobility.' In M. Pacione (ed.) *Population Geography: Progress and Prospect*. London: Croom Helm, 257–283.

Cahn, E. and Barr, N. (1986) *Service Credits: A New Currency for the Welfare State*, Welfare State Programme Discussion Paper No. 8, London: Welfare State Programme.

Caldock, K. (1992) 'Domiciliary services and dependency: A meaningful relationship?' In F. Laczko, and C. Victor (eds.) *Social Policy and Elderly People: The Role of Community Care*. Aldershot: Avebury.

Calnan, M. (1987) *Health and Illness: The Lay Perspective*. London: Tavistock.

Calnan, M. (1990) 'Food and health: A comparison of beliefs and practices in middle-class and working-class households.' In S. Cunningham-Burley, and N.P. McKeganey (eds.) *Readings in Medical Sociology*. London: Tavistock/Routledge.

Cameron, E., Evers, H., Badger, F. and Atkin, K. (1989) 'Black old women, disability and health carers.' In M. Jeffreys (ed.) *Growing Old in the Twentieth Century*. London: Routledge.

Campbell, H. Crawford, V. and Stout, N.W. (1990) 'The impact of private residential and nursing care on statutory residential and hospital care of elderly people in South Belfast.' *Age and Ageing*. 19, 318–324.

Caring Costs (1992) *An Income Policy for Carers*. London: Caring Costs.

Challis, L. and Bartlett, D. (1988) *Old and Ill: Private Nursing Homes for Elderly People*. Age Concern Institute of Gerontology Research Paper No 1. Age Concern England, Mitcham.

Charles, N. and Kerr, M. (1986) 'Issues of responsibility and control in the feeding of families.' In S. Rodmell, and A. Watt (eds.) *The Politics of Health Education*. London: Routledge and Kegan Paul.

Charles, N. and Kerr, M. (1987) 'Just the way it is: Gender and age differences in family food consumption.' In J. Brannen and G. Wilson (eds.) *Give and Take in Families*. London: Allen and Unwin.

Charles, N. and Kerr, M. (1988) *Women, Food and Families*. Manchester: Manchester University Press.

Cicirelli, V.G. (1992) *Family Caregiving*. Newbury Park: Sage.

Clapham, D. and Munro, M. (1988) *A Comparison of Sheltered and Amenity Housing for Older People*. Edinburgh: Central Research Unit Papers, Scottish Office.

Clapham, D. and Smith, S. (1990) 'Housing policy and special needs.' *Policy and Politics*, 18 (3), 193–205.

Clark, D. (1989) 'Living in the third age: A report on U3A discussion groups 1984–1988.' In V. Futerman (ed.) *Into the 21st Century*. Cambridge: University of the Third Age in Cambridge.

Clark, D. (1991) 'Constituting the marital world: A qualitative perspective.' In D. Clark (ed.) *Marriage, Domestic Life and Social Change*. London: Routledge, 139–166.

Clark, W.A.V. (ed.) (1982) *Modelling Housing Market Search*. London: Croom Helm.

Coleman, P. (1991) 'Ageing and life history: The meaning of reminiscence in late life', pp.120–143. In S. Dex (ed.) *Life and Work History Analyses*. London: Routledge.

Coleman, P. and Bond, J. (1990) 'Ageing in the twentieth century.' In J. Bond and P. Coleman (eds.) *Ageing in Society: An Introduction to Social Gerontology*. London: Sage, 1–17.

Collopy, B.J. (1988) 'Autonomy in long term care: Some crucial distinctions.' *The Gerontologist* 28 (suppl.) 10–17.

Comfort, A. (1977) *A Good Age*. London: Mitchell Beazley.

Comfort, A. (1990) *A Good Age*, 2nd Edn. London: Pan Books.

Commission for Racial Equality (1987) *Ageing Minorities: Black People as They Grow Old in Britain*. London: Commission for Racial Equality.

Connelly, N. (1989) *Race and Change in Social Services Departments*. London: Policy Studies Institute.

Connidis, I. (1983) 'Living arrangement choices of older residents: Assessing quantitative results with qualitative data.' *Canadian Journal of Sociology*, 8(4), 359–375.

Cornwell, J. (1984) *Hard Earned Lives*. London: Tavistock.

Cornwell, J. and Gearing, B. (1989) 'Doing biographical reviews with older people.' *Oral History*, 17 (1), 36–43.

Coupe, R.T. and Morgan, B.S. (1981) 'Towards a fuller understanding of residential mobility: a case study of Northampton England.' *Environment and Planning A*, 13, 201–215.

Cox, S. (1984) *Initial Demographic Study*. London: Royal National Institute for the Blind.

Craig, G. (1992) *Cash or Care: A Question of Choice?* York: Social Policy Research Unit.

Creek, G., Moore, M., Oliver, M., Salisbury, V., Silver, J. and Zarb, G. (1987) *Personal and Social Consequences of Spinal Cord Injury: A Retrospective Study*. London: Thames Polytechnic.

Cunningham-Burley, S. (1984) '"We don't talk about it..." Issues of gender and method in the portrayal of grandfatherhood.' *Sociology*, 18 (3), 325–338.

Cunningham-Burley, S. (1985) 'Constructing grandparenthood: Anticipating appropriate action.' *Sociology*, 19 (3), 421–436.

Dalley, G. (1991) 'Beliefs and behaviour: Professionals and the policy process.' *Journal of Aging Studies*, 5 (2), 163–180.

Dalley, G. (ed.) (1991) *Disability and Social Policy*. London: Policy Studies Institute.

Dallosso, H.M., Morgan, K., Bassey, E.J., Ebrahim, S.B.J., Fentem, P. and Arie, T.H.D. (1988) 'Levels of customary physical activity among the old and very old living at home.' *Epidemiology and Community Medicine*, 42(2), 121–127.

Dallosso, H., Morgan, K., Ebrahim, S., Smith, C.W., Bassey, J., Fentem, P.H.F. and Arie, T.H.D. (1986) 'Health and contact with medical services among the elderly in Greater Nottingham.' *East Midland Geographer*, 9, 37–44.

Daniel, S. (1988) 'A code to care for elders.' *Social Work Today*, August 18th p.9.

Dant, T. *et al.* (1988) 'Dependency and old age: Theoretical accounts and practical understandings.' *Ageing and Society*, 8, 171–188.

Darke, J. and Furbey, R. (eds.) (1991) 'Problems of Owner Occupation in Britain'. Unpublished conference proceedings. School of Urban and Regional Studies. Sheffield Hallam University.

Darton, R. and Wright, K. (1992) 'Residential and nursing homes for elderly people: One sector or two.' In F. Laczko, and C. Victor (eds.) *Social Policy and Elderly People*. Avebury: Aldershot, 216–244.

Davies, B. and Ward, S. (1992) *Women and Personal Pensions Equal Opportunities Commission*. London: HMSO.

Davis, R.H. and Davis, J.A. (1985) *TV's Image of the Elderly*. Lexington, M.H.: Lexington Books.

Day, A.T. (1985) *We Can Manage: Expectations about Care and Varieties of Family Support Among People 75 and Over*. Melbourne: Institute of Family Studies.

Department of Health (1988) *Survey of Age, Sex and Length of Stay Characteristics of Residents of Homes for Elderly People and Younger People who are Physically Handicapped in England at 31st March 1988*. London: Government Statistical Service.

Department of Health and Social Security (DHSS) (1988) *Community Care: Agenda for Action*. London: HMSO.

Department of Health (1989) *Caring for People. Community Care in the Next Decade and Beyond*. Command 849, London: HMSO.

Department of Social Security (DSS) (1990) *The Way Forward*. London: HMSO.

Department of Social Security (DSS) (1992) *Social Security Statistics 1991*. London: HMSO

Desprès, C. (1989) 'The meaning of home: Literature review and directions for future research and theoretical development.' Paper prepared for International Housing Symposium, *The Meaning and Use of Home and Neighbourhood*. Alvakarleby, Sweden.

Dex, S. (ed) (1991) *Life and Work History Analyses*. London: Routledge.

DHSS Asian Working Group (1983) *Report of the Stop Rickets Campaign*. London: Save the Children Fund.

di Gregorio, S. (1987) '"Managing" – A concept for contextualising how people live their later lives.' In S. di Gregorio (ed.) *Social Gerontology: New Directions*. London: Croom Helm.

Douglas, M. and Nicod, M. (1974) 'Taking the biscuit: The structure of British meals.' *New Society*, Vol. 30, No. 637, 744–747.

Dowd, J. and Bengtson, V. (1978) 'Ageing in minority populations: An examination of the double jeopardy hypothesis.' *Journal of Gerontology*, Vol. 33(3), 427–36.

Dragadze, T. (1990) 'The notion of adulthood in rural Soviet Georgian society', pp.89–101. In P. Spencer (ed.) *Anthropology and the Riddle of the Sphinx*. London: Routledge.

Ebrahim, S. *et al.* (1987) 'Elderly immigrants: A disadvantaged group.' *Age and Ageing*, 16, 249–255.

Elias, N. (1985) *The Loneliness of Dying*. Oxford: Basil Blackwell.

Ellis, H. (1933) *Psychology of Sex*. London: W. Heinemann.

Evandrou, M. (1992) 'Challenging the invisibility of carers: Mapping informal care nationally.' In F. Laczko, and C. Victor (eds.) *Social Policy and Older People*. London: Gower.

Evandrou, M., Falkingham, J. and Glennerster, H. (1990) 'The personal social services: Everyone's poor relation but nobody's baby.' In J. Hills (ed.) *The State of Welfare: The Welfare State Since 1974*. Oxford: Oxford University Press.

Evandrou, M. and Victor, C. (1989) 'Differentiation in later life: Social class and housing tenure cleavages', pp.104–20. In B. Bytheway (ed.) *Becoming and Being Old: Sociological Approaches to Later Life*. London: Sage.

Evandrou, M. and Winter, D. (1992) 'Informal carers in the labour market in Britain.' Paper presented to the international conference *on Social Security 50 Years After Beveridge*, University of York, 27–30 September 1992.

Falkingham, J. and Lessof, C. (1992) 'Playing God or LIFEMOD – The construction of a dynamic micro-simulation model.' In R. Hancock, and H. Sutherland (eds.) *Microsimulation Models for Public Policy Analysis: New Frontiers*. STICERD Occasional Paper, No. 17, STICERD, LSE.

Falkingham, J. and Victor, C. (1991) 'The myth of the Woopie?: Incomes, the elderly and targeting welfare.' *Ageing and Society*, 11(4), 471–93.

Fallis, G. (1985) *Housing Economics*. Toronto: Butterworth.

Farrah, M. (1986) *Black Elders in Leicester: An Action Research Report on the Needs of Black Elderly People of African Descent from the Caribbean*. Leicester: Leicestershire County Council, Social Services Department.

Featherstone, M. and Hepworth, M. (1989) 'Ageing and old age: Reflections on the postmodern life course', pp.143–57. In W. Bytheway (ed.) *Becoming and Being Old: Sociological Approaches to Later Life*. London: Sage.

Featherstone M. and Hepworth, M. (1990) 'Images of ageing', pp.250–75. In J. Bond, and P. Coleman (eds.) *Ageing in Society*. London: Sage.

Fennell, G., Phillipson, C. and Evers, H. (1988) *The Sociology of Old Age*. Milton Keynes: Open University Press.

Fenton, S. (1988) 'Health, work and growing old: The Afro-Caribbean experience.' *New Community*, 14 (3), 426–433.

Finch, J. (1989) *Family Obligations and Social Change*. Cambridge: Polity Press.

Finsterbusch, K. (1976a) 'The mini survey: An underemployed research tool.' *Social Science Research* 5 (1), 81–95.

Finsterbusch, K. (1976b) 'Demonstrating the value of mini surveys in social research.' *Sociological Methods and Research*, 5 (1), 117–36.

Firth, J. (1987) *Public Support for Residential Care*. London: HMSO.

Forrest, R. (1983) 'The meaning of home ownership.' *Society and Space*, 1, 205–216.

Forrest, R. and Kemeny, J. (1984) *Careers and Coping Strategies: Micro and Macro Aspects of the Trend Towards Owner-Occupation*. University of Bristol, Mimeo.

Forrest, R. and Murie, A. (1985) *The Housing Histories of Home Owners: Some Preliminary Observations*. Mimeo.

Forrest, R. and Murie, A. (1987) 'The affluent home owner: Labour market position and the shaping of housing histories.' *Sociological Review*, 35, 370–403.

Forrest, R. and Murie, A. (1990a) 'A dissatisfied state? Consumer preferences and council housing in Britain.' *Urban Studies*, 27, 617–635.

Forrest, R. and Murie, A. (1990b) *Home Ownership, Differentiation and Fragmentation*, London: Unwin Hyman.

Forrest, R. and Murie, A. (1991) 'Housing markets, labour markets and housing histories.' In J. Allan, and C. Hamnett (eds.) *Housing Markets and Labour Markets*. London: Unwin Hyman, 63–93.

Foster, P. (1991) 'Residential care of frail elderly people: A positive re-assessment.' *Social Policy and Administration*, 25, 108–120.

Fox, A.J. and Goldblatt, P. (1982) *Socio-Demographic Mortality Differentials from the OPCS Longitudinal Study 1971–75*. Series LS, No. 1, London: HMSO.

Fox, A.J., Goldblatt, P. and Jones, D.R. (1983) 'Social class mortality differentials: Artifact, selection or life circumstances?' *Journal of Epidemiology and Community Health*, 39(1), 1–18.

Francis, D. (1984) *Will You still Need Me, Will You Still Feed Me When I'm 84?* Bloomington: Indiana University Press.

Franklin, A. (1986) *Owner Occupation, Privatism and Ontological Security; A Critical Reformulation*. School for Advanced Urban Studies, Working Paper 62, University of Bristol.

Franklin, A. (1990) 'Ethnography and housing studies.' *Housing Studies*, 5 (2), 92–111.

Fry, W.F. (1976) 'Psychodynamics of sexual humour: Sex and the elderly.' *Medical Aspects of Human Sexuality*, 10, 140–141 and 146–148.

Gavilan, H. (1992, June 17) 'Taking control from the frail.' *The Guardian*.

Gearing, B. and Dant, T. (1990) 'Doing biographical research.' In S. Peace (ed.) *Researching Social Gerontology*. London: Sage, pp.129–142.

Gibbs, I. (1991) 'Income, capital and the cost of care in old age.' *Ageing and Society*, 11/4, 373–97.

Gibson, H.B. (1991) *The Emotional and Sexual Lives of Older People*. London: Chapman and Hall.

Gibson, H.B. (1992) *Love in Later Life*. Unpublished.

Giddens, A. (1976) *New Rules of Sociological Method*. London: Hutchinson.

Giddens, A. (1979) *Central Problems in Social Theory*. London: Macmillan.

Giddens, A. (1981) *A Contemporary Critique of Historical Materialism*. London: Macmillan.

Giddens, A. (1984) *The Constitution of Society*. Cambridge: Polity Press.

Giddens, A. (1991) *Modernity and Self-Identity*. Cambridge: Polity Press.

Ginn, J. and Arber, S. (1991) 'Gender, class and income inequalities in later life.' *British Journal of Sociology*, 42, 369–96.

Ginn, J. and Arber, S. (1992a) 'Older women's working lives: Household ties or new opportunities?' Paper presented to the Cambridge Social Stratification Research Seminar, September 1992.

Ginn, J. and Arber, S. (1992b) 'The transmission of income inequality: Gender and non-state pensions.' In K. Morgan (ed.) *Gerontology: Responding to an Ageing Society*. London: Jessica Kingsley Publishers.

Ginn, J. and Arber, S. (1993) 'Pension penalties: The gendered division of occupational welfare.' *Work, Employment and Society*, 7(1), 47–70.

Ginn, J. and Arber, S. (forthcoming) 'Heading for hardship: How the british pension system has failed women.' In S. Baldwin, and J. Falkingham (eds.) *Beveridge: New Challenges*. Brighton: Harvester Wheatsheaf.

GLAD (1987) *Disability and Ethnic Minority Communities: A Study in Three London Boroughs*. London: Greater London Association of Disabled People.

Glendinning, C. (1990) 'Dependency and interdependency.' *Journal of Social Policy*, 19 (4), 469–97.

Glendinning, C. and Craig, G. (1992) 'Rationing vs Choice: Tensions and Options.' Paper presented at the Social Policy Association Conference, University of Nottingham 8 July 1992.

Goffman, E. (1963) *Asylums*. Harmondsworth: Penguin.

Goldblatt, P. (1990) *Mortality and Social Organisation in England and Wales, 1971–1981*. Series LS, No. 6, London: HMSO.

Goodman, J.L. (1976) 'Housing consumption disequilibrium and local residential mobility.' *Environment and Planning A*, 8, 855–874.

Green, H. (1988) *Informal Carers*. OPCS Series GHS, No. 15, Supplement A, OPCS, London: HMSO.

Greengross, W. and Greengross, S. (1989) *Living, Loving and Ageing*. London: Age Concern.

Greenwood, M.J. (1985) 'Human migration: Theory models and empirical studies.' *Journal of Regional Science*, 25, 521–544.

Griffiths, R. (1988) *Community Care: Agenda for Action*. A Report to the Secretary of State for Social Services. London: HMSO.

Grillis, J.R. (1987) 'The case against chronologization; changes in the Anglo-American life cycle 1600 to the present.' *Ethnologia Europaea*, xvii (2):97–106.

Groves, D. (1988) 'Occupational pension provision and women's poverty in old age.' In C. Glendinning, and J. Millar (eds.) *Women and Poverty in Britain*. Brighton: Wheatsheaf Books.

Groves, D. (1991) 'Women and financial provision in old age.' In M. MacLean and D. Groves (eds.) *Women's Issues in Social Policy*. London: Routledge.

Grundy, E. (1989) 'Longitudinal perspectives on the living arrangements of the elderly.' In M. Jefferys (ed.) *Growing Old in the Twentieth Century*. London: Routledge.

Grundy, E. (1991) 'Ageing: Age-related change in later life.' In M. Murphy and J. Hobcroft (eds.) 'Population research in Britain', a supplement to vol 45 *Population Studies*, 33–50.

Grundy, E. (1992) 'Socio-demographic variations in rates of movement into institutions among elderly people in England and Wales', *Population Studies*, 46, 65–84.

Grundy, E. and Harrop, A. (1992) 'Co-residence between adult children and their elderly parents in England and Wales.' *Journal of Social Policy*, 31 (3), 325–348.

Gubrium, J.F. (1986) *Oldtimers and Alzheimer's: The Descriptive Organisation of Senility*. London: JAI Press.

Guillemard, A.M. (1990) 'Re-organising the transition from work to retirement in an international perspective: Is chronological age still the major criterion determining the definitive exit?' Paper presented to International Sociological Association Conference, Madrid.

Guralnik, J.M. (1991) 'Prospects for the compression of morbidity. The challenge posed by increasing disability in the years prior to death.' *Journal of Aging and Health*, 3(2), 138–154.

Gurney, C. (1990) *The Meaning of Home in the Decade of Owner Occupation.* School for Advanced Urban Studies, Working Paper 88, University of Bristol.

Gurney, C. (1991) 'Ontological security, home ownership and the meaning of home: A theoretical and empirical critique.' Paper prepared for *'Beyond A Nation of Home Owners.'* Sheffield City Polytechnic, April 22.

Gurney, C. (1992) 'Talking about the Home.' Paper prepared for British Sociological Association's *Sociology, Architecture and Environment Study Group,* London School of Economics, March 14.

Guttman, D.L. (1987) *Reclaimed Powers: Towards a New Psychology of Men and Women in Later Life.* New York: Basic Books.

Haire, G. (1990) 'Self preservation in hospital: A qualitative study of older patients' views of privacy in hospital wards'. MSc thesis, University of London.

Halpern, J.M. and Wagner, R.A. (1984) 'Time and social structure: A Yugoslav case study.' *Journal of Family History,* 9(3), 229–44.

Hammel, E.A. (1972) 'The Zadruga as a process', pp.335–428. In P. Laslett and R. Wall (ed.) *Household and Family in Past Time.* Cambridge: Cambridge University Press.

Hancock, R. and Weir, P. (1992) 'The changing contribution of the basic state pension towards pensioners' incomes in Great Britain'. Paper presented to the international conference on Social Security 50 Years After Beveridge, University of York, 27–30 September 1992.

Hansard, (1990) written answers, cols. 307–10, 25 July 1990.

Harding, A. (1990) Dynamic micro-simulation models: Problems and prospects, Welfare State Programme Discussion Paper No. 48, LSE.

Harding, T. (1992) *Great Expectations...and Spending on Social Services.* NISW, Policy Forum Paper No 1. London: NISW.

Hareven, T.K. (1982a) *Family Time and Industrial Time.* Cambridge: Cambridge University Press.

Hareven, T.K. (1982b) 'The life course and ageing in historical perspective.' In T.K. Hareven and K.J. Adams (eds.) *Ageing and Life Course Transitions: An Interdisciplinary Perspective.* London: Tavistock.

Hareven, T.K. and Adams, K.J. (eds.) (1982) *Ageing and Life Course Transitions: An Interdisciplinary Perspective.* London: Tavistock.

Harper, S. and Thane, P. (1989) 'The consolidation of "Old Age" as a phase of life, 1945–65.' In M. Jefferys (ed.) *Growing Old in the Twentieth Century.* London: Routledge.

Harris, A. (1971) *Handicapped and Impaired in Great Britain.* London: HMSO.

Harrison, L. and Means, R. (1990) *Housing: The Essential Element in Community Care.* London: SHAC and Anchor.

Haskey, J. (1990) 'The ethnic minority populations of Great Britain: Estimates by ethnic groups and country of birth.' *Population Trends,* 60, 35–37.

Hayward, G. (1975) 'Home as an environmental and psychological concept.' *Landscape,* 20, 2–9.

Hayward, G. (1977) 'An overview of psychological concepts of home.' Paper prepared for *8th Conference of Environmental Design Research Association (EDRA),* University of Illinois, Urbana-Champaign.

Hazan, H. (1980) *The Limbo People: A Study of the Constitution of the Time Universe among the Aged.* London: Routledge and Kegan Paul.

Henwood, M. (1990) 'No sense of urgency.' In E. McEwen (ed.) *Age: The Unrecognised Discrimination.* London: Age Concern.

Henwood, M. (1990b) 'Long-term care insurance: has it a future.' *Health Care UK*, Policy Journals, 97–105.

Henwood, M. (1990a) *Community Care and Elderly People*. London: Family Policy Studies Centre.

Henwood, M. (1992) 'Through a glass darkly: Community care and elderly people.' *Research Report 14 King's Fund Institute*. London: King's Fund Institute.

Herdt, G.H. (ed.) (1982) *Rituals of Manhood: Male Initiation in Papua New Guinea*. Berkeley: University of California Press.

Higgins, J. (1989) 'Defining community care: Realities and myths.' *Social Policy and Administration*, 23, 3–16.

Higgs, P. MacDonald, L. Ward, M. (forthcoming) 'Responses to the institution among elderly patients in long-stay care.' *Social Science and Medicine*.

HM Treasury (1989) *The Government's Expenditure Plans 1989–90 to 1991–92*. Cm 601–621. London: HMSO.

Hockey, J. (1989) 'Residential care and the maintenance of social identity: Negotiating the transition to institutional life.' In M. Jefferys (ed.) *Growing Old in the Twentieth Century*. London: Routledge.

Hodkinson, E. McCafferty, K. Scott, J. and Stoot, R. (1988) 'Disability and dependency in elderly people in residential and hospital care.' *Age and Ageing*, 17, 147–154.

Holland, B. and Lewando-Hundt, G. (1987) *Coventry Ethnic Minorities Elderly Survey: Method, Data and Applied Action*. Coventry: Ethnic Minorities Development Unit.

House of Commons Social Services Committee (1990) *Community Care: Informal Carers*. Session 1989–90, fifth report. London: HMSO.

Hoyes, L. and Means, R. (1991) *Implementing the White Paper on Community Care*. Bristol: School of Advanced Urban Studies.

Illsley, R. (1991) 'Review of Peter Laslett "A Fresh Map of Life"'. *Ageing and Society*, 11, 85–86.

Imhof, A. (1987) 'Planning full-size life career: Consequences of the increase in the length and certainty of our life spans over the last 300 years.' *Ethnologia Europaea* xvii (1), 5–23.

Ineichen, B. (1981) 'The housing decisions of young people.' *British Journal of Sociology*, 32, 252–258.

Ingebretsen, R. (1982) 'The relationship between physical activity and mental factors in the elderly.' *Scandinavian Journal of Social Medicine, suppl.* 29, 153–159.

Itzin, C. (1984) 'The double jeopardy of ageism and sexism.' In D.B. Bromley (ed.) *Gerontology: Social and Behavioural Perspectives*. London: Croom Helm.

Jerrome, D. (1981) 'The significance of friendship for women in later life.' *Ageing and Society*, 1, 175–98.

Jerrome, D. (1986) 'Social bonds in later life – review article.' *Ageing and Society*, 6, 497–503.

Jerrome, D. (1991) 'Social bonds in later life.' *Social and Psychological Gerontology, Reviews in Clinical Gerontology*, 1, 297–306.

Johnson, M. (1976) 'That was your life: A biographical approach to later life.' In J. Mannicks and W. Van Den Henval (eds.) *Dependency and Interdependency in Old Age*. Nijhoff: The Hague. Reprinted in V. Carver and P. Liddiard (eds.) (1979) *An Ageing Population*. London: Hodder and Stoughton, 99–115.

Johnson, M. (1987) 'Towards racial equality in health and welfare: what progress?' *New Community*, 15 (1/2), 128–135.

Johnson, M. (1990) 'Dependency and interdependency.' In J. Bond and P. Coleman (eds.) *Ageing and Society: An Introduction to Social Gerontology*. London: Sage.

Johnson, P. (1988) 'The structured dependency of the elderly: A critical note.' Centre for Economic Policy, Research Discussion Paper No.202.

Johnson, P. (1989) 'The structured dependency of the elderly: A critical note.' In M. Jefferys (ed.) *Growing Old in the Twentieth Century*. London: Routledge.

Johnson, P. and Falkingham, J. (forthcoming) 'A unified funded pension scheme for Britain.' Welfare State Programme Discussion Paper. London: STICERD.

Jones, G. (1987) 'Leaving the parental home; an analysis of early housing careers.' *Journal of Social Policy*, 16, 49–74.

Joshi, H. and Davies, H. (1992) *Child Care and Mothers' Lifetime Earnings: Some European Contrasts*. CEPR Discussion Paper 600.

Joshi, H. and Davies, H. (forthcoming) 'The paid and unpaid roles of women: How should social security adapt?' In S. Baldwin and J. Falkingham (eds.) *Beveridge: New Challenges*. Brighton: Harvester Wheatsheaf.

Judge, K. and Matthews, J. (1980) *Charging for Social Care: A study of Consumer Charges and the Personal Social Services*. London: Allen and Unwin.

Kane, R.L., Kane, R.A. (1991) 'Transitions in long-term care.' In M.G. Ory and K. Bond (eds.) *Ageing and Health Care*. London: Routledge.

Kassel, V. (1975) 'Polygyny after 60.' In K.C.W. Kammeyer (ed.) *Confronting the Issues*. Boston: Allyn and Bacon.

Kaufman, S.R. (1986) *The Ageless Self, Sources of Meaning in Later Life*. Madison, Wisconsin: University of Wisconsin Press.

Keeble, P. (1984) 'Disability and minority ethnic groups: A factsheet of issues and initiatives.' London: RADAR.

Kinsey, A.C., Pomeroy, W.B. and Martin, C.E. (1948) *Sexual Behavior in the Human Male*. Philadelphia: W.B. Saunders.

Kinsey, A.C., Pomeroy, W.B., Martin, C.E. and Gebhard, P.H. (1953) *Sexual Behavior in the Human Female*. Philadelphia: W.B. Saunders.

Knapp, M. (1989) 'Private and voluntary welfare.' In M. McCarthy (ed.) *The New Politics of Welfare*. London: Macmillan.

Knight, B. and Walker, D.L. (1985) 'Toward a definition of alternatives to institutionalization for the frail elderly.' *The Gerontologist*, 25(4), 258–263.

Kohli, M. (1986) 'The world we forgot: A historical review of the life course', pp.271–303. In V.W. Marshall (ed.) *Later Life: The Social Psychology of Aging*. London: Sage.

Kohli, M., Rein, M., Guillemard, A.M. and van Gunsteren, H. (eds.) (1991) *Time for Retirement: Comparative Studies of Early Exit from the Labour Force*. Cambridge: Cambridge University Press.

La Fontaine, J.S. (1985) *Initiation*. Harmondsworth: Penguin Books.

Laczko, F. and Phillipson, C. (1991) *Changing Work and Retirement*. Milton Keynes: Open University Press.

Laing, R. (1960) *The Divided Self*. London: Tavistock.

Laing, W. and Buisson, G. (1991) *Care of Elderly People; Market Survey, 1990/91, Fourth Edition*. London: Laing and Buisson.

Lambert, J., Laslett, P. and Clay, H. (1984) *The Image of the Elderly on TV*. Cambridge: University of the Third Age in Cambridge.

Land, H. (1991) 'The confused boundaries of community care.' In J. Gabe, M. Calnan and M. Bury (eds.) *The Sociology of the Health Services*. London: Routledge.

Larson, R. (1978) 'Thirty years of research on the subjective well-being of older Americans.' *Journal of Gerontology*, 33(1), 109–125.

Laslett, P. (1984) 'The significance of the past in the study of ageing.' *Ageing and Society*, 4 (4), 379–390.

Laslett, P. (1987) 'The emergence of the Third Age.' *Ageing and Society*, 7(3), 133–160.

Laslett, P. (1989) *A Fresh Map of Life*. London: Weidenfeld and Nicolson.

Le Grand, J. (1990) *Quasi-Markets and Social Policy*. Bristol: School of Advanced Urban Studies.

Le Grand, J. and Robinson, R. (eds.) (1984) *Privatisation and the Welfare State*. London: Allen and Unwin.

Leat, D. (1990) *For Love and Money: The Role of Payment in Encouraging the Provision of Care*. York: Joseph Rowntree Foundation.

Levi-Strauss, C. (1966, December) 'The Culinary Triangle.' *New Society*, 937–940.

Lewis, M. (1989) 'Sexual problems in the elderly: II Men's versus women's. A panel discussion.' *Geriatrics*, 44, 75–86.

Lister, R. (1992) *Women's Economic Dependency and Social Security*. Manchester: Equal Opportunities Commission.

Locker, D. (1984) *Disability and Disadvantage*. London: Tavistock.

Lonsdale, S. (1990) *Women and Disability*. London: Macmillan.

Lopata, H. (1973) *Widowhood in an American City*. Cambridge, MA: Schenkman.

Loughman, C. (1983) 'Eros and the elderly: A literary review.' *The Gerontologist*, 20, 182–187.

Macfarlane, A. (1978) *The Origins of English Individualism*. Oxford: Blackwells.

Macfarlane, A. (1986) *Marriage and Love in England: Modes of Reproduction 1300–1840*. Oxford: Blackwells.

Macintosh, S., Means, R. and Leather, P. (1990) *Housing in Later Life*. SAUS Study No 4, Bristol: School of Advanced Urban Studies, University of Bristol.

Maclennan, D., Gibb, K. and More, A. (1991a) *Paying for Britain's Housing*. York: Rowntree Foundation.

Maclennan, D., Gibb, K. and More, A. (1991b) *Fairer Subsidies, Faster Growth*. York: Rowntree Foundation.

Macnicol, J. (1990) 'Old Age and Structured Dependency'. In M. Bury and J. Macnicol (eds.) *Aspects of Ageing*. Egham: Department of Social Policy and Social Science, Royal Holloway and Bedford New College.

Madigan, R., Munro, M. and Smith, S. (1990) 'Gender and the meaning of home.' *International Journal of Urban and Regional Studies*, 14, 625–647.

Marris, P. (1986) *Loss and Change* (Revised Edition). London: Routledge and Kegan Paul.

Martin, J., Meltzer, H. and Elliot, D. (1988) *OPCS Surveys of Disability in Great Britain: Report 1 – The Prevalence of Disability Among Adults*. London: HMSO.

Martin, J. and White, A. (1988) *The Financial Circumstances of Disabled Adults Living in Private Households*. London: HMSO.

Martin, J., White, A. and Meltzer, H. (1988) *Disabled Adults: Services, Transport and Employment*. London: HMSO.

Mason, J. (1987) 'A Bed of Roses? Women, marriage and inequality in later life.' In P. Allatt, T. Keil, A. Bryman and B. Bytheway (eds.) *Women and the Life Cycle*. Basingstoke: Macmillan.

Mason, J. (1988) '"No peace for the wicked": Older women and leisure.' In E. Wimbush and M. Talbot (eds.) *Relative Freedoms: Women and Leisure*. Milton Keynes: Open University Press.

Masters, W.H. and Johnson, V.E. (1966) *Human Sexual Response*. Boston: Little, Brown and Co.

Masters, W.H. and Johnson, V.E. (1970) *Human Sexual Inadequacy*. London: J.A. Churchill.

Mathewman, J. (1991) *Tolley's Social Security and State Benefits 1991–92*. Croydon: Tolley Publishing Company.

Mays, N. (1983) 'Elderly South Asians in Britain: A survey of relevant literature and themes for further research.' *Ageing and Society*, 3 (1), 71–97.

McAuley, W.J. and Nutty, C.L. (1982) 'Residential preferences and moving behaviour: A family life-cycle analysis.' *Journal of Marriage and the Family*, 44, 301–309.

McClone, F. (1992) *Disability and Dependency in Old Age*. Family Policy Studies Centre, Occasional Paper 14, FPSC, London.

McLaughlin, E. (1991) *Social Security and Community Care: The Case of the Invalid Care Allowance*. DSS Research Report No. 4. London: HMSO.

McLaughlin, E. (1992) 'Equal opportunities, community care and the invalid care allowance since 1986.' Paper presented at the Social Policy Association Conference, July 1992.

McFarland, E., Dalton, M. and Walsh, D. (1989) 'Ethnic minority needs and service delivery: the barriers to access in a Glasgow inner-city area.' *New Community*, 15 (3), 405–415.

Means, R. (1987) 'Older people in British housing studies.' *Housing Studies*, 2, 82–98.

Means, R. (1988) 'Council housing, tenure polarisation and older people in two contrasting localities.' *Ageing and Society*, 8 (4), 395–421.

Means, R. (1990) 'Allocating council housing to older people.' *Social Policy and Administration*, 24 (1), 52–64.

Means, R. and Harrison, L. (1992) 'Care and repair.' In F. Laczko and C. Victor (eds.) *Social Policy and Elderly People*. Aldershot: Avebury.

Means, R, and Smith, R. (1985) *The Development of Welfare Services for Elderly People*. Beckenham, Kent: Croom Helm.

Melnyk, C. (1990, March 7) 'Home Truths.' *The Guardian*.

Miles, M. and Huberman, A. (1984) *Qualitative Data Analysis: A Sourcebook of New Methods*. Beverley Hills: Sage.

Mincer, J. (1978) 'Family migration decisions.' *Journal of Political Economy*, 86, 749–773.

Minkler, M. (1989) 'Gold in gray: Reflections on business' discovery of the elderly market.' *The Gerontologist*, 29, 17–23.

Moledina, S. (1987) *Great Expectations: A Review of Services for Asian Elders in Brent*. London: Age Concern Brent.

Morgan, K., Dallosso, H.M., Arie, T., Byrne, E.J., Jones, R. and Waite, J. (1987) 'Mental health and psychological well-being among the old and very old living at home.' *British Journal of Psychiatry*, 150, 801–807.

Morgan, K., Dallosso, H., Bassey, E.J., Ebrahim, S., Fentem, P.H. and Arie, T.H.D. (1991) 'Customary physical activity, psychological wellbeing and successful ageing.' *Ageing and Society*, 11, 399–415.

Morris, J. (ed.) (1989) *Able Lives: Women's Experience of Paralysis*. London: The Women's Press.

Morris, J. (1991) *Pride Against Prejudice: Transforming Attitudes to Disability*. London: The Women's Press.

Morris, J. (1992) 'Personal and political: A feminist perspective on researching physical disability.' *Disability, Handicap and Society*, 7 (2), 157–66.

Mudrovčić, Ž. (1990) 'Socijalna politika – Osnova migrantske politike', pp.553–60. In Nusret Sehic (ed.) *Migracije i Bosna i Hercegovina*. Sarajevo: Institut za medjunacionalne odnose i Institut za istoriju.

Mullen, C. and Swanenberg, F. (1988) *Out of the Twilight: A Resource Pack on Ageism in the Media*. London: BBC Education.

Munro, M. (1987) 'Residential mobility in the private housing sector.' In M. Pacione, (ed.) *Social Geography: Progress and Prospect*. London: Croom Helm 31–61.

Murcott, A. (ed.) (1983) *The Sociology of Food and Eating: Essays on the Sociological Significance of Food*. Aldershot: Gower.

Murray, N. (1985, February 28) 'The central issue is racism.' *Community Care*, pp.19–20.

Musgrove, F. and Middleton, R. (1981) 'Rites of passages and the meaning of age in three contrasted social groups.' *British Journal of Sociology*, 32 (1), 39–55.

Nedeljkovic, Y. (1970) *Old People in Yugoslavia*. Beograd: Institute of Social Policy.

Nissel, M. and Bonnerjea, L. (1982) *Family Care of the Elderly: Who Pays?* London: Policy Studies Institute.

Norman, A. (1985) *Triple Jeopardy: Growing Old in a Second Homeland*. London: Centre for Policy on Ageing.

OECD, (1988a) *1987/88 Economic Surveys: United Kingdom*. Paris: OECD.

OECD, (1988b) *1987/88 Economic Surveys: Yugoslavia.* Paris: OECD.

Office of Population Censuses and Surveys (1980) *Classification of Occupations 1980,* London: HMSO.

Office of Population Censuses and Surveys (1983) *Census 1981. Sex, Age and Marital Status, Great Britain.* London: HMSO.

Office of Population Censuses and Surveys (1984) *Census 1981. Communal Establishments, Great Britain.* London: HMSO.

Office of Population Censuses and Surveys (1989) *General Household Survey, 1986.* London: HMSO.

Office of Population Censuses and Surveys (1990) *General Household Survey, 1988.* London: HMSO.

Office Population Censuses and Surveys (1992) *General Household Survey 1990.* London: HMSO.

Oldman, C. (1991a) *Moving in Old Age.* London: HMSO.

Oldman, C. (1991b) *Paying for Care: Personal Sources of Funding Care.* York: Joseph Rowntree Foundation.

Oliver, M. (1990) *The Politics of Disablement: A Sociological Approach.* London: Macmillan.

Oliver, M., Zarb, G., Silver, J., Moore, M. (1988) *Walking into Darkness: The Experience of Spinal Cord Injury.* London: Macmillan Press.

Olson, L. (1985) 'Older women: Longevity, dependency, and public policy.' In V. Sapiro (ed.) *Women, Biology and Public Policy.* London: Sage.

Osborne, S.P. (1991) 'The management of need: The role of case management and the allocation of resources.' *Local Government Studies,* 17 (1), 5–12 .

Owen, S. and Joshi, H. (1990) 'Sex, equality and the State pension.' *Fiscal Studies,* 11(1), 53–74.

Pahl, R. (1975) *Whose City?* 2nd edition. Harmondsworth: Penguin.

Pahl, R. (1984) *Divisions of Labour.* Oxford: Blackwell.

Palmore, E. (1971) 'Attitudes toward aging as shown by humor.' *The Gerontologist,* 11, 181–186.

Palmore, E.B., Burchett, B., Fillenbann, G.G., George, L. and Wallman, L.M. (1985) *Retirement: Causes and Consequences.* New York: Springer.

Parker, R. (1988) *The Elderly in Residential Care: Australian Lesson for Britain.* Aldershot: Gower.

Parker, G. (1990) *With Due Care and Attention: A Review of Research on Informal Care,* 2nd edition. Occasional Paper No 2. London: Family Policy Studies Centre.

Parker, H. (1992) 'Onwards from Beveridge: Labour market effects of work-tested benefits and their replacement by citizens' incomes.' Paper presented to the international conference on Social Security 50 Years After Beveridge, University of York, 27–30 September 1992.

Parker, G. and Lawton, D. (1990) 'Further analysis of the 1985 GHS data on informal care: The consequences of caring.' University of York, SPRU Paper DHSS 716.

Parkes, C.M. (1972) *Bereavement: Studies of Grief in Adult Life.* London: Tavistock.

Patel, N. (1990) *A Race Against Time.* London: Runnymede Trust.

Payne, J. and Payne, C. (1977) 'Housing pathways and stratification: A study of life chances in the housing market.' *Journal of Social Policy,* 6, 129–156.

Pearl, R. (1930) *The Biology of Population Growth.* New York: A.A. Knopf.

Pfeiffer, E. (1983) 'Health, sexuality and aging.' In J.E. Birren *et al.* (eds.) *Ageing: A Challenge to Science and Society.* Oxford: Oxford University Press.

Pfeiffer, E., Verwoerdt, A. and Wang, H.S. (1968) Sexual behaviour of aged men and women.' *Archives of General Psychiatry,* 19, 753–758.

Pharaoh, C. (forthcoming) 'Primary health care for elderly people from black and minority ethnic groups.' Research Report, King's College London, Age Concern Institute of Gerontology.

Phillips, D.R., Vincent, J.A. and Blacksell, S. (1987) *Home from Home: Private Residential Accommodation for Elderly People in Devon, England.* Sheffield: University of Sheffield Press.

Phillipson, C. (1982) *Capitalism and the Construction of Old Age.* London: Macmillan.

Phillipson, C. *et al.* (eds.) (1986) *Dependency and Interdependency in Old Age.* London: Croom Helm.

Pill, R. (1983) 'An apple a day...Some reflections on working class mothers' views on food and health.' In A. Murcott (ed.) *op.cit.*

Plath, D. (1980) *Long Engagements.* Stanford: Stanford University Press.

Plummer, K. (1983) *Documents of Life: An Introduction to the Problems of Humanistic Method.* London: Allen and Unwin.

Power, C., Manor, O., and Fox, J. (1991) *Health and Class: The Early Years.* London: Chapman and Hall.

Qureshi, H. and Walker, A. (1989) *The Caring Relationship: Elderly People and their Families.* Basingstoke: Macmillan.

Ragin, C. (1991b) 'Introduction: The problem of balancing discourse on cases and variables in comparative social science.' *International Journal of Comparative Sociology,* 32(1–2), 1–8.

Ragin, C. (1991a) 'Issues and alternatives in comparative social research.' *International Journal of Comparative Sociology,* 32 (1–2), 9–17.

Republicki zavod za statistiku Bosne i Hercegovine (1987) *Statisticki godisnjak Bosne i Hercegovine.* Sarajevo: Republicki zavod za statistiku Bosne i Hercegovine.

Rex, J. and Moore, R. (1967) *Race, Community and Conflict.* Oxford: Oxford University Press.

Rhys Williams, B. (1989) *Stepping Stones to Independence: National Insurance After 1990.* Aberdeen: Aberdeen University Press.

Richman, J. (1977) 'The foolishness and wisdom of age: Attitudes toward the elderly as reflected in jokes.' *The Gerontologist,* 17, 210–219.

Rose, D. *et al.* (1991) 'Micro-social Change in Britain: An outline of the role and objectives of the ESRC Research Centre on micro-social change in Britain.' *Working Papers of the ESRC Research Centre on Micro-social Change,* Paper 1, Colchester: University of Essex.

Rosow, I. (1985) 'Status and role change through the life cycle.' In R.E. Binstock and E. Shanas (eds.) *Handbook of Aging and Social Sciences,* (2nd edn.) New York: Van Nostrand-Reinhold.

Ross, E. (1983) 'Survival networks: Women's neighbourhood sharing in London before World War I.' *History Workshop Journal,* 15, 4–27.

Rossi, P.H. (1955) *Why Families Move: A Study in the Social Psychology of Residential Mobility.* Glencoe: Free Press.

Rossi, P. and Shlay, P. (1982) 'Why families move revisited.' *Journal of Social Policy Issues,* 38, 21–34.

Rossiter, C. and Wicks, M. (1982) *Crisis or Challenge.* London: Study Commission on the Family.

Rubin, I. (1977) 'The "sexless older years" – a socially harmful stereotype.' In J.R. Barry and R.C. Wingrove (eds.) *Let's Learn About Aging: A Book of Readings.* New York: Wiley.

Samuel, R. and Thompson, P. (1990) *The Myths We Live By.* London: Routledge.

Sarre, P. (1986) 'Choice and constraint in ethnic minority housing: A structurationist view.' *Housing Studies,* 1, 71–86.

Saunders, P. (1986a) 'Comment on Dunleavy and Preteceille.' *Society and Space,* 4, 155–163.

Saunders, P. (1986b) *Social Theory and the Urban Question,* (2nd Edition). London: Hutchinson.

Saunders, P. (1990) *A Nation of Home Owners.* London: Unwin Hyman.

Saunders, P., and Williams, P. (1988) 'The constitution of the home; towards a research agenda.' *Housing Studies,* 3, 81–93.

Savage, M., Watt, P. and Arber, S. (1992) 'Social class consumption divisions and housing mobility.' In R. Burrows and C. Marsh (eds.) *Consumption and Class: Divisions and Change.* London: Macmillan.

Schorr, A. (1992) 'The personal social services: An outside view.' NISW Mimeo paper.

Seale, C. (1990) 'Caring for people who die: The experience of family and friends.' *Ageing and Society*, 10(4), 413–428.

Shaw, C. (1988) 'Latest estimates of the ethnic minority populations.' *Population Trends*, 51, 5–8.

Sinclair, I. (1988) 'Residential care for elderly people.' In Wagner Report *Residential Care: The Research Reviewed*, Vol. 2. London: National Institute of Social Work/HMSO.

Sinclair, I., Parker, R., Leat, D. and Williams, J. (1990) *The Kaleidoscope of Care: A Preview of Research on Welfare Provision for Elderly People*. London: HMSO.

Singer, I.B. (1982) *Old Love*. Harmondsworth: Penguin Books.

Sixsmith, J. (1986a) 'The meaning of home; an exploratory study of environmental experience.' *Journal of Environmental Psychology*, 6, 281–298.

Sixsmith, A. (1986b) 'Independence and home in later life.' In C. Phillipson, M. Bernard and P. Strang (eds.) *Dependency and Interdependency in Old Age: Theoretical Perspectives and Policy Alternatives*. London: Croom Helm.

Skinner, R. (1988, February 11) 'Young at heart.' *Community Care*. 24–25.

Smith, G. (1980) *Social Need: Policy Practice and Research*. London: Routledge and Kegan Paul.

Smith, T.R. and Clark, W.A.V. (1982a) 'Housing market search behaviour and expected unity theory: 1. Measuring preferences for housing.' *Environment and Planning A*, 14, 681–698.

Smith, T.R. and Clark, W.A.V. (1982b) 'Housing market search behaviour and expected unity theory: 2. The process of search.' *Environment and Planning A*, 14, 717–737.

Smyth, M. and Robus, N. (1989) *The Financial Circumstances of Families with Disabled children Living in Private Households*. London: HMSO.

Sohngen, M. (1977) 'The experience of old age as depicted in contemporary novels.' *The Gerontologist*, 17, 70–78.

Somerville, P. (1989) 'Home sweet home: A critical comment on Saunders and Williams.' *Housing Studies*, 4, 113–118.

Speare, A. (1970) 'Home ownership, life cycle stage and residential mobility.' *Demography*, 7. 449–58.

Spencer, P. (1990) 'The riddled course: Theories of age and its transformations', pp.1–34. In P. Spencer (ed.) *Anthropology and the Riddle of the Sphinx*. London: Routledge.

Stearns, P. (1977) *Old Age in European Society*. London: Croom Helm.

Steinfield, E. (1981) 'The place of old age: The meaning of housing for old people.' In J. Duncan (ed.) *Housing and Identity: Cross Cultural Perspectives*. London: Croom Helm.

Stojak, R. *et al.* (1990) *Socio-ekonomski polozaj starih ljudi u Bosni i Hercegovini*. Sarajevo: Zavod za unapredjenje socijalnih djelatnosti.

Stroebe, W. and Stroebe, M.S. (1987) *Bereavement and Health: The Psychological and Physical Consequences of Partner Loss*. Cambridge: Cambridge University Press.

Stuart, O. (1992) 'Race and disability: Just a double oppression?' *Disability, Handicap and Society*, Vol. 7 (2), 177–88.

Suls, J. (1976) 'Cognitive disparagement theories of humour: A theoretical and empirical synthesis.' In A.J. Chapman and H.C. Foot (eds.) *It's a Funny Thing Humour*. Oxford: Pergamon Press.

Swayne, L. and Greco, A. (1987) 'The portrayal of older Americans on television commercials.' *Journal of Advertising*, 16, 47–54.

Taylor, R. and Ford, G. (1981) 'Lifestyle and ageing.' *Ageing and Society*, 1, 329–45.

Taylor-Gooby, P. (1985) *Public Opinion, Ideology and State Welfare*. London: Routledge and Kegan Paul.

Thane, P. (1978, August 3) 'The muddled history of retiring at 60 and 65.' *New Society*, pp.234–6.

Thienhaus, O.J., Conter, E. and Bosmann, H.B. (1986) 'Sexuality and ageing.' *Ageing and Society*, 6, 39–54.

Thomas, D. (1988) 'Do not go gentle.' In W. Davies and R. Maud (eds.) *The Collected Poems of Dylan Thomas*. London: J.M. Dent and Sons.

Thompson, C. and West, P. (1984) 'The public appeal of sheltered housing.' *Ageing and Society*, 4(3), 305–326.

Thompson, P., Buckle, J. and Lavery, M. (1988a) *Not the OPCS Survey*. London: Disablement Income Group.

Thompson, P., Buckle, J. and Lavery, M. (1988b) *Being Disabled Costs More than they Said*. London: Disablement Income Group.

Thompson, P., Itzin, C. and Abendstern, M. (1990) *I Don't Feel Old: The Experience of Later Life*. Oxford: Oxford University Press.

Thompson, P., Lavery, M. and Curtice, J. (1990) *Short Changed by Disability*. London: Disablement Income Group.

Thomson D. (1983) 'Workhouse to nursing home: Residential care of elderly people in England since 1840.' *Ageing and Society*, 3, 43–70.

Thomson D. (1984) 'The decline of social welfare: Falling state support for the elderly since early Victorian times.' *Ageing and Society*, 4, 451–82.

Thorns, D.C. (1985) 'Age time and calendar time: Two facets of the residential mobility process.' *Environment and Planning A*, 17, 829–844.

Thorogood, N. (1987) 'Race, class and gender: The politics of housework.' In J. Brannen and G. Wilson (eds.) *Give and Take in Families*. London: George Allen and Unwin.

Tinker, A. (1984) *The Elderly in Modern Society*. London: Longman.

Titmuss, R.M. (1958) 'The position of women', pp.88–103. In R. Titmuss *Essays on 'The Welfare State.'* London: George Allen and Unwin.

Titmuss, R.M. (1968) *Commitment to Welfare*. London: George Allen and Unwin.

Townsend, P. (1957) *The Family Life of Old People*. Harmondsworth: Penguin.

Townsend, P. (1962) *The Last Refuge*. London: Routledge and Kegan Paul.

Townsend, P. (1973) *The Social Minority*. London: Allen Lane.

Townsend, P. (1981) 'The structured dependency of the elderly: A creation of social policy in the Twentieth Century.' *Ageing and Society* 1 (1), 5–28.

Townsend, P. (1981) 'Elderly people with disabilities.' In A. Walker and P. Townsend (eds.) *Disability in Britain: A Manifesto of Rights*. Oxford: Martin Robinson.

Townsend, P. (1986) 'Ageism and social policy.' In C. Phillipson and A. Walker, (eds.) *Ageing and Social Policy*. Aldershot: Gower.

Townsend, P., Davidson, N. and Whitehead, M. (1988) *Inequalities in Health and the Health Divide*. Harmondsworth, Middlesex: Penguin.

Troll, L. (1971) 'The family of later life: A decade review.' *Journal of Marriage and the Family*, 33, 263–290.

Tudor-Hart, J. (1971, February 27) 'The inverse care law.' *The Lancet* (i), 405–412.

Turner, B. and Gherardi, S. (1987) *Real Men Don't Collect Soft Data*. Quaderno 13, Dipartimento di Politica Sociale, Universita di Trento.

Twigg, J. (1983) 'Vegetarianism and the meaning of meat.' In A. Murcott (ed.) *op.cit.*

Twine, F. (1991) 'Citizenship and life course interdependence: participation and its implications for old age.' Paper presented to the European Congress of Gerontology, Madrid, September 1991.

Twine, F. (1992) 'Citizenship: Opportunities, rights and routes to welfare in old age.' *Journal of Social Policy*, 21(2), 165–176.

Ungerson, C. (1983) 'Why do women care?' In J. Finch and D. Groves (eds.) *A Labour of Love*. London: Routledge and Kegan Paul.

United Nations (1990) *1987 Statistical Yearbook*. New York: United Nations.

Victor, C. (1991) *Health and Health Care in Later Life*. Milton Keynes: Open University.

Victor C. (1992) 'Do we need institutional care?' In F. Laczko and C.R. Victor (eds.) *Social Policy and Elderly People*. Aldershot: Avebury.

Vincent, J. A. (1973a) 'St.Maurice' pp.200–18. In F.G. Bailey (ed.) *Debate and Compromise*. Oxford: Blackwells.

Vincent, J.A. (1973b) 'St.Maurice: An Alpine Community'. Ph.D. Thesis, University of Sussex.

Vincent, J.A. (1987) 'Work and play in an Alpine community.' In M. Bouquet and M. Winter (eds.) *Who From their Labours Rest?* Avebury: Aldershot.

Vincent, J.A. and Mudrovcic, Z. (1992) 'Ageing populations in the north and south of Europe.' *International Journal of Comparative Sociology* 32 (3–4), 261–288.

Wagner, G. (1988) *Residential Care A Positive Choice*. National Institute for Social Work, London: HMSO.

Waldren, C. (1991) *Predicting Applications and Admission to Residential Care: A Review of the Literature*. Discussion paper 862, Personal Social Services Research Unit, University of Kent at Canterbury.

Walker, A. (1980) 'The social creation of poverty and dependency in old age.' *Journal of Social Policy*, 9 (1), 49–75.

Walker, A. (1981) 'Towards a political economy of old age.' *Ageing and Society*, 1(1), 73–94.

Walker A. (1986) 'Pensions and the production of poverty in old age.' In C. Phillipson and A. Walker (eds.) *Ageing and Social Policy: A Critical Assessment*. London: Gower.

Walker, A. (1990a) 'The benefits of old age?' In E. McEwen (ed.) *Age: The Unrecognised Discrimination*. London: Age Concern.

Walker, A. (1990b) 'Poverty and inequality in old age.' In J. Bond and P. Coleman (eds.) *Ageing and Society: An Introduction to Social Gerontology*. London: Sage, 229–249.

Wandsworth Council for Community Relations (1978) *Asians and the Health Service*. London: CRE.

Warnes, A.M. (1986) 'The residential mobility histories of parents and children, and relationships to present proximity and social integration.' *Environment and Planning A*, 18, 1581–1594.

Watcher, K.W., Hammel, E.A. and Laslett, P. (1978) *Statistical Studies of Historical Social Structure*. New York: Academic Press.

Watson, S. (1988) *Accommodating Inequality*. London: Allen and Unwin.

Weidiger, P. (1975) *Female Cycles*. London: The Women's Press.

Welty, E. (1941) *A Curtain of Green*. London: Doubleday.

Wenger, C. (1989) 'Support networks in old age: Constructing a typology.' In M. Jefferys (ed.) *op.cit.*

Wenger, G. C. (1990) 'Elderly carers: The need for appropriate intervention.' *Ageing and Society*, 10 (2), 197–219.

Wilkin, D. and Hughes, B. (1986) 'The elderly and health services.' In C. Phillipson and A. Walker (eds.) *Ageing and Social Policy*, Aldershot: Gower.

Wilkinson, R. (ed.) (1986) *Class and Health*. London: Tavistock.

Wilson, G. (1987a) *Money in the Family: Financial Organisation and Women's Responsibility*. Aldershot: Avebury.

Wilson, G. (1987b) 'Women's work: The role of grandparents in intergenerational transfers.' *The Sociological Review*, 35(4), 704–720.

Wilson, G. (1989) 'Family food systems, preventive health and dietary change: A policy to increase the health divide.' *Journal of Social Policy*, 18 (2), 167–185.

Wilson, G. (1991a) 'Models of ageing and their relation to policy formation and service provision.' *Policy and Politics* 19 (1), 37–47.

Wilson, G. (1991b) 'Old age and change in home and neighbourhood: personal adaptability to the legacies of social and economic policies.' *Housing Studies*, 6, 263–272.

Winter, D. (1991) *A Cohort Analysis of Chronic Morbidity and Unemployment in the General Household Survey*, Welfare State Programme Discussion Paper No. 59, London School of Economics.

Wolf, D. (1990) 'Households patterns of older women: Some international comparisons.' *Research on Ageing*, 12, 463–486.

Wolf, D. and Soldo, B. (1988) 'Household composition choices of older unmarried women.' *Demography*, 25, 387–403.

Wolpert, J. (1965) 'Behavioural aspects of the decision to migrate.' *Papers of the Regional Science Association* 15, 159–169.

Yeandle, S. (1987) 'Married women at mid-life: Past experience and present change.' In P. Allatt, T. Keil, A. Bryman and B. Bytheway (eds.) *Women and the Life-Cycle: Transitions and Turning Points*. Basingstoke: Macmillan.

Zarb, G. (1991) 'Creating a supportive environment: Meeting the needs of people who are ageing with a disability.' In M. Oliver (ed.) *Social Work: Disabled People and Disabling Environments*. London: Jessica Kingsley Publishers.

Zarb, G. (1992) 'Changes in health care: A British perspective.' In G. Whiteneck and R. Menter (eds.) *Ageing with Spinal Cord Injury*. New York: Demos Publications.

Zarb, G. and Oliver, M. (1993) *Ageing with a Disability: What Do They Expect After All These Years?* London: University of Greenwich/Joseph Rowntree Foundation.

Zarb, G., Oliver, M. and Silver, J. (1990) *Ageing with Spinal Cord Injury: The Right to a Supportive Environment?* London: Thames Polytechnic/Spinal Injuries Association.

Notes on Contributors

Sara Arber is Senior Lecturer in Sociology at the University of Surrey. She is co-author of *Gender and Later Life*, (Sage, 1991), *Women and Working Lives* (Macmillan, 1991) and *Families and Households* (Macmillan, 1992). Her current research is on older women's employment, gender and class inequalities in ageing, informal care and inequalities in women's health.

Janet Askham is a sociologist, whose main research interests include ageing and later life, family and marital relations, and care and services for frail, ill or disabled people. She is Assistant Director of the Age Concern Institute of Gerontology at King's College London.

Kate Bennett is a research officer at the Health Services Research Unit, Department of Psychology, University College of North Wales, Bangor. She was previously a research fellow on the Nottingham Longitudinal Study of Ageing in the Department of Health Care of the Elderly, University of Nottingham Medical School. Her research interests are in the area of health psychology.

David Clapham is a Reader at the Centre for Housing Research at the University of Glasgow. He has undertaken research on a wide range of housing topics including an evaluation of sheltered housing in Scotland and is joint author of *Housing and Social Policy* (Macmillan, 1990).

Maria Evandrou is Lecturer in the Department of Epidemiology and Public Health, University College London Medical School and also Research Fellow on the Welfare State Programme, STICERD, London School of Economics. Her areas of research include; equity and the distribution of Personal Social Services, health and service use amongst elderly people and the socio-economic position of informal carers.

Jane Falkingham is a Research Fellow on the Welfare State Programme, STICERD, London School of Economics. She is co-author of *Ageing and Economic Welfare* (Sage, 1992). Her areas of research include; economic implications of an ageing population in advanced industrialised economies and less developed countries, pension policy reforms, and the income and standard of living within the elderly population.

H.B. Gibson is the Emeritus Head of the Psychology Department at the University of Hertfordshire (previously Hatfield Polytechnic) and continues there as a Senior Research Fellow. He is aged 77 and has been widowed for some years. He is active in various organizations concerned with the study of ageing and the welfare of older people, such as the University of the

Third Age in Cambridge. He is author of six books, and numerous book chapters and papers in learned journals.

Jay Ginn has been a contract research fellow in the Sociology Department at the University of Surrey since 1989. She co-authored *Gender and Later Life* (Sage, 1991) which used secondary analysis of the General Household Survey to study elderly people's health, income and access to informal care. She is currently working with Sara Arber on an ESRC-funded project analysing older women's labour force participation and pension entitlements.

Craig Gurney is Lecturer in Urban Sociology and Politics, School of Urban and Regional Studies, Sheffield Hallam University. His main interest concerns the meanings attached to 'home' and home ownership. He is currently registered for a Ph.D. at the School of Advanced Urban Studies, University of Bristol. He is a graduate of Sheffield City Polytechnic and the University of Sussex.

Lesley Henshaw has a degree in Sociology, an LLM, and a Ph.D in Law from University College of Wales. Her research has included a study of the use of the Welsh language in the courts, including comparison with the use of the Irish language in Irish courts; also work on Magistrates' Courts. She joined the Age Concern Institute of Gerontology at King's College London as a Research Associate to study service provision to elderly people from black and minority ethnic groups.

Paul Higgs is the Eleanor Peel Lecturer in Social Gerontology in the Division of Geriatric Medicine at St. George's Hospital Medical School, London. He studied sociology at the University of North London and received his Ph.D in Social Policy from University of Kent in 1988.

Glennys Howarth is the T.H. Marshall Fellow at the London School of Economics, studying the work of Coroners' and their staff in the social and legal processing of bodies and bereaved. Prior to this she worked on a project, funded by the Nuffield Foundation, concerned with ageing and the maintenance of independence amongst the oldest old.

Robin Means is Lecturer in Social Policy, School of Advanced Urban Studies, University of Bristol. He is co-author of *Housing: the Essential Element in Community Care* (Anchor/SHAC, 1990) and co-editor of *Implementing Housing Policies* (Open University Press, 1993). He is presently joint manager of a research project, funded by Joseph Rowntree Foundation, to study the impact of the community care reforms on service users in four contrasting localities.

Kevin Morgan is Lecturer in Gerontology, Department of Health Care of the Elderly, University of Nottingham Medical School.

Željka Mudrovčić is Assistant to Professor in the Department of Sociology at the Faculty of Political Sciences, University of Sarajevo. She is Honorary Visiting Research Fellow in the Department of Sociology at the University of Exeter in 1992.

Moira Munro   is Senior Lecturer in Economics at the Centre for Housing Research. Her main research interests are the meaning and use of the house, the interaction between housing and labour markets and housing finance and subsidies.

Maryrose Tarpey   has a degree in Sociology and Social Administration from University College Dublin. She has pursued a research career, with an emphasis on qualitative work and the evaluation of various social and community services. She has a particular interest in the accessibility of such services to people from black and minority ethnic communities, and joined the Age Concern Institute of Gerontology at King's College London as a Research Associate to work on this topic.

Christina Victor   is Senior Lecturer in Public Health at St. Mary's hospital Medical School in London and Director of Research for Parkside District Health Authority. She is author of *Health and Health Care in Later Life* (Open University Press, 1991) and Old Age in Modern Society (Croom Helm, 1987).

John Vincent   is Lecturer in the Department of Sociology at the University of Exeter and was a British Academy exchange visitor to the Academy of Science and Arts of Bosnia and Hercegovina in 1991.

Gail Wilson   is Lecturer in Social Policy and the Elderly at the London School of Economics. She has worked on the distribution of resources within households and the evaluation of community care for older people, and is currently involved in research on aspects of advanced ageing, elder abuse, ageing across Europe and interprofessional issues in the management of community services. She is co-editor (with Julia Brannen) of *Give and Take in Families* (Allen and Unwin, 1987).

Gerry Zarb   is a Senior Research Fellow at the Policy Studies Institute. He has worked on several research projects on disability issues and consumer perspectives on health and social services, and is author of the first major study of ageing with disability in the U.K. – *Ageing with a Disability: What do they expect after all these years?* (Joseph Rowntree Foundation, 1993). He is currently working on an evaluation of a national initiative on the provision of domiciliary care in the independent sector.

Subject Index

Name Index

Acton, William, on female sexuality 105, 106
Ahmad, A., on ageing, disability and race 42
Allen, I., Hogg, D. and Peace, S., on community care legislation 215
Altman, I. and Werner, C., on meaning of home 126
Anderson, M., on extended families in Britain 94
Anthony, K. on 'favourite homes' 123
  on perceptions of 'broken homes' 122
Arber, S., on individualistic approach 155
Arber, S., Gilbert, M. and Evandrou, M., on state support for those living alone 155
Arber, S. and Ginn, J. on ageing and class/gender/ethnic differences 13, 24, 42, 46, 115, 142, 153–4
  on attitudes to personal care 23
  on caring by spouse 156–7
  on classification of carers 153
  on disability 16, 153–4
  on elderly as proportion of population 110
  on employment after retirement age 13
  on extended families in Britain 94, 159
  on negative images of elderly people 11
  on independence of women 48
  on informal care by friends and neighbours 197
  on institutional care 157, 193
  on pensions 21, 33, 47, 74
  on preferability of care 'at a distance' 152
  on remarriage 157
  on state support for those living alone 155
Arendell, T. and Estes, C., on health costs in US 150
Aristophanes, *Ecclesiazusae* 106–7
Askham, J. *et al*, on ageing, disability and ethnicity 42, 171, 182

Badger, F., Atkin, K. and Griffiths, R., on ethnicity and ageing 171
Baldwin, S., on employment impact of caring 215
Baldwin, S. and Parker, G., on government policy and carers 215, 216, 218
Bashevis Singer, Isaac, on 'old love' 107–8
Basic Income Research Group 220
Batty, M., on changing spending patterns of elderly 11
Begum, N., on ageing, disability and race 28, 42, 43
Bellow, Saul, *Mr Sammler's Planet* 108
Belsky, J., on retirement and sex roles 113
Bengston, V.L., on qualitative and quantitative research 95
Bennett and Morgan, on retirement and sex roles 113
Benson, M., definition of *snaga* 99
Bertaux, D., on qualitative and quantitative research 95
Bhalla, A. and Blakemore, K., on ethnicity and ageing 171
Bhaskar, R., and structuration 144
Blakemore, K., on ageing and identity 172
Bland, R., on attitudes to rises in prices 58
Bond, J., Gregson, B. and Atkinson, A., on nursing homes 192
Bone, M., Gregory, J., Gill, B. and Lader, D., OPCS Retirement Survey 207, 210, 211, 212–13
Booth, T., on unnecessary institutionalisation 199
Bosanquet, N. on demographic change and long-stay provision 190
  on social care markets 204
Bosanquet, N., Laing, W. and Propper, C., on retirement income 47
Bosanquet, N. and Propper, C., on equity release schemes 218
Bourdieu, P., and structuration 144
Bowlby, J., on bereavement 65

Bowling, A. and Formby, J., on nursing homes 192
Braithwaite, V., on costs of caring 151
Brecher, E.M., on sexuality and ageing 113, 116, 117
British Household Panel Study 18
Brody, E., on 'Women in the middle' 166
Brok, A.J., on sexuality 106
Brown, J., on pensions policy 202
Brown, R., on treatment and individual need 169–170
Bryant, C. and Jary, D., and structuration 144
Bulmer, M., on housing and support networks 73, 74, 75
Bury, M. and Holmes, A., on very old and institutional care 28, 193
Butler, A., Oldman, C. and Grieve, J., research on elderly entering specialised housing 135
Butler, R.N. and Lewis, M.I., on sexuality of elderly 105, 114
Byers, J.P., on 'management' of lone parents 114

Cadwallader, M., on moving house 133
Cahn, E. and Barr, N., on social care markets 204
Caldock, K., on class and caring 150
Calnan, M. on attitudes to diet and health 65
  on food and family preferences 67
Cameron, E., Evers, H., Badger, F. and Atkin, K., on ageing and disablement 28
Campbell, H., Crawford, V. and Stout, N.W., and incontinence levels 196
Caring Costs on Invalid Care Allowance 216
  on strategic incomes policy 222
Challis, L. and Bartlett, D., on private nursing homes 190, 197–8
Charles, N. and Kerr, M., on food and social relations 24, 65, 67
Chaucer, Geoffrey, *The Merchant's Tale* 107
Cicirelli, V.G., on attitudes to independence 47, 49